100

10653315

Public Relations in Practice

Despite recent international expansion in the public relations industry, public relations is still often regarded as peripheral to the overall tasks of a successful organization. Yet a well-executed public relations programme can play a vital strategic role within many different types of organization. *Public Relations in Practice* presents a complete picture of public relations work, and provides a guide to its use which will be invaluable to senior company executives, as well as to students and practitioners.

The book contains fourteen recent case histories of effective public relations campaigns and looks at the strategic thinking that lay behind them. Choosing from a wide range of examples – from BT to Barnardos, from Shell UK to the Government of Brunei – it illustrates the gains that public relations can offer and the variety of strategic uses to which it can be put.

The cases making up the text have been supplied by experienced public relations professionals and are intended to help the reader gain a greater understanding of the role and potential of carefully planned public relations. The cases are presented in common format and each is accompanied by a discussion of its main features, highlighting the key lessons to be learned.

Public Relations in Practice
A casebook

Edited by Danny Moss

London and New York

First published 1990
by Routledge
11 New Fetter Lane, London EC4P 4EE

Simultaneously published in the USA and Canada
by Routledge
a division of Routledge, Chapman and Hall, Inc.
29 West 35th Street, New York, NY 10001

© 1990 Danny Moss

Typeset directly from the publisher's w-p disks by
NWL Editorial Services, Somerset, England, TA10 9DG

**Printed and bound in Great Britain by
Biddles Ltd, Guildford and King's Lynn**

British Library Cataloguing in Publication Data
  Public Relations in Practice.
  1. Great Britain. Public relations
  I. Moss, Danny, *1954–*
  659.20941

ISBN 0–415–05528–8
ISBN 0–415–04342–5 pbk

Library of Congress Cataloging in Publication Data
Public Relations in Practice : a Casebook / edited by Danny Moss.
    p.   cm.
  Includes bibliographical references.
  ISBN 0–415–05528–8. – ISBN 0–415–04342–5 (pbk.)
  1. Public relations – Case studies. 2. Public relations – Great Britain –
Case studies. I. Moss, Danny, 1954-   .
HM263.P76567   1991   90-32593
659.2–dc20   CIP

To Bernadette

for all her support and patience
during its writing and editing

Contents

Contents

Plates

Figures

Contributors

William Beaver was educated in the US and at Oxford University. After a Research Fellowship there, he joined J. Walter Thompson advertising agency where he was a Senior Representative for Corporate & Community Communications. He then spent five years as Director of Publicity for Barnardos before joining Pergamon AGB in 1989 as Group Director of Public Affairs.

Sam Black, MBE, FIPR, FBIM, MJI, FBCO, MSEE (Hon.), FRSA, is an independent Public Relations counsellor of international repute. He is an Honorary Professor of Public Relations at the University of Stirling, Scotland, where he inaugurated the Masters Programme in Public Relations in 1988. He is also a visiting Professor in Public Relations at the College of St Mark and St John, Plymouth. Amongst his notable appointments during a career in public relations that has spanned over forty years, are Secretary-General of the International Public Relations Association (IPRA) 1977–80 and President of IPRA in 1982. He is the recipient of both the President's medal from the Institute of Public Relations (IPR) and IPRA. In 1969 he was awarded the MBE by Her Majesty Queen Elizabeth II for 'services to export'. Sam Black is also the author of a number of textbooks including, *An Introduction to Public Relations* and *Exhibitions and Conferences from A–Z*.

David Budge is a Director of PR Consultants Scotland. He leads the account team which started work on the original Livewire pilot scheme in 1982. In 1986 he was awarded the IPR Swords of Excellence for the public relations work on Livewire. Prior to joining PR Consultants Scotland in 1982, he worked in London and Australia in public relations, advertising and marketing.

Bill Daring graduated with an MSc in Marketing from UMIST in 1978 after a short career as a scientist. He worked as a freelance qualitative market researcher before setting up Burgess Daring Advertising and Public Relations Ltd, Manchester, in 1980. The agency now specializes in integrated communications programmes for business to business, consumer and high technology clients.

Philip Dewhurst is a Director of GCI Sterling. Prior to joining Sterling in 1987, he spent four years as Head of Public Affairs for the Chemical Industries Association. He was elected a Fellow of the Institute of Public Relations in 1989.

Anne Dunne is Lecturer in Public Relations at the University of Stirling. Anne has six years' experience of public relations and marketing management and worked for the Lilley Group as PRO during its crisis period.

Avril Macdonald, MIPR, MAIE, joined British Telecom West of Scotland district as Press and Public Relations Manager in 1987. She joined from Countrywide Communications, where she was Senior Account Executive, and prior to her move south to join the Banbury-based PR company, was editor of the *Glasgow South and Eastwood Extra* for four years. She started her career in communications and PR in Dundee, and has free-lanced for national daily newspapers.

John Macdonald, Dip. CAM, MIPR, Director, PR Consultants Scotland, Aberdeen, was educated at Aberdeen Grammar School and Aberdeen College of Commerce. He worked as a journalist in London between 1973 and 1978 when he moved into public relations as Chief Press Officer for the British Overseas Trade Board. In 1983 he joined the Scottish Development Agency as Senior Public Relations Executive and worked there until joining PR Consultants Scotland in late 1986, to head their new Aberdeen office.

Alan Mole is a Director of Shandwick International and Shandwick Asia Pacific. He joined the Group in 1978 and was, in succeeding years, Managing Director of Shandwick Public Relations, Shandwick Consultants and Shandwick Communications respectively. He has been in charge of the work Shandwick has undertaken for the Government of Brunei Darussalam from the start. He has also carried out projects for the Government in the Republic of Cyprus and the Royal Palace in Morocco. He entered public relations in 1961 and, prior to Shandwick, was a Director and Senior Consultant in several other UK established firms.

John Morton is an Account Executive with TMA Communications, public relations consultants, based in Glasgow. After graduating from Glasgow University in 1985 with an MA, he spent three years in sales and marketing in one of Scotland's largest motor groups. He joined TMA in January 1989 and specializes in corporate public relations.

Tony Peck, FRSA, MIPR, FIEx (Grad) – Chairman Infopress, was educated at Kingswood and Queen's College, and is a Fellow of the Royal Society of Arts, a liveryman of the Worshipful Company of Broderers, Clerk to the Institute of Heraldic and Genealogical Studies and a Fellow of the Institute of Directors. Following an early career in the theatre and television, Tony Peck pursued a career in marketing and public relations, specializing in financial and corporate communications.

Diane Thompson, after starting her career in food marketing with the Co-operative Wholesale Society, spent five years as Wallcoverings Marketing Manager with ICI Paints Division. She then took up an appointment as a Senior Lecturer in Marketing and Advertising at Manchester Polytechnic where, during a seven-year period, she also ran her own successful advertising agency. She returned to the commercial world as Marketing Director for Sterling Roncraft, a wholly-owned subsidiary of Sterling Drug USA in 1986, and is currently Managing Director of Sandvik Saws and Tools UK Ltd.

Moreen Traverso is a marketing planner with the European division of Citibank in London, responsible for marketing planning for European financial services and has over ten years' experience in a variety of corporate communications positions in the energy and financial services sectors. She completed a sponsored MBA at Cranfield School of Management in 1987 and 1988, specializing in industrial marketing, business strategy and public relations.

Neville Wade is a director of Welbeck Golin/Harris Communications, which became part of Shandwick plc in June 1989. He is responsible for corporate and business-to-business clients and has worked in public relations for over twenty-six years. This experience covers both in-house and consultancy appointments. He is a Fellow of CAM and of the IPR of which he was President in 1983. Currently he is a trustee of the Public Relations Education Trust and chairs the PRCA Education Committee.

Jon White is a public relations practitioner with seventeen years' experience as an in-house public relations manager, consultant and teacher. He has worked as a consultant with Legal and General, the National Westminster Bank, BP, and the Canadian government's Department of Health and Welfare. He has headed Cranfield School of Management's teaching activities in public relations, public affairs and corporate communications since 1986 and holds a PhD in psychology from the London School of Economics and Political Science.

John Williams was educated at Oxford University. From there he joined the J. Walter Thompson advertising agency as a graduate trainee and stayed for eleven years. In 1986 he joined Valin Pollen, a specialist corporate communications company embracing PR, design and advertising services. He is currently head of the Research and Planning Department and led the team that produced and helped launch Barnardos' new identity.

Foreword

Peter Gummer
Chairman Shandwick plc

There have been rapid changes over the past ten years in the public relations market. We have seen the growth of international consultancies, the prominence of in-house positions at board level, and the influx of graduates into public relations as a first career.

Public relations is now an accepted part of the corporate strategy of any major business. Our clients demand professional public relations and it is up to the industry to satisfy the increased demand for trained people.

Never has the need been greater, with the demand for public relations consultancy services continuing to grow at 20 per cent per annum in Europe, North America and the Pacific Basin. The only real limit on growth is the number of committed professionals who can service the demands of the client.

From our own experience, there is an increasing demand for access to an international public relations network of regional specialists. The sophistication of electronic media, cable and satellite television has resulted in an insatiable demand for news, with business targets becoming an obvious source. The growth of an international media ensures world-wide coverage of any crisis situation or major news story. No company, however small, can afford to neglect the implication of these developments. News has to be managed.

The business world is shrinking fast with the growth of transnational operations, the deregulation of financial markets, closer ties between governments and cross-border bids and deals. It is now crucial for any progressive company to communicate effectively and quickly with its audiences. This internationalism of the media and of business creates further demands on public relations practitioners and presents them with new challenges. We need international 'thinkers', people who can understand the global implications of a strategy, but who are also aware of the importance of regional and cultural differences around the world.

In any business or profession there is always a tension between necessary qualifications and the importance of 'on the job' experience. We need to put this relationship on a surer footing. There are moves towards formalizing entry into public relations through examination, yet, as any practitioner knows, public relations demands of its successful consultants the ability to draw on a range of experiences and abilities, many of which may not be readily tested by examination. Constant updating and improvement of professional skills through 'on the job' training and short residential courses must be the way for the industry to proceed.

I welcome this new UK public relations casebook which I believe will prove invaluable for existing practitioners, students and second career recruits. It provides those of us who work in the business with an opportunity to learn from the experience of our colleagues, and for newcomers a chance to look past the limiting textbook definitions and discover something about the tremendous scope of public relations.

Peter Gummer, 1989

Shandwick is currently the world's largest independent public relations company with seventy-four offices in Europe, North America and the Pacific Basin, servicing over 5,000 clients.

Acknowledgements

I would like to offer my sincere thanks to all those practitioners who have taken the time and trouble to contribute the case studies that have made this book possible. I would also like to thank those client organizations who assisted in the preparation of case materials, and who took the trouble to supply additional information and illustrative materials. Finally I would like to acknowledge the assistance of my colleague Anne Dunne, who provided a case study herself, drawing on her earlier experiences in industry, and assisted in the preparation and editing of the manuscript.

Danny Moss, 1989

Introduction

Despite the remarkable growth in expenditure on public relations in recent years, and the efforts of the profession to improve understanding of its work, public relations still largely fails to receive the recognition and status afforded to other management disciplines. In recent years the Institute of Public Relations (IPR), the Public Relations Consultants Association (PRCA), as well as many individual practitioners themselves, have made strenuous efforts to educate the public, and the business community in particular, about the true nature of their work. However, despite their efforts, the profession is still largely perceived as primarily concerned only with media relations or gaining publicity, by the vast majority of people. Although the 1980s have undoubtedly witnessed an increase in awareness of the wider scope of public relations work, the image of the profession has not improved significantly.

The Summit meeting in Reykjavik in 1986, between US President Ronald Reagan and Soviet Premier Mikhail Gorbachev, perhaps did more to raise awareness of public relations than any event in recent history. The Summit was claimed to be a 'public relations' triumph for the Soviet Premier with the media throughout the world reporting it as 'A public relations victory' for the Soviet Union. As a result of the Summit and the media attention it received, public relations became recognized as an important new strategic 'weapon' in the battle for international advantage between the two superpowers.

Since the Summit, the term 'public relations' has been applied increasing by the media to describe the machinations of the protagonists in virtually any public issue. In fact, the media have taken to attaching the label to virtually any form of publicity or public statement issued by organizations almost irrespective of its purpose. In this sense, the term is often used in a pejorative sense, with the implication being that public relations involves some attempted 'sleight of hand' or merely an attempt to put a 'gloss' on the true facts, rather than being concerned to improve the presentation of the relevant information and facilitate an improved understanding of the issues in question.

The importance of good communication and presentation skills has, however, come to be increasingly recognized both by industry and government.

For example, when Mrs Thatcher, the British Prime Minister, announced her 'reshuffle' of British Cabinet posts in her government in 1989, a number of ministers were said to have been moved or to have lost their jobs because of the government's need to improve the communication of its policies with the voting public.

While it is important not to belittle the very real importance of effective communication and presentation skills, the preoccupation with this single aspect of public relations work should not be allowed to detract from the important strategic role that a well-executed public relations programme can play in supporting the activities of many organizations.

An important function of this book is to help present a more complete picture of public relations work. The cases illustrate the wide scope of its work, and also illustrate the genuine contribution public relations can make to the successful achievement of the objectives of the respective organizations discussed within the cases. In fact, one of the chief benefits of the cases, lies in their examination of the underlying strategic thinking that lay behind the programmes that were developed and implemented.

Although this book cannot, in itself, hope to change attitudes toward the profession, it is hoped it can at least contribute towards a better understanding of the true nature and scope of modern public relations work. The profession has steadily evolved over the years and now employs some of the most talented people working in either industry or the public sector. Many Chief Executives have come to recognize the importance of effective public relations, and it is often a portfolio which is seen as the primary responsibility of either the Chief Executive himself (or herself) or of a senior Board Director.

It is perhaps only through the continued efforts of all practitioners to uphold the highest standards of professional practice, that attitudes will gradually change towards the profession. Practitioners must recognize that only by example, will they gradually re-educate the public, and more importantly the media, as to the true nature and value of public relations practice.

Using the case studies

This book aims to provide both practitioners and students of public relations with the opportunity to learn from the experience of actual case studies that illustrate the state of current thinking and practice within the industry. The cases contained within the book provide examples of the application of public relations in a wide range of contexts and illustrate something of the scope of modern public relations practice. They have been supplied by practitioners who, both individually and collectively, can claim to have experience of virtually all facets of public relations work.

The cases illustrate the various stages in the development and implementation of effective communications solutions to the respective situations faced. The reader will be taken through the various stages, from initial problem analysis and the identification of key issues, to the identification of relevant target audiences or publics and the selection and implementation of specific programmes of activity. In each case the outcomes of the programmes are described and, where appropriate, the methods used to evaluate the programmes discussed. Each case is preceded by a brief 'case preview', which provides an overview of the case and some of the key principles of public relations to which it relates.

However, the cases are not intended to be purely case histories, valuable as they are in this respect, but they are also intended to stimulate discussion as to the effectiveness and appropriateness of the programmes undertaken. Students, in particular, are encouraged to consider the alternative approaches that could have been adopted, and how the outcomes might have changed given different circumstances or the adoption of different approaches to handling the issues involved. For the benefit of the student and less experienced reader in particular, each case is followed by a case discussion section, which highlights the key lessons to be learned from each case. A number of discussion questions and exercises are also provided at the end of each case. These are intended to stimulate debate, and provide the basis for further work by students, related to each case.

While the respective cases describe one particular solution to the problems presented, there is rarely only one way in which any particular problem could have been tackled. The circumstances at the time, the budget available or the specific client requirements, as well as the particular consultant's interpretation of the situation, can all influence the particular approach adopted. Readers may find it useful, therefore, to consider, albeit with the benefit of hindsight, the alternative ways in which the problems could have been tackled. In such an essentially dynamic and constantly evolving field as public relations, it is quite possible for any two practitioners to successfully tackle an identical problem in significantly different ways. Often, however, specific factors such as the time constraints involved, or the particular audiences to be addressed, may suggest a particular course of action .

One of the chief benefits of case studies is the ability to carry out post-mortems and consider each case in the light of alternative scenarios. Sometimes the particular circumstances under which the respective practitioners were forced to work at the time may have largely dictated the particular strategy adopted. Case studies have the advantage of allowing the student of public relations the chance to review each situation objectively, and without the pressures that the respective practitioners might have experienced at the time. Therefore, they provide both the student of public relations and the current practitioner with an excellent opportunity to draw upon the experience of those who were actually involved in tackling the respective problems. It is hoped that, through studying these cases, both practitioners and students will be able to enhance their own understanding of the profession.

Barnardos: relaunching Britain's biggest children's charity

John Williams and Dr William Beaver

Preview

The 1980s witnessed a dramatic increase in the number of organizations opting to undertake changes to their corporate identity. Often such changes involved the expenditure of huge sums of money in changing virtually every visual manifestation of the organization. However, a corporate identity change involves far more than the alteration of the visual identity of an organization. To be effective, it must strike at the very heart of the organization – its philosophy, modes of operation and beliefs about itself. The corporate design or logo seeks to encapsulate the essence of an organization in the form of a memorable and distinctive visual symbol.

Corporate identity is essentially concerned with an organization's personality and its *raison d'être*. It therefore often requires quite fundamental changes in the way an organization both operates and communicates with its audiences before the image held of the organization can be changed. By implication, changes in an organization's image do not happen overnight and often require quite profound changes to an organization's policies which must then be communicated to, understood, and accepted by the relevant audiences.

The catalyst for embarking on a change in corporate identity often comes from the recognition that the reality of an organization is no longer matched by perceptions held of it. Thus, the aim of many corporate identity programmes is to find a new and more appropriate way of communicating what the organization stands for to both internal and external audiences.

The first, and often most important, audience for a corporate identity change are the employees of the organization in question. Unless they understand and accept the proposed changes, any external communication programme designed to launch and establish the new identity will be of limited value and may at best have only a short term impact.

Corporate identity change is not confined only to commercial organizations – non-profit-making organizations can equally seek to readjust their identities. Dr Barnardo's, one of Britain's oldest charities, had come to recognize that its image, which still reflected the traditional practices and values first established by its Victorian founder, had become outdated and no longer reflected the true scope of the work it was undertaking in the 1980s. This case examines how Dr Barnardo's sought, through a change of corporate identity, to reposition itself and update the perceptions held of it by the public.

Background

Issues, need and opportunity

Until 18 October 1988 there was a serious and growing divide between the work Britain's largest childcare charity was doing and what the public thought it was doing. The story of its founder, Dr Thomas John Barnardo, and his work of rescuing orphans from 1866 to 1905 has been, and still is, an inspiration to millions in Australia, Canada, the Republic of Ireland, New Zealand and the United Kingdom.

Dr Barnardo's innovative childcare was matched only by his ability as a tireless, imagination-capturing communicator. He so carefully positioned Barnardos as *the* children's charity, the 'Ever Open Door', where 'No Destitute Child is Ever Refused Admission', that well over 90 per cent of all Britons would 'actively support' its work today (Abacus 1985; MORI 1986) but almost an equal percentage would do so for the wrong reasons. They still associate Barnardos with caring for orphans.

In reality, Dr Barnardo's had moved dramatically. Improving health standards coupled with the advances in birth control, meant that there were simply fewer and fewer orphans. They had ceased to be the major social problem Dr Barnardo set up his organization to alleviate. Instead Dr Barnardo's evolved its caring into new, related areas. Gone were the large children's homes for normal young people, to be replaced by over 160 UK 'projects' in areas of need. Dr Barnardo's now helps more than 16,500 disabled or disadvantaged young people and their families within their communities, employs 4,000 staff, has a known volunteer force of 126,000, runs 300 charity shops and must raise a million pounds a week. Nevertheless, people remain more interested in the charity's past, something of particular concern to those inside the organization.

In its first employees' audit (1986) staff put 'shifting the orphan image' as their highest concern. It was interfering badly with the work. The charity was faced with two tasks:

- a strong obligation to tell donors more effectively what they were contributing to;
- a need to erase any stigma about being helped by Barnardos.

An opportunity was seen for a dramatic restatement of the real Barnardos mission which could:

- invigorate fundraising efforts and remotivate volunteers;
- reforge links with those wanting to find better ways to help children in their own communities;
- remove all stigma of being helped by Barnardos;
- create a platform from which the charity could begin campaigning for improved laws and services for young people with special needs.

Goals and objectives

Dr Barnardo's had taken a step to addressing its image problems when it appointed its first Director of Publicity in 1983. This proved the basis for building a more professional approach to communications.

As approved by the governing council, the goal was to replace the orphan image with an accurate perception of the charity's innovative childcare work in the community today. Barnardos set about re-examining and restating its core values and, at the same time, determined to revise its corporate identity.

The corporate identity objectives were to:

- use the change of identity as a PR platform to relaunch the charity for the first time in its 120-year history.
- change the charity's visual and written identity to convey the reality of Barnardos at a glance.

The current identity was dated, heavy, and applied without consistency. To bring the charity's visual persona into line with its newly set corporate goals, the Publicity Director was convinced a new identity was crucial, and proposed employing a corporate communications agency with a strong design unit to research and implement a new identity. Senior management were cautious at first: the link between image (about which they cared passionately) and identity had to be explained and promoted. Once convinced, they were enthusiastic and supportive.

The external appointment to undertake the identity change (at a budget of no more than £50,000) and to implement it throughout the organization (for no more than £40,000) was approved in February 1988 and Valin Pollen was appointed.

Tackling the brief

Before setting about designing a new identity, Valin Pollen set itself four tasks:

1. To confirm the assumptions in Barnardos' brief through further research among external audiences.
2. To gain an objective picture of Barnardos' identity, culture and self-image,

through an internal audit.
3. To evaluate through desk research the existing charity 'market' and in particular other corporate identities.
4. To write, and get agreement on, a corporate identity brief that would also form the basis of a PR strategy to launch the new identity.

External research

External research was confined to four qualitative group discussions among the general public.[1] Within a fully commercial project, the qualitative findings would have been supplemented by quantitative large-scale research. However, due to the desire to keep down the costs, plus a high level of confidence that the conclusions supported past research, this stage was not pursued.

The results of the research were that Dr Barnardo's was held in high esteem, but that it did have a dated image. It was seen as a *caring* organization that upheld an 'open door' policy which meant that no one was ever turned away. Nevertheless, respondents associated Dr Barnardo's exclusively with orphans and, overall, it was seen to be a rather old-fashioned charity.

The then current logo was shown and discussed. It was recognized, but felt to communicate a message of protective isolation, contradicting Dr Barnardo's own operational philosophy of finding solutions *within* the family and the community. It was also felt that it did not distinguish Dr Barnardo's sufficiently from other childcare charities which were thought to have 'caught up' in image terms. What was a pioneering identity twenty years age, was no longer so.

Internal audit

The central part of the research phase was an internal audit of Dr Barnardo's existing identity, culture and communications. This involved:

- analysis of all existing physical manifestations of Dr Barnardo's from letterheads and advertisements to collecting boxes and shop fronts, in order to assess the consistency and style of presentation, as well as cataloguing the range of different applications of a new identity;
- evaluating what these applications *communicated* about Dr Barnardo's both in the written word and the choice of imagery;
- extensive visits to various childcare projects and appeals programmes in London, Birmingham and Liverpool, as well as to the Head Office in Barkingside;
- thirty in-depth interviews with members of the council of Dr Barnardo's, its full-time Directors and staff drawn from the Childcare, Appeals and Shops divisions.

The results of this internal audit exposed an underlying tension between ideals, ambitions and focus of different parts of the organization. This was most marked between those concerned with childcare and those concerned with fund-raising. This was, in turn, reflected in an identity that was inconsistent in its application and sentiment. Both 'Barnardos' and 'Dr Barnardo's' were being used as the charity's name. Types faces varied, slogan's abounded. There was a clear need to rationalize the identity, even if the logo itself did not change.

This lack of consistency in the identity reflected a lack of coherence within the organization and confirmed the need, not only for a new identity, but also for the 'core values' exercise – involving extensive consultation through internal discussion groups, seminars and meetings, to act as a means of rededication and refocusing of the organization.

The interviews with staff did produce consistent themes to form the basis of these core values. In addition, they provided a view on Barnardos' work, and a culture, that contrasted markedly with public perceptions.

Above all, staff endorsed the modern reality of charities by wanting to be seen as *professionals*, delivering a service that was as efficient and expert as it was concerned and caring. Indeed they stressed their active involvement in meeting needs, and rejected the notion of being seen as 'passive care-givers', full of good intentions and little else.

Staff were clearly aware that the external image did not fit with the reality. The childcare staff were concerned that the orphan image was not only inaccurate, but could also work against some of its projects with the handicapped and others with special needs. Not only could the stigma of the 'orphan' label be attached to anyone Dr Barnardo's was helping, but there was evidence that parents in need were discouraged from seeking help on the mistaken assumption that the only approach of Dr Barnardo's was to take the child away and place it in a home.

There was, however, an ambivalent response to this image from the appeals staff. While they conceded that the orphan image was outdated, it provided a powerful and clear fund-raising appeal and they expressed some concern that the reality of Barnardos' work today did not necessarily provide the clarity of message, nor as palatable stories, as did the orphan image.

This division between the two main sides of the charity was accentuated by a decentralization of organization and communication, with the result that it was failing to speak with one voice.

Summary of the key issues

The result of extensive study highlighted several key issues to address:

- A public view of Dr Barnardo's rooted in 'orphans' and unaware of the charity's actual work.
- A corporate identity that was inconsistently applied with a logo that re-inforced public perception that charity worked only for young children

held protectively in isolation from the community.

- An ambivalence among the staff about what Dr Barnardo's should be seen to represent.
- Fragmentation of the charity's culture both between regions and the centre, as well as between divisions, particularly Appeals and Childcare.
- A public image that was old-fashioned, undynamic and low profile.

Key decisions

Valin Pollen's conclusion confirmed and built on Dr Barnardo's original brief. The charity and its agency went on to agree the following implications:

- Dr Barnardo's should be relaunched as what it actually was – a modern pioneering, broadly-based charity. The image of Dr Barnardo himself had become sentimentalized as a 'do-gooder'. The reality was that he was a campaigning and radical figure. The charity should rediscover these roots, while at the same time laying to rest the 'orphan' myth.
- This approach would require being honest about Dr Barnardo's role – what it did, and what it did not do. It would also require confronting and challenging public perceptions. It could and should do this, in the spirit of Dr Barnardo, by exploiting its national standing and taking a more 'campaigning' stance. While this was accepted as a challenge to Appeals to find as effective a message as 'give to orphans' it was felt that this was a challenge that could not be shirked.
- Dr Barnardo's should adopt a clear, central positioning for itself within the charity 'market-place' that not only accurately reflected its activities and core values, but also identified added values and a unique approach to its service that would give it a competitive advantage in the search for support and funds.
- The relaunch should be built around the redesign of its logo and the creation of a new and fully-integrated corporate identity system. The role of the new identity would be to:
  - create a single, unifying culture and mission for the charity;
  - distinguish Dr Barnardo's more clearly from other childcare charities;
  - signify a change in direction for the charity;
  - refocus the image of Dr Barnardo's from one of isolation and protection to one of partnership and community involvement;
- The relaunch should be underpinned by the adoption of the core values and agreed positioning throughout the whole organization of the charity.
- To add further impetus to the message of change, the name of the charity would be formally changed from 'Dr Barnardo's' to simply 'Barnardos'. This move, supported by staff in research, was seen to be an important symbolic gesture to distance the charity from its orphan past, as well as

providing a practical PR 'hook' on which to hang the relaunch story.

The communications strategy

The strategy for the relaunch of Dr Barnardo's provided the basis for redefining the whole charity, as well as providing the basis of the brief for the design of the corporate identity and the platform for the strategy for the PR programme which launched it. A single integrated strategy, identifying one set of messages against a consistent set of audiences, was essential to the success of the campaign. To complement this, it was important that the communications programme needed to be equally integrated.

Positioning/essential message

The essential message summarized the positioning and set a target for what the PR programme should communicate about what Dr Barnardo's does and what it stands for:

> Dr Barnardo's is a 'solutions charity'; it helps children with handicaps or who face deprivation to find the tools to build a better life, and it helps communities come to terms with their fears of handicaps in order to build a better society. The charity's foundation is its belief that everyone is capable of achieving their full potential.

Target audiences

The role of the corporate identity and the communications programme was to achieve this positioning of Dr Barnardo's with a wide-ranging group of audiences. While one positioning and communications *strategy* had to be adopted for all groups, identifying and segmenting them was important to developing the right communications *programme* for each audience. The several audiences divided on one key dimension, those *within* the charity organization and those *without*.

Internal audiences

These comprised:
- The charity's (voluntary) council.
- The full-time directors and Head Office staff at Barkingside.
- The main divisions: Childcare, Appeals and Shops.
- The volunteers, particularly those on regional appeals committees.

External audiences

- The general public, as donors, as possible users of one of the charity's services and as opinion formers.
- The government, both local and national.
- The media and commentators.
- Other charities.
- Other social welfare agencies.

Desired responses

In setting the essential message, three key responses were sought from the external audiences:

- 'Dr Barnardo's isn't (just) orphans now'.
- 'They're still caring – but now about children with a whole range of handicaps'.
- 'If they think these children are worthy, perhaps I should too'.

Tone

The style and tone of communications had to be as influential as the messages themselves. All media needed to convey the modernity, and serious professionalism inherent in the Barnardos approach.

The new corporate identity design

From this communications brief, the design team distilled four tasks for the new identity:

1. To capture the spirit of the charity's philosophy and activities.
2. To help explain Barnardos' work.
3. To project Barnardos as a modern, professional charity.
4. In doing this, to avoid sentimentality and self-pity.

Three core themes were explored in the initial design proposals:

- friendship;
- partnership;
- teamwork.

The initial design reflecting these themes came close to the desired solution, but took several weeks and several meetings to evolve the final version (see Figure 1).

A change of colour from red to green was recommended. Red was felt to be alarming, whereas green was more friendly. It represented life, growth and health, as well as being the international safety colour. (It is interesting to note that, at the time, in spring 1988, the environmental connotations were barely acknowledged.)

The figures were designed to be androgynous and symbolic, neither men nor women, neither adults nor children, allowing the widest interpretation of their role. At the heart of these symbols was an image of partnership, helping, optimism, and above all, accomplishment. As one council member put it, 'They are helping the child over the "d" for difficulties'.

The design team had had to move quickly. Work started on the design brief at the end of March 1988, the first presentation of designs to the Barnardos council took place on 10 May and a final agreement on the revised design was reached on 12 June, leaving just four months to implement the design in time for the relaunch, scheduled for 18 October.

The public relations strategy and programme

The development of the new corporate identity was central to Barnardos' strategy for its relaunch. Changing the identity, and seeking to change so fundamentally the impressions of Barnardos that the new identity represented, would provide the platform from which all other communications could be launched. It was the focal 'hook' of the relaunch.

To maximize the impact of the new identity, it was agreed desirable to have one single date on which it was launched, with the organization changing overnight, as far as practical.

Therefore the occasion of the Barnardos Annual Conference, on 18 October 1988, was chosen. Plans were agreed to organize the largest conference since the 1930s to bring together staff and volunteers from all divisions and regions, as well as corporate sponsors and the media. Following this decision, Dr Barnardo's President, The Princess of Wales, agreed to unveil the new identity and address the conference.

However, it was understood that the new identity was only the means to the end of effecting a repositioning of the charity. There the *quality* of the coverage, rather than the quantity would be the best guide to its success. Another key decision was to target mass media – the national press and broadcast media, rather than segment the audience through specialist press, as this would provide the most efficient coverage of the specialist target groups.

Internal strategy

The messages behind the new identity needed to reach all the target audiences listed earlier, but the internal task of reaching staff and volunteers had to be handled with particular sensitivity. While it was agreed that the new identity would be kept secret and revealed to the external audiences for the first time

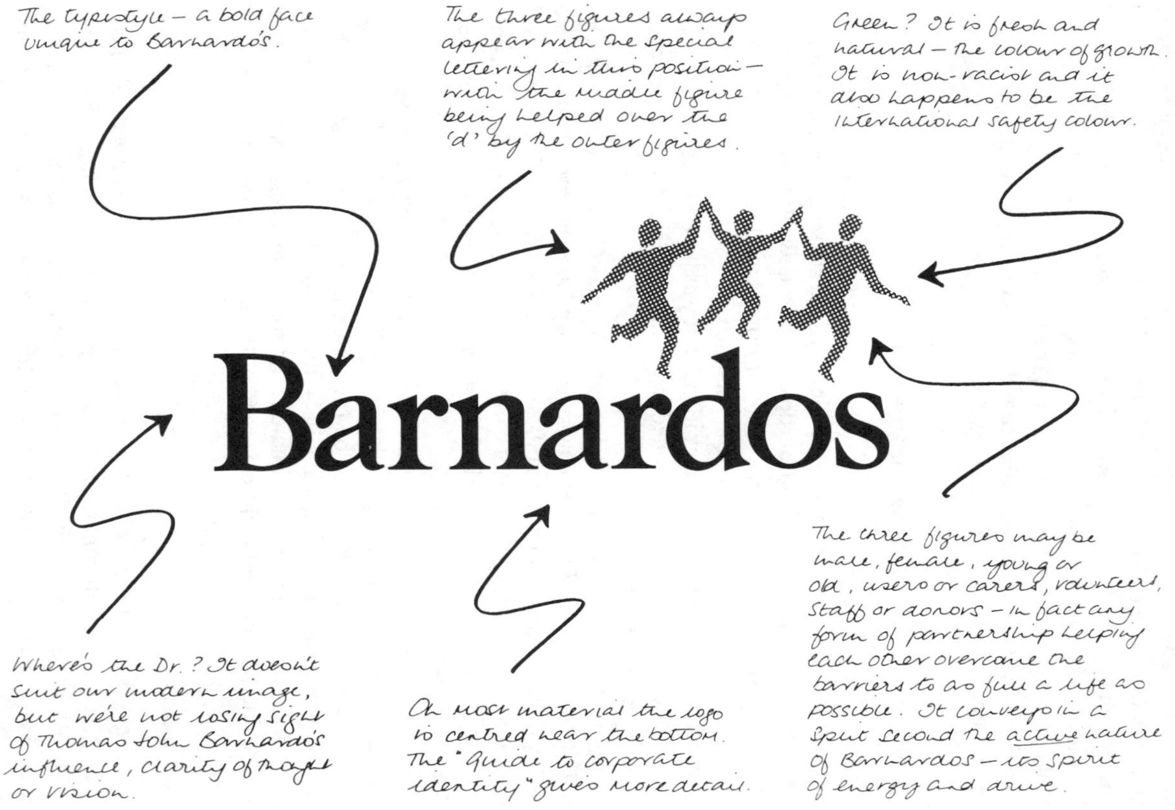

Green? It is fresh and natural – the colour of grass. It is non-racial and it also happens to be the international safety colour.

The three figures always appear with the special lettering in this position – making the middle figure being helped over the 'd' by the outer figures.

The typestyle – a bold face unique to Barnardos.

The three figures may be male, female, young or old, white or coloured volunteers, staff or donors – in fact any form of partnership helping each other overcome the barriers to as full a life as possible. It conveys a spirit around the active nature of Barnardos – its spirit of energy and drive.

On most material the logo is centred near the bottom. The 'Guide to corporate identity' gives more detail.

Where's the Dr.? It doesn't suit our modern image, but we're not losing sight of Thomas John Barnardos' influence, charity of thought or vision.

Figure 1 The current Barnardos logo

on 18 October, it was practical and desirable to win over the internal audience in advance.

This was for several reasons:

- There was likely to be some resistance to the change – the old logo had existed for twenty years – and the new logo and the core values it represented needed careful explanation;
- Winning the hearts and minds of as wide an audience as possible was essential to achieve the objective of bringing the organization closer together under a common mission and set of shared values;
- To make the relaunch work, the staff and the volunteers needed to work as ambassadors for the 'new look' Barnardos, confidently able to explain what the changes and the relaunch signified. Their support and enthusiasm was vital.

Altogether, the internal audience was the primary and crucial audience for the new identity and the new core values.

Therefore, at the heart of the internal PR strategy was a requirement to avoid presenting an abrupt *fait accompli* and instead, unveil gradually, the thinking behind the change, the values involved and then the change itself.

Internal PR programme

The actual development of the logo design was the start of the internal communication. Both the senior directors and the Barnardos council were active participants in the decision-making process, and this allowed Valin Pollen to explain in detail its thinking to a relatively broad audience and help achieve a consensus of support and enthusiasm for the change at the top of the organization.

For those not participating in the decision, a structured flow of information was created. Once the identity had been agreed by the council and senior directors, the decision was made to show it on a need-to-know basis, but otherwise to keep it under wraps. The only exception to this was that the design was researched among a number of volunteers.

One particular concern was raised in Scotland, where a view was expressed that the colour green, associated with the Catholic faith, particularly in Glasgow, would cut across the normally ecumenical appeal of the charity. Rather than argue on this potentially emotive issue, some research was carried out among the general public in Scotland which found that in the context of Barnardos, green carried no religious significance.

In April a video was made and distributed which featured the senior director and Valin Pollen account director explaining the value of the corporate identity review in the context of the core values discussions and the need for Barnardos to re-present itself to the public.

This was supported by a special publication, *Planning for Profile*, which was issued at key stages in the development of the new identity: core values were explained and articulated in August. The October issue presented the launch with practical answers to concerns and queries raised. Four thousand of each issue were mailed direct to staff, with additional copies supplied for volunteers.

The internal newspaper, *Barnardos News*, was revamped and its December/January issue reported on the launch and helped keep up the momentum.

Just before the launch day, Tessa Baring, Chairperson of the Council, sent a letter to volunteers, parents and others connected with the charity, explaining the reasons for the relaunch.

The day before the launch day, all staff received a briefing pack and background materials, allowing them to explain the changes as they were happening.

Just after the launch day, *Barnardos Today* in its new livery, was mailed to 1.5 million supporters and donors, to explain the new identity and act as the charity's autumn mail-shot.

The external PR programme

The logistics of the media relations programme presented a huge administrative challenge, as dozens of journalists were identified as potentially interested in the story, covering TV, radio, national and regional press, general and women's magazines, specialist charity and social services journals, and embracing social services correspondents, news journalists and features editors.

For several weeks before the relaunch date, itself strictly embargoed, Barnardos' PR staff were 'talking up' the story using the hook that Britain's largest and best-known charity was about to get rid of the doctor. They targeted news features, using confidence about news coverage as a persuader. The Chief Executive also met with each 'quality' social services correspondent and specialist press editor to ensure an understanding of the serious intent behind the relaunch event.

By 17 October, Channel 4 News, BBC and ITN had already filmed childcare feature packages and both breakfast television stations had broadcast standard archive footage ready for use as prelaunch trailers on the morning itself.

While the knowledge that the Princess of Wales might make a major speech at the conference strengthened the likelihood of major coverage, a photo-opportunity for the press and daytime television news was seen as a desirable measure. A sailboat, with the new logo on its main sail, was commissioned, sailing through Tower Bridge (which was opened specially) on the morning of the conference. On board was Bruce Oldfield, an ex-Barnardo boy, together with several young people the charity helps today. All were wearing new logo sweatshirts.

At the conference itself, the Princess's involvement meant that the charity was working under the royal rota system which requires that all the media must share their copy and footage with colleagues unable to get a place as one of the lucky eleven (the size of a half rota). However, Barnardos was also able to invite additional journalists as guests of the charity for the day.

At the same time as the London event, eight regional launches (using new look charity shops, helium logo balloons, tee shirts and local celebrities) took place across the UK. Each had a different flavour. For example, in Belfast volunteers on stilts took a festival atmosphere into the city centre, while in Newcastle there was a ceremonial flag lowering and hoisting of the new colours. Following the national pattern, local news opportunities were matched with pre-arranged feature coverage, adding local radio to the desired media mix.

Syndicated articles – written by a *Woman's Own* journalist who waived copyright – were sent to every free sheet across the UK.

All childcare and appeals managers were given in-house media and PR training in the year before the launch and they were encouraged to take advantage of the opportunities, put into place centrally and regionally, and to make their own contact at a local level.

The external programme not only needed to maximize the impact of the launch, but also to extend interest and the heightened profile of Barnardos as long as possible towards Christmas, the key charity-giving period. The month of November provided three opportunities:

- A gala Bruce Oldfield fashion show in the presence of the Prince and Princess of Wales.
- The Princess appearing at a celebrity luncheon honouring 'champion children'.
- A fifty-minute BBC TV documentary on the charity, scheduled for early November.

The first two opportunities provided excellent 'windows' in which to display the new identity. Following briefings by Barnardos the BBC documentary producer decided to feature a segment focusing on the development of the new identity and the reasons behind it, culminating in a presentation by Valin Pollen to the Princess of Wales which was filmed in September 1988. The documentary itself effectively positioned the charity at the centre of the modern childcare 'market', and a second showing in May 1989 provided an excellent bonus.

The role of campaigning had been identified as an important way to follow through on the success of the launch itself. In December the charity launched a sharply focused campaign, combining parliamentary lobbying with widespread media coverage, on the needs of young people leaving care. Called 'I can't go back to my Mum and Dad', the report is widely acknowledged to have brought about a change in the government's thinking. May 1989 saw the launch of a more sustained campaign due to run to the end of the year.

The role of advertising

The use of advertising was important to the relaunch, and to the overall success of the PR programme. It provided the opportunity for Barnardos to raise its profile further, extending the period in the public eye beyond the immediate days after the launch conference. The advertising consisted of a 'manifesto' advertisement in the daily quality press on the day after the conference, followed by a series of three case histories demonstrating the range of Barnardos' activities and its approach to achieving solutions. The campaign was not intended to directly appeal for money but to emphasize and reinforce the PR messages behind the relaunch. The fact of advertising itself was significant. A budget of £175,000 for an eight week period, though modest, was the highest ever spent by the charity in a concentrated period. The nature of the advertisements received coverage and comment in their own right, notably in a piece in the *Guardian* shortly before Christmas, and the direct style of the advertisements indicated that Barnardos was talking about itself in a new way both internally and externally. All this reinforced the PR impact of the launch.

Results and evaluation

As outlined earlier, the relaunch of Barnardos was seen as the start of a process of changing attitudes to, and understanding of, the charity. Nevertheless, the relaunch can be analysed both in terms of the immediate impact of the relaunch as well as in terms of the longer-term benefits.

Media coverage

The immediate coverage of the relaunch was boosted by two factors. First, the subject matter of the Princess of Wales's speech captured the imagination of the media. Second, it was by luck a relatively quiet newsday. The result was that the reporting of the speech, and the relaunch, dominated broadcast media on the day (from the lunchtime to evening news) and received extensive press coverage the following day. What was significant, however, was that the context of the speech was correctly reported and the message was got across that Barnardos had changed its look, its name and, implicitly, its work. In particular, the dropping of the 'Dr' was picked up and proved a successful news 'hook' (also the sailboat featured on the ITN news).

The story received ninety minutes of television broadcast coverage (national and regional combined) and saturation column inches, including significant uptake of syndicated material.

The following extracts from the national press coverage the day after the launch conference demonstrated that the strategic messages were getting through:

Dr Barnardo's, which is shrugging off its Victorian 'orphan' image, shedding the 'Dr' and transforming itself into a modern organisation.

(Guardian)

spearheading a campaign to help Dr Barnardo's to erase its Victorian 'orphan' image and focus the nation's attention on the plight of Britain's most needy youngsters.

(The Times)

The Princess, President of Dr Barnardo's, was launching a new image for the charity which is in future to be known as Barnardos.

(Daily Telegraph)

It's dropping the 'Dr' from its title, adopting a new logo and trying to get over to the public the variety of ways it helps young people and their families.

(Daily Mail)

the charity, which now will be known simply as Barnardos. It is determined to shed its Victorian Orphan image.

(Daily Express)

It is trying to show the public that it is not just about orphanages.

(Daily Mirror)

...dropped the 'Dr' in its title and taken on a new logo in an attempt to shed its Victorian 'orphans image'.

(Today)

In addition to the immediate news coverage, there were pieces specifically about the background to the charity's relaunch in the *Guardian*, the *Daily Telegraph*, the *London Evening Standard* and the *New Statesman and Society*, as well as specialist social care journals.

Media relations

The relaunch not only raised Barnardos' profile with the media, but also built and extended relations with individual journalists. The result was that Barnardos became a more likely contact for a comment or response to a story and helped build the profile of the charity.

Public response

One measure of the public interest in the relaunch can be gauged by the dramatically increased public correspondence. There were 84,000 letters in November, 23,000 above the previous year. No precise calculation of the impact of the relaunch on fund-raising had been made in advance. The level of direct donation was expected to rise, but all expectations were exceeded in the months following the relaunch, when donations were 11 per cent above budget in October, and up 27.8 per cent in November. In fact, by the end of November these donations above budget had covered the entire cost of the corporate identity programme.

Staff response

No formal research was conducted among staff after the launch, but reports back from all regions were positive and individual criticisms of the new identity were few. The level of coverage during the relaunch proved the best possible justification for the exercise.

Public attitudes

In addition to the physical evidence of increased donations, quantified market research was conducted in January 1988, with the repeat of a tracking study, by the MORI research company. The previous study had been conducted in November 1986.

This was not a perfect 'pre' and 'post' benchmark study. Ideally the research should have run in the summer of 1988 (it was not conducted then for reasons of budget) to give an accurate reading of current opinion immediately before the relaunch. There were therefore some negative shifts of opinion, notably among those agreeing that Barnardos 'provides a lot of information about itself'. This was interpreted as a demonstration that in the intervening two years Barnardos had lagged behind other charity communication activity, as well as reflecting an increasing hunger from the public for information. There were, however, some encouraging movements. Barnardos is now less regarded as 'old-fashioned' than was the case in 1986 (16 per cent agreeing in 1988, against 23 per cent in 1986). It is also more well known as a charity that provides services to families as well as to children (35 per cent agreeing against 23 per cent in 1986). The overall conclusion from the research is that although Barnardos has made a good start, there is still much communication work to be done.

Conclusion

This case study will in reality not be completed for several years. It will take that long for the general public to come to understand the full range of

Barnardos work and to set aside the orphan image, the legacy of Barnardos' founder. However, the PR programme behind the relaunch, both in its strategy, its planning and its execution, have given the charity the best possible basis on which to achieve its ends.

Case discussion

Although Barnardos is a non-profit making organization, as this case study demonstrates its problems were every bit as demanding as might be encountered in handling the public relations for any commercial organization and required the same degree of professionalism and strategic thinking for a solution as a situation involving a commercial organization might demand, if not more so. The process of developing its strategic communication programme required the same careful in-depth analysis of the issues and targeting of key publics as are demanded in handling projects for commercial organizations. The techniques employed were broadly similar to those that might be used in handling any complex communications problem. For Barnardos, a charity that had been established for some 120 years, the problem of updating its image and changing perceptions of the organization, both externally and internally stemmed, at least partially, from its very entrenched values and the long-established perceptions held of it by the general public.

The first key lesson to take from the case is that the image of any organization does not change overnight, even if it is possible to change its visual identity on a single day. Valin Pollen recognized that the change of visual identity, in particular Barnardos' name and logo, could only be the first stage in a far more extensive and longer term process of changing people's understanding and perceptions of the organization. However, the change of visual identity and the consolidation of its previously inconsistent application, provided a platform from which to launch the public relations programme directed both at external and internal audiences. It was an important symbol of the charity's commitment to promulgate its new and more up-to-date image.

The change of identity was an important catalyst for more fundamental change within the organization itself, among its vast number of voluntary workers and supporters, and ultimately, among the general public. It is important to recognize that Barnardos, as with similar organizations, is essentially a very person-centred organization. The perceptions held of it by the general public and specialist audiences are heavily influenced by their contacts with its large number of workers (both employees and and voluntary workers), who act as ambassadors at many different levels. The production of a comprehensive information pack for staff enabled them to respond to the inevitable enquiries that followed the change of identity, and was an important part of the communications strategy. Although the advertising and specific PR campaign played an important part in establishing awareness of the change of identity,

Barnardos recognized that acceptance of the reality of the modern Barnardos by different audiences, would only be brought about through their actual experiences of a 'new-look Barnardos' over time.

The success of the PR strategy developed by Valin Pollen owed a good deal to the careful research and internal audit undertaken at its outset, which resulted in considerable emphasis being placed on internal communication within the strategy. In an organization whose image was steeped in the traditional values, first established by its charismatic founder, the introduction of any change could not be achieved easily. When this problem was overlaid with the tensions existing between its different divisions, it is perhaps surprising that the change of identity went as smoothly as it did. This was largely due to the carefully structured approach to involving the staff throughout the organization, and particularly at senior levels, in the process of identity change. The internal PR strategy was perhaps the most critical element in the programme.

Any change of identity involves some degree of risk as to how it will affect perceptions of the organization. For Barnardos this was a particular cause for concern amongst the Appeals Division, who were worried about its impact on fund-raising for the charity, especially during the crucial Christmas period. The long-established 'orphan image', although generally accepted as being outdated, still held a strong emotional appeal with the public, whose donations were vital to the charity's activities. There was legitimate concern that the decision to change the identity might lead to confusion amongst the donating public and adversely effect the charity's receipts. Nevertheless, the decision was taken to proceed, as the longer-term benefits of re-positioning Barnardos as a modern, professionally-run and 'solutions-based charity' were seen to outweigh any short-term worries over the effects on fund-raising. In fact, although the change of identity presented the Appeals Division with a challenge, it also offered them an opportunity to 'market' Barnardos in a far more relevant manner.

It must be borne in mind that the charity 'market' is every bit as competitive as many consumer goods markets. Barnardos has to compete for support and donations with an increasing number of local, national and international charities, and must seek to differentiate itself from its competitors and ensure its appeal is perceived as relevant to the needs of a modern caring society. The orphan image, while well established and instantly recognizable, was increasingly becoming less appropriate to the problems of society today. While the changing nature of today's social problems had been reflected in the scope of Barnardos work, this was not reflected in its image. This gap had to be bridged if the charity was to maintain the longer-term loyalty of the public.

One perhaps less significant, but none the less interesting aspect of the identity design, was the potential problem raised by Barnardos Scottish workers over the use of the colour green in the new logo. Although the concerns raised about the potential alienation of Protestant support, due to the association of the colour green with the Catholic faith, were proved unfounded; it nevertheless highlights how important attention to detail is in the researching of any new identity. Perhaps more surprising is the fact that research (in September 1988) failed to reveal any significant associations between the proposed green colour and environmental issues. In the light of the dramatic increase in sensitivity to 'green' issues in recent years, this highlights just how quickly public perceptions can change as a result of external circumstances. Perhaps one of the most important lessons to be drawn from this case is that in designing a new corporate identity, preparatory research is essential and must be exhaustive and, at times, even inspired. All possible connotations and associations need to be thoroughly explored before finalizing the design.

Although the change of identity formed only the first stage in what will be an on-going programme to change perceptions of Barnardos, undoubtedly this first stage has been a success. The media exposure, both in terms of the quality and quantity of coverage was highly satisfactory, with the key messages being picked up and carried in the vast majority of the reports of the launch conference. Perhaps of equal importance, given the need to build on and sustain awareness of the new identity, was the opportunity to renew and reinforce contacts with key journalists that will facilitate future media coverage. Ultimately, of course, the success of the programme must be judged by its impact on the perceptions of the key target audiences, including potential donors, Barnardos' staff and potential beneficiaries of its work. Although it will be some time before a final judgement can be made, the initial results were obviously very encouraging.

The case also illustrates the importance of ongoing research to monitor public perceptions of an organization. Without benchmarks against which to measure the impact of a PR programme on final audiences, evaluation (when confined to media coverage) is restricted to measuring the effectiveness of the *process* of communication, but not necessarily its effects on the target audiences.

In general, this case has shown not only the important stages in the redesign of a corporate image, stressing the crucial importance of internal as well as external communications, but it also illustrates that the principles of effective public relations apply equally in the non-profit making sector as they do to commercially-orientated organizations.

Student discussion questions and exercises

1. Consider how important a well known visual identity is for Barnardos and identify the main potential advantages and disadvantages of its change of identity. Consider also how you would propose to evaluate the impact that the change of identity has had for Barnardos.
2. Draw up a list of charities and voluntary organizations operating in any one or two fields (for example, Childcare, Animal Rights, Environmental Protection) and try to identify the key values and messages that characterize

and differentiate each, and which each seeks to communicate.

3. Examine any two recent charity fund-raising campaigns, identify the key emotive appeals that each have tried to convey and the specific target audiences to which they are aiming to appeal. Evaluate how effective you feel the two campaigns were, in terms of communicating their respective messages to their likely target audiences.

Note

1. The group discussions involved in-depth interviews lasting one to two hours with groups of up to eight people led by an experienced moderator.

The launch of the Prudential's corporate identity

Moreen Traverso and Dr Jon White

Preview

The Prudential Corporation, one of the UK's leading financial institutions, in many ways faced a similar problem to Barnardos – their image no longer adequately reflected the changing nature of their business. Not only had the Prudential's business undergone significant changes over the years, but it was entering a period of even more dramatic changes in the financial services market which would involve it in new areas of business, dealing with new customers and facing challenges from new competitors. The Prudential saw a change in its corporate identity as a means of bringing together the organization's different operations under a single unifying corporate banner that would reflect the modern reality of its activities. The Prudential's management believed that this would, in turn, help strengthen its ability to compete more successfully in the new financial services market.

Many organizations, such as the Prudential, find that, as they have expanded their operations over the years, the perceptions held of them no longer reflect the true reality of the organization. This is a problem which can affect both internal as well as external audiences. In the Prudential's case, the significant changes taking place in its business environment made it vital for the organization to reposition itself to take advantage of the opportunities offered by the new market for financial services in the UK. Equally, it had to prepare itself to combat the new sources of competition it would soon inevitably face from the banks and building societies in particular. The launch of a new corporate identity cannot be expected, in itself, to change audience perceptions of an organization immediately. However, it often provides a platform from which a far more extensive communications programme can be successfully mounted.

Some questions have been raised in recent years about the true value of the often highly expensive changes in visual identity introduced by many major companies. However, design can play a very powerful role in shaping the physical environment and potentially provides public relations practitioners with a very powerful tool for reaching target audiences and influencing their perceptions and decisions. The launch of a new identity is normally an important symbolic event that can serve to remotivate internal staff and alert other audiences of the changes underway. Hence the launch event itself can be of critical importance to the success of a subsequent public relations programme and, invariably, is the subject of very careful and detailed planning. Equally, the process of implementing a new identity, which can often take a number of years to complete, has to be carefully managed and monitored.

This case also illustrates something of the process of developing and implementing a new corporate identity and the problems that can often surround gaining internal agreement for a proposed change to an organization's identity.

Background

In September 1986 the Prudential Corporation unveiled its new corporate identity to the world at large. In the space of one week the UK's leading insurance company attracted more press publicity than at any other time in its 140-year history.

The scale and nature of the launch took many by surprise. It was a high risk and expensive move calculated to generate a sufficiently high degree of controversy to enable the Prudential to reposition its business. City opinion formers and the international financial press welcomed the move as confirmation of the Prudential's intent to realize its potential as a leading financial services provider.

Within the company the new image had a powerful impact on Prudential staff. In recent years new businesses, products and technologies had been introduced to take advantage of a rapidly changing competitive and regulatory environment. The new look served to focus attention and reaffirm a common purpose and identity for the corporation.

The Prudential Corporation

The Prudential Corporation is the third largest UK financial institution by capitalization (National Westminster and Barclays being slightly larger). The Corporation was formed in 1978 by the then directors of the Prudential Assurance Company Ltd. This company was founded in 1848 when it pioneered the sale of life assurance to the working classes of Victorian Britain.

From this base (which gave the company access to millions of individuals) the Prudential has grown to become the largest single investor in British industry, the UK's third largest property owner and a significant player internationally in the reinsurance and investment management businesses. These activities are carried out through subsidiaries of Prudential Corporation which acts as an investment holding company.

Today the mission of the Corporation is to be the leading provider of services in its core business of insurance, medium- to long-term savings and estate agency. It sees its competitors as being those companies which use large customer bases to sell financial services. Such businesses include banks, building societies, insurance companies and even high street retailers with their own charge cards.

The company structure

The company is organized into seven core business areas:

1. *The UK Individual Division* sells savings and protection products, pensions, unit trusts, mortgages and personal insurance services through a 12,000-strong salesforce. It is largely through the activities of this salesforce, selling to people at home, that the public image ('The Man from the Pru') was formed.

2. *Prudential Property Services (PPS)* was set up in 1985 to provide the Corporation, through acquisition, with a profitable estate agency chain in the UK. Through this additional distribution outlet, the Prudential, in common with its major banking, building society and life insurance competitors, is developing its ability to cross-sell a range of financial services related to the sale and/or purchase of homes. In 1988 PPS almost doubled in size and became the largest estate agency in Europe. In the UK the Prudential's expansion has been extremely rapid over 800 branches nationwide.

3. *Corporate Pensions Division* provides corporations, local authorities and affinity groups with a full range of pension services. These include 'with profit' insured contracts, unit linked managed funds or separately managed portfolios.

4. *The International Division* operates in over thirty countries throughout the world through a variety of subsidiaries, branches and agencies. The classes of business written include life and pension contracts and a range of general insurance (often termed property and casualty insurance) both for the individual and the commercial buyer.

5. *Mercantile and General Reinsurance (M&G)* is the UK's biggest reinsurance company with two-thirds of its premium income derived from overseas subsidiaries. Through reinsurance, insurers can pass on a proportion of the risks accepted from policy-holders and hence offer a far wider range of cover than could be possible from their own resources. M&G reinsures both life and general business, dealing with over 2,000 insurance companies world-wide. Its business is highly technical and made more complex and risky by catastrophes like hurricanes and, of late, the longer-term impact of AIDS.

6. *Prudential Portfolio Managers (PPM)* is a wholly-owned investment management company which today ranks as one of the largest British-based investors in the world's stockmarkets. It invests in a range of assets – stocks

and shares, property, foreign currencies and financial futures – on behalf of policy-holders, major corporate and financial clients (including other subsidiaries and divisions of the Prudential itself). Out of assets of over £30 billion managed world-wide by the Prudential, some £22 billion is invested by PPM.

7. *Prudential Holborn* was set up in 1987 to meet the financial services needs of high net-worth individuals. It provides a comprehensive range of investment, savings and protection products (for example, Personal Equity Plans, unit trusts and life assurance) designed to meet the fast-moving taxation and stockmarket conditions. Sales are made primarily through financial intermediaries.

Management structure and organization

Each of these business area divisions has its own Board of Management. The Chief Executive on each of these boards is usually an Executive Director of the main board of the Corporation. On a day-to-day basis they report to the Group Chief Executive, Brian Corby, who is also a main board member. In addition, the board has sixteen non-Executive Directors of which the Chairman, Lord Hunt of Tanworth, is one.

The current structure of the Prudential and its operating divisions has evolved over the last decade since the formation of the Prudential Corporation in 1978. When Brian Corby was appointed Chief Executive in 1980 the decision was taken to decentralize what was a very hierarchical organization into individual operating divisions with substantial operating autonomy from the centre. One side effect of this development was the promotion, over time, of the individual operating divisions services with little thought given to the overall image of the Corporation as a whole. The Prudential's non-Executive Directors were particularly concerned by this development. In 1985 the extent to which the business areas should be allowed to conduct their own activities without regard to the effect on other areas and the Corporation as a whole became an issue for debate at board level. It was around this time that the decision was made to bring in specialist public affairs expertise to help formalize and manage the Corporation's internal and external communications activities.

The establishment of a public affairs function

In 1985 David Vevers was chosen for the position of Public Affairs Manager. His background was in wholesale financial services as PR Director of a major merchant banking organization. Until this time the Prudential had limited its corporate public relations activities to media relations. It employed two press officers and three staff writers and made no use of PR consultants. Contact with the media was, in the main, reactive, with the Prudential providing expert spokespersons to talk about different product areas when requested.

Individual operating divisions conducted their own marketing activities and there was little corporate involvement in this process. Upon Vevers's appointment, Brian Corby made it clear to him that he had to find a way of 'getting everything under one banner' and to 'rein in' the operating divisions. Privately, Vevers calculated that he had about six months to come up with a response and a maximum of two years in his post to establish both his own position and that of the public affairs function in the Corporation.

Vevers summed up the situation he found as follows:

It was the first time that management had really considered how they communicated both internally and externally. We started a process of looking at all the identities used within the Corporation. We listed all their different names and those of their products to see how they related. In reality, we found they didn't.

The Prudential had under-estimated the need for a unified image that correctly portrayed the underlying spirit of the company. Our name was strong and yet it did not appear in any consistent way in the identities created by the operating companies. As a result, our customers, and even many of our staff, didn't fully understand what the Prudential stood for.

This point was not lost on the board who had been spending considerable financial and managerial resources in broadening the Prudential's core business activities into other financial services areas. Significant changes in the regulatory environment meant increasing opportunities to expand the Corporation's product range. Furthermore, a traditional inward-looking industry was being opened up to new competition such as the banks and building societies, who were also beginning to present themselves to their public in a strong, clear way. At the time, the Prudential was planning to move into new product areas such as unit trusts and estate agency. Some of these services could not be sold through direct contact with the public (the Prudential's traditional strength) and would require the use of intermediaries, direct mail and advertising instead.

The introduction of the corporate identity programme

The need to project a consistent image and capitalize on the Corporation's strengths was therefore seen of increasing importance. However, Vevers saw the main impetus for the change as not the result of any long-term strategic rethink, but rather arising from internal and organizational problems within the Corporation.

Vevers had spent a lot of time after joining the Prudential getting the views of a wide range of people within the company – at all levels and from different functional areas – to find out how they viewed the company. He was struck by the 'down-market' image of the Prudential, and how little they knew of the totality of the business. As he commented, 'You could sense they were almost embarrassed by its success.'

Coming from the outside, he was able to take a fresh view of the situation and saw the biggest priority as being to increase the staff's own confidence in the Prudential. There was essentially a good story to be told. The challenge was to find a way of getting it across.

Vevers recommended that the best approach was to introduce a corporate identity programme and to buy in the skills of a top firm in this field. Wolff Olins were chosen for this task. The central issue to be addressed was whether each business should try to create an image in the market-place which was uniquely its own or whether there should be a single unifying identity which emphasized the name Prudential.

The importance of research

The team made use of existing market research material to find out what people outside the organization thought the name stood for. It showed that people generally knew the Prudential's name, but were not sure what the Corporation's range of products and services were. For example, they thought the Prudential was an insurance company first and foremost and there was a good deal of confusion as to whether it was involved in property services and unit trusts.

When asked about the character of the Prudential, the most common reply was that the company was honest, responsible, old-fashioned and staid. Vevers concluded that there were some good perceptions that could be built upon, but that the more negative characteristics needed to be converted into positive ones. The Prudential's personality was described as convenient, big, lumbering and lower middle class. 'Convenience' would continue to be a major attribute. Not least because of thdescribed as convenient, big, lumbering and lower middle class. Conveniencee company's commitment to service in the home and making its services easily understood. But a new image had to be created that was dynamic, not lumbering. The perception of being 'lower middle class' was a hangover from its origins, when it sold penny-a-week insurance policies. It was important to project an image that now appealed to all classes, particularly at the higher end of the market.

The perceptions in the City, whose job it is to understand the company and its business, were, not surprisingly closer to the reality. Financial commentators and business analysts understood and accepted that the Prudential was at the leading edge of the financial services revolution. Equally important, they saw the company as having the right management and resources to become a major winner against the competition.

As a result of the research it was concluded that the name 'Prudential' was a major asset which had potential, if properly managed, to retain the goodwill of current customers and the capacity to help attract new ones.

Objectives for the corporate identity programme

To help bring these different audiences' perceptions into line with the reality of the image that the Prudential was trying to project, the following objectives were set for the identity programme:

- To bring together all the companies within the group under a common banner and in a way which was appropriate to the Prudential's development as a major financial services provider – not just an insurance company.
- The new identity had to be flexible enough to be used across all the company's services.
- The new identity, using the Prudential name, should provide an endorsement of the quality of the services provided.
- The new identity had to be distinctive and to differentiate the Prudential from its competitors.

The identity design solution

The design solution to meet these communication objectives 'combined two key strengths – the Prudential's name and what it embodied. As one of the four cardinal virtues – alongside Justice, Fortitude and Temperance – Prudence represented the very principle the Corporation stood for – wise conduct. The design incorporated the 'mirror', representing the ability of the wise man to see himself as he really is, the 'snake' which is an ancient symbol of wisdom and the 'arrow', which hits the target straight on. The aim of the design team was to bring these traditional components of the Prudential's symbol up to date and incorporate them into a new and striking visual identity. The eventual design solution was judged to do exactly this, and managed to convey the spirit they sought (see Figure 2).

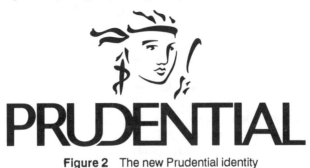

Figure 2   The new Prudential identity

Managing the decision-making process

The concept of the new identity and the form it took did not, however, meet with universal approval from senior management. Vevers suspected, as indeed proved to be the case, that it would be more difficult to sell the concept of the new corporate identity internally than to the outside world.

It was the experience, drive and personality of the senior consultant, Wally Olins, in positioning the programme as a key factor in the future success of the Corporation that eventually won the day. Both Vevers and Olins agreed that they must have the courage of their convictions to prevent the identity being compromised.

Timing was also a crucial factor. The formal decision to proceed with a new identity was taken in June 1986, after several months of discussion with individual board members and senior management. During this period (in anticipation of a positive outcome) Vevers and a small team of public affairs staff worked with the consultants to prepare detailed plans to launch the identity to staff and the public as soon as possible. Within the company, only they knew the nature and scale of the programme that it was intended to launch. Vevers recognized that an element of surprise was crucial – he also recognized that if approval was sought in advance for the 'razzmatazz' that would accompany the launch, it was likely to be turned down as being too radical and extravagant.

The crucial and deciding factor was the gaining of the Chief Executive's support and commitment to the new identity and the plans for its launch. The Chief Executive recognized that the new identity involved more than merely a change in the corporate symbol, it was far more to do with the style in which the company intended to go about its business. It was his singlemindedness which persuaded the rest of the board to go along with the plans.

The decision to launch in September – some three months after the formal decision on the identity and just three weeks before the 'Big Bang' in the City (the date on which the new Financial Services Act deregulating the City came into operation) – was based on a number of considerations. The long-awaited Financial Services Act was in the process of being finalized and there was far greater awareness amongst consumers of the need to deal with solid, reputable and experienced financial advisers. Also the Prudential's competitors were stepping up their marketing activities with the building societies moving into insurance services for the first time in their history.

The speed of execution and a high profile launch were seen as essential prerequisites for success. It was also important to act quickly to prevent some managers from raising renewed doubts about the programme. Vevers appreciated that to try to do all the detailed preparatory work *prior* to the launch would cause unnecessary delay. He decided therefore it should be phased in over a period of time.

The public affairs team identified eight types of application for the identity: stationery, forms, publications, advertising and sponsorship, sales support, signs and the design of premises. Immediately following the launch guidelines were laid down for the way publications would be produced. Guidelines for the other applications came on-stream over the next year. The time-scale for the total programme was estimated at around three years.

The launch of the new identity

The launch of the new identity to the staff and public took place in the third week of September 1986. During that time about a third of the Prudential's UK staff were invited to London to see a special one-hour presentation. Bringing this number of staff to twelve shows was a major undertaking; it involved using planes, trains and coaches to transport staff to the London venue from their places of work and back again within the same day. It was decided that all managers within the company should attend, together with a cross-section of other staff. Some 600 staff attended each presentation. Afterwards, managers were expected to return to their own locations and brief the remaining staff within forty-eight hours.Special materials were prepared for this purpose including videos and speakers' notes and brochures to be handed out to each member of staff.

The London presentations consisted of two parts; a summary by the Chief Executive of the changes taking place in the financial services market-place, and an explanation by the Public Affairs Manager of the rationale behind the new identity. The latest state-of-the art technology was employed for the presentations to create an impactful and motivational occasion for the staff attending. In addition to inviting the press and VIPs to these presentations, Vevers also took the somewhat unusual step of inviting key competitors to attend. Vevers was in little doubt that the identity programme was 80 per cent targeted at staff rather than external audiences. He summed up the objective of the launch for the staff as, '... to have them walk out of these presentations two feet taller than when they went in'.

The implementation of the identity programme

In the spring before the launch a new unit was created in the Public Affairs Department to manage the the implementation of the corporate identity programme. It was headed by Gwes Lloyd, who had many years of experience in different functional areas within the Prudential, and therefore knew how best to go about getting things done within the company. The unit's brief was to make sure the identity programme was introduced throughout the organization in a sensible and methodical manner and that the standards being set were being applied consistently. It was not an easy task; for example, the Prudential's in-house designers resented this new unit 'vetting' their work. Their resistance was eventually overcome after public affairs involved them in developing the new graphic guidelines.

The marketing and sales areas were also somewhat sensitive as traditionally they had commissioned outside design groups for creative support. Again, however, the new unit was able to demonstrate that they could give advice which was valuable and their prime concern was purely to ensure that the principles underlying the identity were being maintained. Over time all materials bearing the corporate identity were routed through this unit as a matter of routine procedure.

The identity programme also resulted in the rebranding of some 450 Prudential Assurance offices throughout the UK and the subsequent rebranding of all branches of the Prudential estate agency chain.

Evolution of the public affairs function

The introduction of the corporate identity programme was the first key task for the public affairs function under Vevers. As such, it achieved two main objectives: first, it helped place public affairs and its head on the 'corporate map'; second, it established a means of exercising quality control over the communications media used by the Corporation. In practice, this meant that Public Affairs could take the opportunity to become involved early on in the creative process when new products, advertising or other communications activities were being planned.

For example, Vevers chairs the committee which co-ordinates all advertising commissioned by the various marketing departments within the Prudential. However, this still fell short of Vevers's ideal for Public Affairs, which would see it manage all corporate advertising. His vision of the role for the Public Affairs Department was for it to become the guardian of the Corporation's image. This would necessitate exercising influence, if not control, over all ways in which the company communicated with both internal and external audiences.

In the past two years the Public Affairs function has expanded and now has responsibility for such areas as community affairs, sponsorship, employee communications, investor relations as well as corporate identity management and media relations. It employs a staff of around thirty people and has a budget in the region of £10 million.

In addition, the department has received external recognition. In 1987 it won the Grayling Award for the best in-house department in a large company and was also awarded the IPR Sword of Excellence for its handling of the internal communications work associated with the launch of the new identity to its 25,000 UK staff. Furthermore, in a recent survey of journalists from the business and financial media, the Prudential's media relations activity was rated very highly.

Nevertheless, the mission of the public affairs function within the Prudential is continuing to evolve in line with the changing requirements of the business and management. Vevers summed up the situation as follows:

We still need to work harder at ensuring that management understand the pivotal role of the function within the organisation. We have moved a long way from the idea of being the 'servant' to the divisions within the Group whose sole responsibility is to passively deliver their message to the outside world. But we must continue to refine and communicate our objectives to ensure the contribution that Public Affairs makes is long-lasting and worthwhile.

Case discussion

This case, together with that of Barnardos, examines the issue of corporate identity change. Although both the Prudential and Barnardos are very different organizations, and operate in entirely different fields, the process and problems involved in changing identity bear many similarities. In both cases the starting point for the development of a new identity was careful research of both external and internal audiences, to establish the perceptions of the organizations and to gain an understanding of the core values and culture of each organization.

In both cases internal audiences were as important if not more important than external audiences to the success of the change of identity, and were the subject of particular attention throughout the whole process. Both organizations had to overcome internal resistance to their respective changes in identity, and both saw the main benefits of a change of identity in terms of bringing the various parts of the respective organizations together through the development of a new and more appropriate visual identity.

In the Prudential's case, its rapid growth into new areas of business, spurred on by the changes in the regulatory environment covering the financial services sector, brought with it a new set of competitors in the form of the banks and building societies, who were themselves investing heavily in positioning themselves to take advantage of the new market opportunities. Prudential's rather old fashioned and staid image was seen as being inappropriate for its move into new and dynamic areas of financial services, in which it would have to compete hard for a market share.

Research revealed that Prudential's main problems were essentially internal. Staff had a low opinion of the company, lacked self-confidence, and did not fully understand the totality of the business. Inevitably, such attitudes were being communicated to customers. The fact that this situation had arisen, illustrates just how difficult it can be for the management, especially during times of considerable change, to appreciate how an organization perceives itself, or what effect employee attitudes towards the organization have on the perception of it held by external audiences.

This case also highlights the importance of recognizing the value of an established name such as Prudential. As with consumer brands, corporate names convey a unique set of values and connotations about an organization to both customers and other audiences. As such, they represent a considerable investment, often made over many years, by their respective owners. As a result, organizations are naturally reluctant to abandon or even see small changes made to their names, and only do so after very careful consideration, and often in the face of considerable internal hostility. Prudential, as with many other organizations, chose to retain its existing name, but to update visual presentation. Although Barnardos opted for an actual change to its name, dropping the 'Dr', it still retained the essential component of its original name.

A key lesson to emerge from both cases is the recognition that a corporate identity consists of far more than merely its visual manifestations. The name and corporate logo act essentially as visual symbols that embody what the organization stands for and provide an instant point of reference for audiences. Although the importance of visual symbols must not be underestimated, it is the underlying way in which an organization performs its activities, and people's experience of them, that ultimately determines its image. As both cases illustrate, the development of a visual identity must start with a clear definition of the core values of the organization to be represented. The process of reducing what may be a complex set of values to a relatively simple but meaningful visual form, then becomes one for expert designers.

Both Prudential and Barnardos experienced problems in gaining universal internal approval for their proposed new identities. As both cases illustrate, the task of selling a new design concept to internal audiences, and gaining their commitment for a new identity, often proves the most difficult part of the process. As in the Prudential's case, the key to successfully overcoming internal resistance to change often lies in winning the support and commitment of the Chief Executive, who can act as a 'concept champion' within the organization. Without such powerful support, the integrity of a design concept may suffer at the hands of opposing factions within an organization, and its power to help bring together disparate parts of an organization may be compromised.

Both the Prudential and the Barnardos cases illustrate the importance of the launch of a new identity as a 'springboard' for change within an organization. The launch event provided, in both cases, the platform for gaining extensive media coverage. However, the launch, in itself, was only the first stage in the process of changing external and internal perceptions of the respective organizations. The implementation of a change of identity, in its fullest sense, cannot take place overnight, although some organizations may choose to implement the change in visual identity literally overnight. The decision as to how the change will be introduced largely depends on practical, logistical and cost factors involved. In Prudential's case it was decided to phase in the changes over a period of between one and three years.

Prudential recognized the importance of ensuring the consistent application of the new identity to all aspects of the organization. The special unit established with the responsibility for vetting all aspects of its communications and assisting the different parts of the organization in the application of the new identity, was clearly necessary given the many applications of the identity and vast array of materials to be handled.

Finally, this case shows how a change in corporate identity can be used to establish a new direction for an organization, and bring about a better understanding within an organization of its position in relation to both the markets in which it operates and society as a whole. In Prudential's case this was reflected in the growing importance attached to its public affairs function.

Student discussion questions and exercises

1. Examine any two organizations which have introduced a change of identity in recent years. Compare and contrast how effectively you feel their approach has proved, and what core values they have sought to communicate about themselves.
2. Consider the advantages and disadvantages of introducing a change of visual corporate identity in a phased manner or as a single 'overnight' programme.
3. For a selected organization, draw up a list of all the ways in which it communicates with its publics, to which a change in identity would have to be applied.

Cutting the gas bill: a public relations campaign for Sheffield Forgemasters Holdings

Tony Peck

Preview

In 1986, Sheffield Forgemasters Holdings, one of the UK's largest producers of steel castings and forgings, faced a difficult battle to try to extract more reasonable terms of trade and pricing policies from British Gas who, at the time, were preparing themselves for privatization.The case illustrates how an effective industrial and political lobbying campaign was mounted which eventually forced concessions from British Gas.

The practice of lobbying whether in a political or industrial context, is often misunderstood. The general public, in particular, tend to associate it primarily with physical protests and demonstrations. Although lobbying can sometimes involve such physical demonstrations of opposition to policies or on issues, it normally involves the careful seeding of information with potentially influential individuals or groups, in order to influence their opinions and gain their support.

Many of the basic principles that apply to political lobbying are equally relevant in an industrial context. The identification of key opinion formers and the timely and skilful presentation of arguments to them, are invariably critical to the success of the campaign. In Forgemasters' case, because of the powerful monopoly position of British Gas, it was vital to enlist the support of other large industrial gas users whose support would be critical to give added credibility to the presentation of Forgemasters' case.

The case also illustrates the value of independent and authoritative opinion in persuading both the media and the public of arguments involved in a case. Forgemasters' commissioning of an independent expert report into British Gas's pricing policies was then used to stimulate a debate in the media over British Gas's policies with respect to its industrial customers. Such reports can often prove a powerful 'public relations' weapon, helping to gain media coverage and ultimately sway public and political opinions.

Forgemasters were able to successfully capitalize on the vulnerability of British Gas (with privatization pending) to the widespread concern over its monopoly position in the supply of gas; a fact that highlights the importance, when conducting a campaign of protest or opposition to an organization's policies, of targeting the campaign, wherever possible, at the most vulnerable point of the organization's defences. Equally, the case illustrates the importance of not only sustaining the arguments within the media, but also, wherever possible, enlarging the platform of support for the case being presented.

Introduction

At the time of writing, a public relations (PR) campaign aimed at trying to achieve less uncompetitive industrial gas prices, initiated by Infopress Ltd in October 1986 on behalf of its client Sheffield Forgemasters Holdings Ltd, has reached a sustained climax – the referral of British Gas (BG) plc, via the Monopolies and Mergers Commission (MMC), to the EC Directorate of Competition.

The outcome of the EC ruling on the issue of whether BG is still continuing to charge unfairly for industrial gas supply is still awaited. Whilst a favourable ruling is important to Sheffield Forgemasters, it is to some extent irrelevant viewed solely from the PR point of view, as either way the opportunities for Infopress to extend the campaign further are excellent due to the sustained and carefully structured PR programme that responded to the events, influenced the creation of further events, and promoted the outcome in favour of the client. Classical PR techniques were employed throughout the campaign – the commissioning of an influential report, extensive media relations, political lobbying and industrial lobbying.

The campaign, in response to the initial contact from its client Forgemasters, succeeded in achieving its principal objective of a lower and somewhat less uncompetitive gas price, but also had the effect of making its client's name, previously virtually unknown, internationally recognized as the voice of industrial gas users, as well as raising their corporate visibility.

Background

Forgemasters, established in 1982, following a merger between divisions of British Steel and Johnson Firth Brown, is the only UK manufacturer of very large (in excess of 100 tonnes) high-performance steel castings and forgings for use in industries including nuclear, oil, power generation, aerospace and defence. The Forgemasters group, consisting of eleven UK subsidiaries, is headed by Chief Executive Phillip Wright, who was appointed in 1985 with the brief to turn the loss-making group into a profitable enterprise. Forgemasters had a history of massive losses in common with most of the steel industry in the early 1980s and Mr Wright was appointed because of his strong track record of turning companies around into profit – notably at Aurora between 1979 and 1985, and previously at Edgar Allen Balfour.

Soon after taking up his post at Forgemasters, Phillip Wright became aware that the company was paying more money than its competitors for gas used in the precision manufacturing and refining processes involved in steel production. In total BG were being paid £6 million a year by Forgemasters (approximately 6 per cent of turnover) who were buying enough gas to heat approximately 25,000 to 30,000 homes a year, equivalent to the size of a small town.

Wright tried to negotiate with BG in the summer of 1986 for a price reduction per gas therm from 32.5p to 28p, arguing that as one of BG's largest industrial customers, he was entitled to a reduced bulk purchase industry rate. This would assist his company's efforts to become profitable and enhance its ability to fight off European competition in the competitive market for specialist forged steel products.

There was in fact a bulk industry rate for gas in existence known as the interruptible supply rate. Mr Wright was aware of this, but was unable to qualify for this rate because Forgemasters had no oil-fired capacity, enabling steel production to continue in the event of a gas cut, or interrupted supply. Forgemasters had even arranged to borrow the money to buy an oil-fired back-up system against the expected savings in gas prices they would make at the lower interrupted supply rate – estimated at between £2 and 3 million in the first twelve months. However, BG would not confirm they would supply gas at the interrupted rate, even if Forgemasters installed the oil-fired back-up system. Nor would they indicate what price they would charge if they did supply interrupted gas at all. The reasons for the lack of co-operation still remain a mystery, but Mr Wright believes they are due to an unwillingness to be deprived of the large amount of revenue from Forgemasters. BG also insisted on monthly payments of approximately £500,000 within three days of invoice, which was a particular drain on Forgemaster's financial resources, given the nature of the specialist steel products industry, which required the costing of products up to two years ahead of delivery. Despite repeated efforts, BG refused to co-operate on either issue.

It was at this point that Mr Wright contacted Infopress with the brief to develop a short term PR campaign to a budget of £10,000, which would establish positive media coverage for Forgemasters, making public its discontent with BG's pricing policies. Infopress had acted for Forgemasters during an earlier sixteen-week strike which had affected the company, helping to establish clear lines of communication between management, the work-force and the local media, that helped ensure the more balanced reporting of the events within the press.

Issues/problems faced

There were issues and problems connected with the pricing policies of BG, providing both ammunition to fire in a PR campaign, but also problems to overcome. The key issues were as follows:

- Britain was the only European country where gas prices had risen steadily over the preceding two years – useful background information for press briefings on behalf of Forgemasters.
- BG had refused to inform Forgemasters what rates it was charging other large gas customers, pleading confidentiality and implying an absence of a proper pricing policy – another positive point for the media.
- The government's privatization plans for BG were imminent. It was clear the government, BG and the advertising industry were all set to make profits from privatization. It was not clear that large BG customers would benefit at all.
- Gas pricing arrangements for major industrial users in the USA, and specifically for one of Forgemasters' major competitors in that country, were far more economical because of the opportunity for users to negotiate on price due to the existence of competitive suppliers – not as was the case in the UK.

Mr Wright and Infopress identified that the two chief problems to be tackled were:

- How to change the operating policy of a major monopoly supplier upon whom one is totally dependent.
- How to influence an organization embarked on the road to privatization, backed by Government, and whose name would soon to be on everyone's lips as a result of the heavily advertised 'Tell Sid' campaign.

Objectives and programme – the first stage

The consultancy began work in October 1986. A concise three-stage PR strategy was recommended within the £10,000 budget. The strategy was designed to create fast influential news, and involved:

- Political lobbying;
- the organization of coverage in a leading national newspaper;
- television representation on a respected current affairs programme.

The backbone of the campaign was to feed off BG's strong media profile from the privatization campaign, and use both the prominence and weaknesses of the privatization issue to build a media platform for Forgemaster's grievances.

As a result of the budget restrictions, Infopress chose not to communicate directly with trade journals and local newspapers, arguing that too early a use of such media would diminish the story's importance for the national press, and pointing out to their client that success with the national media on behalf of Forgemasters would lead to local and trade press coverage at a later stage. A suggestion, in fact, that was borne out in practice.

Political lobbying

Mr Wright had already approached his local MP, Richard Hickmet, prior to contacting Infopress. Mr Wright was advised to continue the dialogue with politicians in order to try to influence opinion in favour of Forgemasters' case. Mr Hickmet had written to the Secretary of State for Industry, Peter Walker, and a copy of the letter was sent by Peter Walker to Sir Denis Rooke, Chairman of BG.

Political lobbying was also used to influence the content and angle of the proposed national newspaper article. Several letters were sent to MPs, explaining Forgemasters case against BG and outlining the PR campaign. A number of luncheons were arranged for MPs, with Mr Wright in attendance,[1] to enable advice to be shared – it was at one of these that it was decided that it would be appropriate and useful to lobby OFGAS, the gas industry's regulatory body.

Involving a national newspaper

Infopress advised Forgemasters that the *Guardian* would be the best newspaper to approach on the issue because of its campaigning style and circulation to a readership most likely to be sympathetic to Forgemasters' claims against BG. John Hooper, a *Guardian* writer, was approached on 3 October, and provided with full information on the background to the Forgemasters–BG issue, and its importance to Forgemasters and British industry generally.

Mr Hooper considered the story both weighty and topical enough to be of interest to *Guardian* readers and the detailed story was published on 9 October. The piece made much impact, covering the points outlined earlier in this case study, and centring on the line of argument that BG's pricing policy was hindering Forgemasters' attempts to remain competitive. Both Phillip Wright and Forgemasters' heavy engineering division Chief Executive, David Fletcher, were quoted, adding emphasis to the story. Because of the impact of the *Guardian* article, which led to follow-up coverage in Sheffield newspapers, and the effectiveness of the political lobbying carried out, BG offered Forgemasters a reduction in price per therm from 32p to 28p for a period of three months. This was viewed by Phillip Wright as progress, and indicative of the influence that can be brought to bear on issues by an effectively planned PR campaign. However, Forgemasters knew it was still paying well over the odds, and viewed the concessionary offer as falling short of what was needed to be competitive against overseas companies.

The recommendation to try to pursue television coverage for Forgemasters on a current affairs programme was the final part of the initial proposed PR strategy. 'World in Action' was targeted because of its reputation for strong investigative journalism, its high and appropriate viewing figures, and advantageous timing – 8.30p.m. The programme producer, David Mills, was contacted. He was already aware of the Forgemasters issue as a result of the *Guardian* story, and expressed interest in meeting Phillip Wright and Infopress to discuss the matter further. A format for a programme was agreed in November 1986 and the consultancy continued to regularly liaise between Msrs Wright and Mills, advising Mr Wright on television presentation skills and assisting Mr Mills's requests for story angle permission and filming sequence clearance. The programme was shown on 8 December, its theme 'Who will benefit from the sale of British Gas?' fitted perfectly with the core theme of the PR programme – to feed off the BG's media profile from the privatization issue. Forgemasters dominated the programme, with quite spectacular film footage of the shop floor with furnaces in the background, from where David Fletcher spoke on the size of Forgemaster's gas bill. He outlined his fears that privatization would lead to an actual increase in gas prices once government control was removed. Phillip Wright also figured prominently, arguing that privatization was a nonsense if it failed to encourage a competitive economic climate.

The programme was well received by a wide range of academics and industrialists, and marked the end of the three-stage PR programme. The programme had successfully enhanced Forgemasters' public image and created awareness of its complaint against BG. This had been achieved with the budget of £10,000.

Objectives and programme – the second stage

On 21 January 1987, BG informed Forgemasters that it was increasing the rate per therm from 28p to 32p, backdated to 1 January. This clearly came as a shock to Forgemasters, who recognized that the campaign against BG's pricing policy would have to be resumed, and also broadened and intensified. Infopress were asked to develop a longer-term PR strategy, with a budget of £50,000 to include fees and operational expenses. The objective was, as with the earlier programme, to establish as much positive media coverage for Forgemasters as possible, highlighting its discontent with BG's pricing policy.

Forgemasters were advised that the issue should be broadened by harnessing the concern that existed amongst other large industrial users of gas, for example, the steel, chemical and engineering industries, together with their representative trade associations. The approach of feeding off the privatization issue was to continue, but it was suggested that an additional 'weapon' was needed to help publicize Forgemasters' arguments on a broad national scale. The programme proposed and accepted by Mr Wright was as follows:

- Commission a report by an independent expert into BG's pricing policies, using the publicity surrounding the report as press relations material for the national media and, if the results were favourable, use the report as a basis for an official complaint to the Office of Fair Trading (OFT).
- Target Forgemasters' grievances against BG pricing policy at the national press, national energy correspondents, energy correspondents of the quality local press, the energy trade press and selective TV and radio programmes, but extend the PR argument to an issue being fought on behalf of other large industrial gas users.
- Continue active political lobbying to influence politicians on behalf of Forgemasters, conveying the message that BG privatization was simply creating a private monopoly from a public monopoly, with no real benefit for British manufacturing companies.
- Broaden the lobbying activity to involve the representative bodies of other large industrial gas users.

The report into gas pricing was considered to be the crux of the PR programme. Reports can be tremendous publicity tools, creating a framework for sustained news, and are often able to influence events on behalf of clients.

The broadening of the media relations programme to energy correspondents at a local press level, and to the energy trade press, was thought necessary to alert industrialists to the Forgemasters' campaign, in order to gain their support. The extra time and expense involved in the extended press relations campaign, together with additional TV current affairs work and radio interviews was met by the increased budget. Additionally the need to 'beef up' over an extended period of time would be necessary to meet with the weekly and monthly publication dates of the journals involved, and was justified by the extended shelf-life of many of the energy trade magazines. Local press would continue to be briefed to ensure they covered the story as a strong local issue.

Political lobbying had proved fruitful during the first stage of the campaign, eliciting advice from politicians that had provided useful tactical information for Mr Wright. Broadening the campaign required the continued use of such techniques. The need to influence representative bodies of other industrial gas users was also an important requirement, as without positive support from other manufacturers Forgemasters would lack sufficient influence to change opinions. All lobbying activity and communications were first cleared with Forgemasters' legal advisers and solicitors, to ensure that neither the consultancy nor Forgemasters issued statements which could be counter-productive or give rise to litigation.

The use of direct mail techniques were considered, but rejected. Targeting BG's senior management or shareholders was considered a waste of time, given the previous experience of negotiations with BG. Sending direct mail to other industrialists was also rejected, as it would not carry the same weight as newspaper editorial comment and would hence not warrant the time and expense involved. Corporate advertising could have been used, but was rejected on expense grounds – a full-page advertisement in the *Daily Telegraph* would have cost £27,500, excluding production costs, and would have less credibility than editorial coverage.

The programme

The four principal activities undertaken, the commissioned report, media relations, political lobbying and industrial lobbying are examined separately, although obviously occurring simultaneously during the campaign period from February 1987 to December 1988.

The report into gas prices and follow-up activities

The first question to be tackled was who should prepare the report. Infopress had previous experience of working with economic specialists and advisory groups, and recommended Graham Bannock and Partners Ltd because of their expertise in the preparation of influential documents covering economic trends. The report written by Professor Victor Morgan was commissioned in March 1987 and published on 20 May. Entitled *Pricing and other policies of British Gas plc in relation to the supply of contract gas*, it was painstakingly researched, and concluded that there was a fundamental inconsistency between BG's previous public statements and those pursued by the company in its dealings with Forgemasters.

The report claimed that BG was distorting competition against public interest, proven by the absence of any apparent relationship between prices charged by BG for contract supplies and its costs. It also said that BG as a monopoly supplier to the British market was unfairly penalizing Forgemasters, a massive user, because it knew that Forgemasters had little bargaining power.

Professor Morgan's report was used throughout the campaign as an effective PR 'weapon'. It provided at times a communications tool to generate media coverage, support for the complaint to the OFT, background information for politicians, and helped rally support from industrial gas users and their representative trade associations. The detail of the report was so supportive of Forgemasters' complaints against BG that the consultancy recommended holding back its issue to the press until the complaint to the OFT had been completed, to avoid dampening the full impact of the news story. Instead a news release, summarizing the report's findings and announcing Forgemasters' intentions to make a complaint to the OFT was issued in advance of the report publication, to create a groundswell of press coverage.

The submission to the OFT was made on 26 May 1987, with Professor Morgan's report attached as the basis of the submission. It argued that BG was using its monopoly position to pursue a gas contract pricing policy discriminating against British industry generally, and Forgemasters in particular. The complaint was upheld on 25 November by Sir Gordon Borrie, Director General of Fair Trading, who referred the case directly to the Monopolies and Mergers Commission (MMC), with an instruction that it should report back within nine months – a timescale fifteen months shorter than a typical MMC referral, which normally takes two years. This news was duly publicized in the sustained media relations programme.

During the period between the complaint to the OFT and its referral to the MMC, the consultancy had been actively pursuing the campaign of media relations, political and industrial lobbying. This activity had stimulated additional complaints to the OFT from other industrial gas users, that played their part in securing the impressive nine-month deadline for an outcome from the MMC. Considerable publicity was achieved during the MMC hearing. Other industrial gas users gave evidence and Infopress assisted in the preparation of case material and presentations.

The MMC report was duly published on 19 October 1988, upholding the complaints by Forgemasters and others. It found extensive discrimination by British Gas in the pricing and supply to contract customers, and made four recommendations to encourage competition in the supply of gas, and restrain BG from discriminatory policies:

- British Gas was to publish a price schedule to supply firm and interruptible gas to contract customers, and not to discriminate in pricing or supply.
- British Gas was not to refuse to supply interruptible gas on the basis of the use made of the gas, or the alternative fuel available.
- British Gas was to publish further information on common carriage terms.
- British Gas must contract for no more than 90 per cent of any new gas fields.

The results confirmed the success of the tactic of commissioning the report. The report, supported by additional activities outlined shortly, was used to the widest possible extent, and played a key role in achieving the objectives set for the PR programme on behalf of Forgemasters, as well as providing the basis for the complaint to the MMC.

Additionally, a complaint was made to the EC Directorate of Competition. This course of action had been advised by the solicitors, Turner Kenneth Brown, if the OFT outcome proved favourable. Such a referral would not affect the PR campaign, and could only further assist the aims of industrial gas users. Planning for this course of action was initiated during 1987, and the complaint was lodged with the Directorate on 27 November, after it was known the complaint to the OFT was to be referred to the MMC.

Media relations

A broad spectrum of media relations activity was undertaken to maximize the coverage for Forgemasters from February 1987. Fifty key energy correspondents on national, trade and local newspapers were identified, and the first press release, headed 'Independent economic report accuses British Gas of anti-competition practices' was issued in April. This outlined the main arguments in Professor Morgan's report in advance of its publication. Substantial coverage in newspapers including the *Independent*, the *Guardian* and *The Times*, who all outlined Forgemasters' plans to take the complaint to the OFT, MMC and eventually the EC. The release was followed up with a second story issued just before the Easter weekend, which also received strong coverage.

A monitoring company was appointed to record transcripts of TV and radio coverage for Forgemasters, and both Phillip Wright and David Fletcher undertook media presentation skills training. In late April the Channel 4 Business Programme confirmed that they would run a major story on Forgemasters complaint to the OFT. This was shown in June and Phillip Wright was introduced as 'the most prominent of the complainants against British Gas'. More than two minutes of positive coverage for Forgemasters followed, with Mr Wright explaining the basis of the submission to the OFT and MMC.

On 21 June Forgemasters and Mr Wright were covered on the Money Programme, and on 9 July a further news story was prepared, whilst background briefings were given for *The Financial Times*, *The Times*, the *Guardian* and the *Independent*, before its distribution to wider media, increasing its chance of coverage by the nationals.

Further TV coverage was achieved for Forgemasters on 27 July, on the BBC2 'Newsnight' programme, as a result of written communication from Infopress, enclosing Professor Morgan's report. Using by now a well-established theme, the programme was gently critical of privatization generally, arguing that turning public utilities, such as gas, into private monopolies was likely to increase instances of poor service and overcharging. Phillip Wright was introduced in a brief interview as 'leading the attack on British Gas'. In August the consultancy started discussions with the *Observer*, feeding them information on behalf of Forgemasters and other companies considering complaints to the OFT. This resulted in a major story on Sunday, 16 August.[2]

It was also decided to try to use the Annual General Meeting (AGM) of British Gas on 27 August to promote the Forgemasters' case to the media. This was BG's first AGM and therefore was a national news item in its own right. Due to the success of the industrial lobbying activities, the consultancy advised that a person of repute and standing be nominated as a Director of BG before the AGM, to represent industrial gas users. The decision was taken to ask Sir Ian Macgregor, for several reasons, not least his strong media profile and his experience as Chairman of British Steel. Mr Macgregor's acceptance was promoted in a press release, and British Gas chose to circulate all its shareholders informing them of this move before the AGM. As a result of this activity, the AGM on 27 August was widely publicized, and attended by national journalists, who gave their subsequent news stories a slant towards the case of Forgemasters and the industrial gas users.

By September 1987 five national newspapers had devoted 'leader' columns in support of the Forgemasters campaign and against British Gas. The frequency of national press coverage had promoted other large gas users to write to the letters columns in support of Forgemasters, and creating more publicity. A further press release was issued on 25 November to maintain the pressure. There was also exclusive coverage on radio programmes such as 'The World at One' and 'File on Four', as well as on local radio and television.

The outcome of the MMC report in October was promoted and achieved strong coverage on behalf of Forgemasters. The story appeared in nine daily national newspapers, with additional leader comment in *The Financial Times* on 20 October. By December a news story was issued saying the Forgemasters was considering suing BG for overcharging, due to the abuse of its monopoly. This also received broad national coverage, and a writ was issued in January 1989.

Political lobbying

The consultancy advised that Richard Hickmet, MP and barrister, should be retained by Forgemasters as an adviser, due to his knowledge of the issues. Mr Hickmet continued to provide strategic advice throughout the campaign and, kept fully briefed of the PR programme at all stages, he corresponded with BG on behalf of Forgemasters. In terms of direct communication with MPs, the consultancy identified eighty MPs, broadly interested in energy, and mailed them with extracts from Professor Morgan's report.[3] Copies of the report were also sent to the Secretary of State for Energy, Cecil Parkinson, and his parliamentary private secretary.

In July Mr Wright wrote to Mr Parkinson, and informed him of the decision to call for Mr Macgregor's appointment to the board of BG. Mr Parkinson was also asked for a meeting to discuss Forgemasters' complaint and share knowledge in respect of the legislation that might be needed to force BG to act more responsibly.

Communication was also established in July with John Wybrow MP, who was at that time a special adviser at Downing Street. He was informed of the decision to proceed with the complaint against BG to the EC.

Face to face briefing of MPs was initiated at the end of July. The consultancy wrote to Tony Blair MP, who had contributed measurably to the public debate on BG pricing policy, enclosing background detail on the Forgemasters case, and Richard Hickmet was consulted on the format and timing of a major briefing to be staged at the end of October. This event, held at the Wig and Pen Club on 28 October, was attended by eight senior back-bench MPs and the consultancy briefed them on the Forgemasters' issues. Recommendations for political action were mooted – questions in the House, a private members bill, and a meeting with Cecil Parkinson to discuss general privatization issues. In November further contact was made with Cecil Parkinson, via MPs that had attended the briefing luncheon. The consultancy arranged a further event for MPs at Lockets on 16 November. This was attended by fourteen MPs, including Michael Fallon, Cecil Parkinson's private secretary. As before, concise briefing notes were provided by the consultancy for MPs. By the end of November it was clear that Mr Parkinson could see the strengths of the Forgemasters case.

On 13 April 1988 a House of Commons dinner was organized, hosted by Phillip Wright, to update a group of sixteen MPs on Forgemasters developments relating to the referral. Yet a further event was held at Lockets on 22 December, attended by twenty-two MPs, to canvass proposals for future pricing policies a couple of months after the publication of the MMC report. James McKinnon, Director General of OFGAS, was invited to be the guest speaker. By 21 December Sir Denis Rooke had at last agreed to meet Phillip Wright to discuss Forgemasters long-standing grievances.

Industrial lobbying

The involvement of the key industrial gas users and their representative bodies was crucial to the success of the PR programme. BISPA, the British Independent Steel Producers' Association, were liaised with regularly, and their production of gas price surveys on behalf of the industry were influential in increasing the pressure being exerted against BG. BISPA also gave evidence to the MMC. Infopress had established a positive link with the OFGAS press office at the outset of the campaign, and ensured a stream of regular communication reached James McKinnon, the Director General of OFGAS, throughout the campaign, ensuring that OFGAS were always aware of the views of industrial gas users.

The British Management Data Foundation (BMDF) were also contacted regularly, and a meeting to discuss BG energy prices, with specific reference to Forgemasters, was held on 14 May 1987. At this meeting BMDF declared its support for the Forgemasters campaign, and stated that its many influential members would do likewise.

The report prepared by Professor Morgan was circulated with press material to all interested parties.[4] In June, a meeting at the OFT was attended by directors of the Gas Consumers Council (GCC), with the Forgemasters complaint on the agenda.

Communication continued with industrial gas users throughout 1987, support and sympathy being shown by organizations and industrial bodies including Tunnel Refineries, Euramax Aluminium Ltd, Rigid Paper Products, The National Farmers Union, The Chemical Industries Association and Union Carbide. The Chemical Industries Association submitted details of their own members' gas prices to the OFT in June. In August BISPA recommended that its members write to the OFT about their experiences with gas prices. During the same month, all industrial organizations supportive of Forgemasters who were shareholders in BG were contacted by the consultancy, and requested to support the nomination of Mr Macgregor as a non-executive director of the BG board. In September seven key industrial companies were contacted by the consultancy, with a request to write to *The Times* in support of a letter published from Phillip Wright. Meanwhile, additional companies added their support to the campaign, by providing gas price details for Mr Wright.

Industrial lobbying also resulted in the sending of many independent letters to Sir Denis Rooke, expressing their dissatisfaction, whilst the Forgemasters submission to the EC Directorate of Competition was followed up with correspondence to industrial companies where supporting evidence was requested to back the case, should the need arise.

In November 1988 the consultancy advised that a letter be sent to sympathetic industrial gas users from Phillip Wright, asking them to monitor the press closely and write to OFGAS Director General James McKinnon, if they felt that he was not acting strongly enough on their behalf.

The results

BG, at the time of writing, is faced with claims for damages and overcharging from Forgemasters. If the claims are successful, BG will be landed with a substantial bill. It claimed in evidence to the MMC that, if forced to reduce prices, its profits would be cut in the first year by as much as £240 million. The outcome of the submission to the EC Directorate of Competition is still awaited. Until the outcome, BG is under consistent pressure from industrial gas users, and its pricing policies are obviously being implemented delicately.

The Forgemasters PR campaign achieved a number of positive results. As well as meeting the original PR objective – to establish positive media coverage for Forgemasters making public its discontent with BG's pricing policies – it also succeeded in creating the following benchmarks:

- A reduction in gas therm prices.
- A positive OFT referral.
- A positive MMC report, achieved within short time-scales, requesting specific action from BG to benefit industrial gas users.
- A submission to the EC Directorate of Competition, the outcome of which is still awaited.

- Widespread support and endorsement for Forgemasters' case amongst MPs.
- Widespread support and recognition for Forgemasters amongst industrial gas users, many of whom made their own OFT, MMC and EC submissions, adding further weight to Forgemasters' reputation as a prime mover behind industrial complaints concerning BG's pricing policy.
- A strong media profile for Forgemasters, which it continues to retain, hitherto being only really known to its customers.

In terms of press coverage, 266 cuttings about Forgemasters were generated between April 1987 and January 1989, covering national, trade and local press (see Plate 1). Eighty of these – well over 25 per cent – were from national daily or Sunday newspapers. Additionally, there were sixty-six general industry cuttings, prompted by the PR campaign on the outcome of the MMC report.

Television and radio coverage were also impressive, with sixty-eight mentions for Forgemasters being monitored on local and national television and radio. National television accounted for twenty mentions, including coverage on ITV's 'News at Ten', and BBC's 'Six O'Clock News'. Additionally, there were twenty industry-related items, six of which were on national television.

The PR campaign on behalf of Forgemasters was successful in managing to influence the course of events for two main reasons. First, the implications of Forgemasters' grievances were of national importance to many industries, creating a unified PR campaign, not a competitive one. And second, the techniques used by Infopress, were designed to complement each other, creating sustained opportunities to influence the respective bodies at national level.

Case discussion

The public relations programme on behalf of Sheffield Forgemasters illustrates the problems faced in campaigning on behalf of any individual company or organization against a large state-controlled or quasi-state-controlled body or, for that matter, against government itself. The individual company, almost irrespective of its size, often finds it very difficult to make headway without appealing to an issue capable of mobilizing national, or at least wider industry, support. The success of the Forgemasters' campaign hinged on the ability to show that its complaints against British Gas were not peculiar to Forgemasters alone, but affected many other industrial gas users. It was vital to build up a groundswell of support amongst industry for the campaign in order to exert sufficient pressure on both BG and the government.

Undoubtedly Forgemasters were helped in their cause by the sensitivity of the public and media to the operation of BG, in light of its pending privatization. However, whilst the privatization issue helped to maintain the interest in the Forgemasters case, it still required a carefully orchestrated public rela-

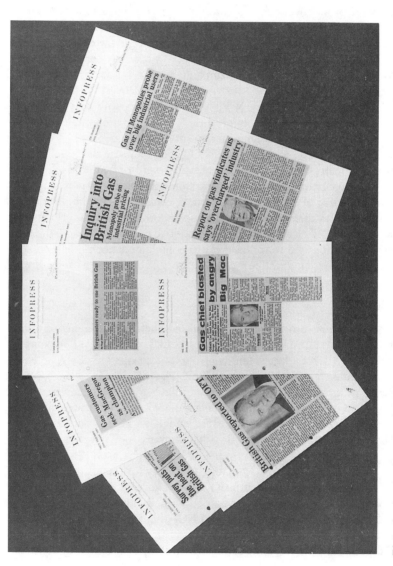

Plate 1 A selection of national press cuttings achieved for Forgemasters during the public relations campaign
Note: the photograph shows cuttings from *The Times, The Financial Times, Daily Telegraph, Guardian, Sunday Times, Independent* and the *Sun*.

tions programme to bring about the desired response from BG itself, as well as from the appropriate government ministeries. In seeking concessions from such a powerful national utility as BG, with monopoly control over the supply of gas, it was inevitable that Forgemasters would encounter staunch opposition from BG, who clearly recognized that loss of the case would potentially open the flood gates to similar claims from other large-scale gas users. In addition, BG no doubt appreciated that the loss of the case would also prove damaging to their image with government, with the public in general, as well as with the City. In the latter case, an enforced reduction in gas prices would ultimately affect the attractiveness of investment in the shares when the company was a privatized company (it is notable that in their defence to the MMC, BG cited the potential loss of revenues if forced to reduce their prices). The Infopress campaign recognized that it would be insufficient to base the attack purely on BG's natural monopoly of gas supply, and a sustained programme, based on independent and authoritative evidence of unfair practice, was essential.

The success of the programme depended on the marshalling of opposition on a number of fronts – at industry level, within government, and within the media – in order to maintain the pressure on BG and keep the issue on the boil. The programme succeeded, through the use of a series of complementary activities, in bringing together a coalition of interested parties, united in their common opposition to BG's policies with respect to industrial gas users. Faced with such a climate of opposition, it was believed that BG would be forced to make concessions and, ultimately, would be faced with the prospect of substantial damages being awarded against them. The presentation of the arguments as one of interest to many industries and of national importance, rather than simply to Forgemasters themselves, helped ensure the support of MPs and the media in particular.

The case illustrates just how powerful an influence for change the media can prove. The extensive coverage gained in both the press and on broadcast media could not be ignored by government, industry and, of course, BG themselves. The commissioning of an independent and authoritative report into BG's pricing policy was clearly a crucial step, providing as it did independent corroboration of Forgemasters' allegations against BG, as well as providing a further valuable source of media coverage. Although the issue was potentially very newsworthy in itself, it was still important to carefully manage the presentation of the arguments to the media, in order to maximize the coverage and impact of the story. It was also critical that the arguments presented should carry weight with key opinion leaders, particularly at government level. The media relations programme also had to maintain interest in the story throughout the time taken to complete the investigation; first by OFT, and subsequently following the referral to the MMC. This was helped by involving wider industry and political support through lobbying, which provided the basis for a sustained flow of stories to the media, whilst maintaining the prominent position of Forgemasters at the head of the campaign.

The success in sustaining the media relations programme also illustrates the importance of developing media opportunities, wherever possible, on a multi-media basis. By exploiting opportunities for both press and television coverage, the campaign was able build up a momentum of interest in the issue that helped ensure it remained high on the news agenda. As the case demonstrates, the media often 'feed off one another' for news stories. A story appearing first in the regional or national press, or on regional or national television or radio, may be picked up by other media (albeit, using a different approach to the story) if it is considered to be sufficiently newsworthy to warrant further coverage. The practitioner's skill often lies in the way he presents the story to the different media, in order to stimulate multiple interest in it.

Ultimately the success of the programme depended on the outcome of the MMC ruling and the still-awaited response from the EC Directorate of Competition. The submission to the latter highlights the importance of recognizing the increasing importance of the European dimension in the affairs of industry in the United Kingdom. An effective public relations programme can often play a vital role in helping to determine the agenda for consideration by public or government bodies both in the UK and in Europe, and can create the climate of support in which a favourable outcome is more likely to result.

A number of valuable lessons can be identified as emerging from this case. First, it illustrates the importance of careful analysis to identify the main vulnerabilities of any organization against whom a campaign is to be launched. The aim of this analysis should be to find a platform on which to base the campaign, and should take account of the potential sources of support and the likely responses of the media. Second, where possible a campaign should seek to build a strategic alliance of interests. This may help in stimulating media interest in the issue, and may be newsworthy in itself. Third, independent and authoritative opinion can prove valuable in gaining credibility and support for a case being put forward. Where this takes the form of an 'expert' report or investigation, it can be a valuable means of gaining media coverage in itself. Fourth, the success of any campaign ultimately hinges on the presentation of the facts of the case rather than sentiment. Public relations can help ensure that the relevant facts receive the widest possible exposure and are clearly understood by the decision-making bodies and those able to influence them. Fifth, where it is intended to win political support for an issue, it is important to target those potentially sympathetic MPs at an early stage, and to ensure they are fully briefed on the facts and the timetable involved. Finally, in developing a media relations programme to support a campaign it is important to recognize the value of careful targeting of potentially sympathetic journalists (in both the press or broadcast media), and tailoring the presentation of the issues to the particular editorial interests of the respective media. Media relations programmes should also, where appropriate, seek to exploit opportunities for mutually supportive coverage in both the press and in the broadcast media. However, it is also important to recognize the relative strengths of the different media.

Broadcast media coverage is particularly valuable in widening awareness of an issue, whereas the press is usually able to provide more in-depth analysis of an issue. As a result, the press often plays a more important role in stimulating initial debate, and setting the agenda for discussion about an issue, than the broadcast media. Hence, both press and broadcast media coverage can play important and mutually supportive roles in any campaign, albeit often in different ways and at different stages in the development of the arguments.

The approach taken in campaigning on behalf of Forgemasters can be usefully compared with the following case which examines the campaign carried out to try to influence changes in the copyright laws on behalf of photographers.

Student discussion questions and exercises

1. Consider how important you feel the privatization issue was to the success of the campaign on behalf of Forgemasters, and which elements of the programme were most influential in its ultimate success.
2. Consider how a campaign on behalf of domestic consumer users of gas against a tariff increase would be mounted, and how it would differ from the Forgemasters case.
3. Prepare a news release that might have been sent out on behalf of Forgemasters on completion of Professor Morgan's report into BG's pricing policies. Also draw up a media distribution list for the release.

Notes

1. The invitations to attend the luncheons were made to MPs who were members of the All-Party Energy Committee.
2. In negotiating broadcast media coverage the lead-times involved ranged from two to three weeks in the case of 'World in Action', to the day before the broadcast in the case of 'Newsnight'. Press coverage lead-times ranged from approximately seven days in the case of major feature articles in the *Observer* and *Guardian*, to the day or evening before for news coverage in the national daily newspapers.
3. Dodd's Parliamentary Companion provided a valuable source of reference in identifying potentially sympathetic MPs.
4. The companies targeted for industrial lobbying were identified through trade associations, by recommendation from existing supporters of the campaign, and by reference to contributors to the letters columns of the newspapers.

Case four

Changing legislation: a lobbying project on behalf of photographers

Neville Wade

Preview

Political lobbying has recently come under increasing scrutiny and has been the subject of considerable criticism both in the UK and particularly in the United States, where political lobbyists exist in large numbers and are an accepted part of the political scene. In the UK, although political lobbying has always existed, it has tended to develop in a different manner from the US, and the professional lobbyists have not so far really become a 'fact of political life'. Lobbying has, however, become a far more professional activity and an increasing number of specialist parliamentary public relation consultants have begun to offer their services to a wide range of organizations.

This trend can be attributed to a number of factors. First, the increasingly active role of government in legislating on issues affecting all aspects of our lives has focused attention on the need to take a closer interest in the proposed policies of the government of the day. This has been reflected in the increased media coverage and editorial comment devoted to parliamentary affairs. Second, organizations have perhaps more than ever come to recognize the often crucial influence of government policies on the economy, industry and society as a whole, and the need to try to influence these policies. Third, organizations have realized the increasing need to take account of European legislation, emanating from Brussels, but which has equal effect throughout all EEC countries. Finally, the media undoubtedly have played a significant part in increasing the awareness and interest in parliamentary affairs and are themselves often the chief advocates of parliamentary lobbying activity. The progress towards the single internal market in Europe in 1992 will undoubtedly only serve to fuel the interest in lobbying activity, both on an individual country and on a European basis.

Many political lobbying campaigns are unsuccessful simply because they fail to recognize the crucial importance of timing in the parliamentary process. Sometimes a campaign of active lobbying is only begun when the legislation in question has already reached its first or even final reading stage in the Houses of Parliament, by which time it is often far too late to effect any significant changes to it. To be effective it is vital that key politicians and civil servants are targeted at an early stage in the passage of any proposed legislation and ideally before it has been fully drafted.

This case examines a lobbying campaign carried out on behalf of photographers in the UK, and illustrates some of the more important principles of effective political lobbying. Photographers in the UK have for many years complained that the Laws on Copyright left them disadvantaged compared to other artists and authors, with respect to the protection afforded to their work. In 1981 the Committee on Photographic Copyright (CPC) was formed to represent the interests of photographers. The CPC campaigned actively to obtain fairer treatment for all photographers and, in particular, sought to influence the new government Bill on copyright intended to replace the Copyright Act of 1956. The success of their campaign was due to the marshalling of influential support among MPs and the Lords through the effective and timely presentation of their case.

Background

The Committee on Photographic Copyright was formed in 1981 to represent the interests of photographers in the debate on new copyright legislation. It was particularly concerned with the protection of photographers' work, which under the existing law was treated quite differently from artistic work. It was formed by representatives of nine professional groups, who recognized that the copyright issue affected all photographers, including the amateur snapshooter. The member organizations represented on the CPC included: The Association of Fashion, Advertising and Editorial Photographers, The Institute of Journalists, The National Union of Journalists, and The Royal Photographic Society. Amongst these organizations there already existed a considerable manpower resource which, between them, possessed a considerable number of influential contacts. However, this resource required to be effectively organized and co-ordinated in order to bring influence to bear on the legislative process. Having presented evidence to the Whitford Committee, which had been formed to consider the government's 1981 Green Paper, the committee made proposals for certain clauses to be included in the new Bill which would replace the existing Copyright Act of 1956. This bill, which was redesignated a Lords Bill, received its first reading in the House of Lords on 28 October 1987, and in November, in readiness for its second reading, the CPC decided to enlist the professional advice on its lobbying activity from Welbeck.

Issues and objectives

The chief issue of concern to photographers was to safeguard their rights over their 'intellectual property' and to give them 'moral' rights over the use of their work. To this end it was deemed necessary to try to secure amendments to some of the clauses in the proposed Bill on Copyright, Designs and Patents. The most important amendments sought were:

- Duration of Copyright: The Bill proposed to maintain the copyright period (fifty years from the author's death) for *all* creative work *except* for photographers when the fifty-year term would merely date from the year the photograph was taken.
- First ownership of copyright: The Bill sought to withhold copyright from employed photographers and to deny all photographers the moral right not to have their work subjected to unjustified modification.
- Fair Dealing: The Bill would have excluded review and news reporting from the clause on Fair Dealing.

The strategy

The CPC had considerable knowledge of the law on photographic copyright and firm ideas on how the Bill should be amended to give more protection to photographers. However CPC required advice on how best to present their case during the Bill's passage through both Houses of Parliament. It was agreed that Welbeck should take on a counselling role, employing its Public Affairs advisers, one of whom was a Peer and another being an MP, whilst CPC themselves would prepare various documents in support of their arguments with Welbeck's guidance. In light of the budget constraints, this would allow the work to be carried out in a cost-effective manner.

Implementation

Influencing the House of Lords

CPC were advised that securing press publicity would be important as a support for briefing material that was to be sent to elected peers. A press release was prepared and issued, while at the same time a letter was sent to *The Times* from the Chairman of CPC. The latter appeared on 12 November, the day of the second reading debate in the House of Lords.

Before the debate a list of the peers intending to speak was obtained. Unlike the House of Commons, members of the House of Lords who wish to speak in a debate notify the Whip's Office, and a list is prepared from which the order of speaking is agreed between the parties. This list is openly available, a fact that is perhaps not widely known. CPC were advised on the preparation of the briefing letter, which was dispatched to selected peers at their home addresses, an essential requirement for House of Lords mailings.[1] The mailing list was prepared by research through directories and appropriate reference materials.

Following the debate, the Hansard report was marked-up by Welbeck to identify those peers who had spoken in support of the photographer's case and they were approached on an individual basis by members of CPC. The Bill had been introduced by Lord Young, the Secretary of State for Trade and Industry. The Committee stage, before the whole House lasted for seven Sitting days (30 November to 31 January), and was delegated to Lord Beaverbrook, a junior minister with whom CPC kept in touch by correspondence. During this period draft amendments were prepared by CPC and mailed to sympathetic peers along with a short covering letter. It was agreed that the strategy was not to press for amendments if the government would agree to reconsider them. Lord Beaverbrook sensed that the feeling of the House was sympathetic to the photographer's case, and promised to reconsider certain amendments including the most important amendment concerning the duration of copyright for photographs. Government decided to have an unusually long interval before the report stage, to allow the department time to redraft parts of the Bill.[2] The Report stage commenced on 23 February and took a further three days, during which time the government introduced their own amendment to give photographers the same copyright protection as other artistic works (fifty years from the death of the photographer rather than from when the photograph was taken). This concession secured for CPC its most important objective before the Bill left the House of Lords.

Throughout the period whilst the Bill was before the House of Lords, Welbeck continued to monitor the Hansard reports for CPC, supplying copies of the amendments as soon as they became available. In addition, contact was constantly maintained with the government and opposition Whip's Offices and the business managers of the House on the issues of timing and other details concerning the Bill, and with peers of all parties (including the frontbench spokesman) on further points arising out of debates.

Influencing the House of Commons

The Bill's second reading in the House of Commons took place on 28 April 1988, a full month after it had left the Lords. This interval enabled contact to be made with MPs known to be interested in photography[3] and a letter from CPC was sent to them to explain the special need of photographers for additional protection of their works. The letters seem to have had the desired effect of bringing CPC's concerns to the attention of a number of MPs, with the result that the problems of photographers were pointed out during the debate by four back-bench MPs from both sides of the House. At Welbeck's suggestion one senior Conservative MP wrote to the minister (John Butcher) urging him to reconsider certain of the Bill's provisions.

The Bill was considered by Standing Committee E, which sat on eighteen occasions from 10 May to 21 June, usually twice daily on Tuesdays and Thursdays. The Standing Committee was comprised twenty-one MPs, and a list of these was obtained shortly after the Committee of Selection had decided on their membership and the date for the first sitting.[4] CPC was thus able to send detailed briefs with proposed draft amendments to all its members before the Committee held its first meeting. CPC were supplied with the details of the Committee Room and time of sittings, with advice on how to gain access to the meetings. It is not generally known that such meetings are in fact open to the public. Throughout the sitting of the Committee Welbeck supplied CPC with daily copies of any official reports and printed amendments and counselled as to what further action to take.

During the Committee stage of the Bill, government ministers took the line that sufficient concession had already been given in the House of Lords and declined to accept further amendments concerning photographs. Hence it was necessary for CPC to step up their campaign and the minister was asked to meet a delegation from CPC. Welbeck advised that this should be headed by a Conservative MP, who was identified as a keen photographer. At the same time written and oral representations were organized by photographers to their respective MPs in their constituencies. As a result of this sustained pressure, government agreed eventually to amend the Bill to exclude photography from the clause on Fair Dealing. This strengthened photographers' copyright on the use of their creative material, particularly in the case of press reporting. This important amendment was achieved during the Final Report stage and amounted to a major breakthrough.

Results

As a result of the sustained campaign the Bill was amended in several ways during its passage through Parliament, giving photographers far more adequate copyright protection than when the Bill was originally drafted. The Bill received Royal Assent on 15 November, and The Copyright, Designs and Patents Act thus passed on to the Statute book in a form that largely met with CPC's objectives. In total seven of the eighteen amendments suggested by CPC were incorporated in the Bill, these included the following crucial issues:

- A photograph is now defined as an 'artistic work'.
- The 'author' of a photograph is defined as the person who creates it.
- The first owner of copyright in a commissioned photograph is the author.
- Photographic works are excluded from the Fair Dealing Clauses.
- Photographs have the same copyright protection as the authors of other artistic works (fifty years from death).
- Photographers have the moral right to be identified as the author, and the right to object to derogatory treatment of the work.
- Photographers have the right to protect their work from being distorted or

mutilated (that is, through cropping of the photograph).

Summary

There are no formal rules about the timing and best approach to lobbying – every case is different. As far as the CPC were concerned, it was a process that started with evidence given to the Whitford Committee which reviewed the initial Green Paper. If some very urgent piece of legislation is required, as for example with the legislation on security and anti-terrorist measures that was rushed through Parliament following a spate of terrorist incidents, the business managers can impose a short timetable. Increasingly, with particularly complex Bills, the trend has been to introduce the Bill in the House of Lords, as was the case with the Copyright Bill. There are generally less time pressures on the Lords, and with complex subjects greater consideration can be given to the proposed legislation. Additionally, peers are not professional parliamentarians, often having specialist knowledge from their own backgrounds, and represent a broad cross-section of experiences, which can be brought to bear on any subject. New life peers are occasionally created, not necessarily as an honour, but to introduce new expertise into the House. An obvious further example of Bills that are normally given special consideration by the Lords are those affecting the legal profession, on which Law Lords and other peers will debate the issues.

Staff commitment

The involvement by Welbeck in advising and supporting CPC involved at various times, a director, a senior executive (the consultancy's public affairs adviser), a retained outside consultant, plus secretarial assistance.

Case discussion

A number of valuable lessons can be learnt from this case concerning campaigns designed to influence government; perhaps the most important being the need for lobbyists to understand the nature of the parliamentary process and the timing involved. In trying to influence the nature of legislation under consideration, it is crucial to begin the process at as early a stage as possible, and particularly before legislation reaches the Report stage of its passage through Parliament. It is important to assess the strength of sentiment in Parliament regarding a piece of legislation, and to set realistic goals for the campaign. It may be unrealistic to expect a Bill to be actually radically changed or even stopped from becoming law, particularly when the government of the day has a large majority, as at present. However, it may be possible to secure significant amendments to the legislation, as in the case of the Copyright Bill, if

Parliament can be shown that it will have perhaps unforeseen, and potentially detrimental, consequences for some sections of the public. In lobbying for a change to legislation it may be necessary to accept a compromise solution, as government will rarely be prepared to accept the defeat of legislation they have introduced.

The essence of effective lobbying lies in marshalling support amongst sympathetic MPs and peers, and particularly from those members of either House whose opinion is respected, and who carry some influence amongst their fellow members. The starting point for any lobbying campaign must be detailed research to identify facts that can help sway opinion and win over support. These must be carefully presented to MPs or peers, and particularly those who it can be expected will be most sympathetic to the cause. Knowledge of the working of Parliament allows a lobbyist to identify the members appointed to sit on committees considering any particular Bill. Detailed research can also allow those members most likely to sympathetic to the lobbying campaign to be identified. Often the mystique surrounding the working of the parliamentary system is exaggerated; however, ignorance of the system can severely handicap or destroy attempts to mount a successful lobbying campaign.

In the case of CPC, a coalition of groups with a vested interest in seeing changes in the legislation provided a useful resource of contacts, and demonstrated that opposition to the Bill as framed came from a broad range of interests. This was was clearly a significant factor in persuading peers and MPs to re-examine the legislation and accept the need for some amendments.

Student discussion questions and exercises

1. Consider why is it important to understand the timetable for the passage of legislation through the Houses of Parliament? Identify the sources of information from which the timetable for any Bill can be obtained.
2. Identify the different forms that a lobbying campaign can take and consider the role that the public relations practitioner can play in trying to ensure its success.
3. Select a recent piece of legislation that has passed through Parliament and compile a list of MPs or peers who would have been targeted in any lobbying campaign that might have been mounted with respect to the interests of any of the parties involved.

Notes

1. Unlike the House of Commons, it is not permitted to mail peers in bulk as the facilities do not exist, and organizations making this error will be told to collect their mail.
2. In the case of the Copyright Bill there was no time constraint and, unusually, the business managers in Parliament allowed a lot of time for its passage, recognizing the complexity of the Bill. In particular, an exceptional if not unprecedented period was

allowed between the Committee and Report stages so that the DTI could reconsider major elements and table its own draft amendments as government changes.

3. CPC were able in this case to advise which Members of Parliament were keen photographers. Had this not been the case then it would have had to be laboriously researched in reference books such as *Dodd's Parliamentary Companion* and *Who's Who*.

4. The Committee of Selection chooses members to sit on Standing Committees and the list is published.

Environmental crisis: CFCs and the ozone layer – how ICI handled a major public issue

Philip Dewhurst

Preview

The management of an organization's responses to 'issues' arising in its operating and external environments have, in recent years, assumed increasing importance for organizations throughout the world. Social and political pressures have forced organizations to recognize their obligations to act in a more socially responsible manner, and to respond to environmental sensitivities in the societies in which they operate. No organization can, nowadays, afford to ignore the potential concerns of the general public, consumers, the media and governments, over their operating policies.

One of the chief issues of concern in many parts of the world during the 1980s has been that of environmental protection. During 1988 public concern over this issue reached a peak in the UK, fuelled both by a series of man-made disasters, and the 'crusading' stance taken on the issue by the media. What is perhaps most remarkable about this issue is the speed with which it captured the public's attention, influencing not only public attitudes but also purchasing behaviour.

The 'Green Movement' emerged during the late 1980s as a major force for change in societies throughout the world. While public concern over the environmental protection issue is not entirely new, it has escalated at an unprecedented rate in recent years. A major force behind this growing concern over the state of the environment, has been the increasing number of highly active environmental pressure groups, often highly skilled in developing their media relations, who have undoubtedly been instrumental in raising both media and public interest in this issue.

The environmental issue that perhaps attracted more attention than any other in 1988, concerned chlorofluorocarbons (CFCs) – chemicals, which some scientists claimed were causing serious damage to the earth's ozone layer. This issue was seized upon by the media, and concern over CFCs rapidly assumed crisis proportions for those organizations associated with their use or production. ICI, as Europe's largest producer of CFCs, naturally found itself in the 'firing line', and was forced to respond to the concerns being voiced.

Not only was its position with regard to CFC production threatened, but its world-wide reputation as a responsible, socially-concerned organization was placed in jeopardy.

The regular monitoring of emerging issues has become an important part of the external or public affairs function of many large organizations. The early identification of important issues of increasing public concern can alert an organization as to their likely implications for its operations and allow it to take action to avoid the issue escalating into one of crisis proportions. However, it is perhaps impossible always to forecast how some issues may develop, or, as in the case of CFCs, how quickly an issue may become one of widespread concern. ICI was faced with a potential crisis, largely as a result of the speed with which the issue came to the boil.

This case examines how ICI sought to respond to this crisis. It illustrates the principle that, in today's society, organizations must not only *recognize* their obligation to act in a socially responsible manner, but they must be *seen* to do so if they wish to maintain the goodwill of the public, governments and customers alike. ICI's ability to emerge from the crisis in a positive light was due to the goodwill it had built up over the years, together with its frank and open handling of the situation. This helped ICI to eventually reposition itself as leader in the race to find more 'environmentally-friendly' substitutes for CFCs.

Background

The 1980s witnessed a heightening of public interest and concern over the issue of environmental protection in the UK as well as throughout the world. By the late 1980s, 'green issues', as they came to be called, had moved to the top of both the public and political agendas. Concern over the environment reached a high point in the UK in 1988. Mrs Thatcher, the Prime Minister, was reported as having turned 'green', placing environmental issues among those of chief concern to her government. A series of 'headline-catching' incidents occurred which served to further heighten public awareness and concern over environmental issues. These included: the death of North Sea seals as a result of a mysterious virus; a chemical waste ship turned away from British shores; and the Alaskan oil spillage. These all contributed to the growing public concern at this time over the damage being done to the environment.

During 1988 public and media attention began to focus particularly on the damage being caused to the earth's ozone layer, which shields the earth from the harmful effects of the sun. A group of man-made chemicals called chlorofluorocarbons, used in aerosols, refrigerators, air-conditioners and plastic foams were implicated as the principal culprits.

Some leading scientists had been aware of the potential damage being caused to the earth's ozone layer for some time. However, little conclusive evidence as to the cause of the problem had been established. The hypothesis, that chlorine released by CFCs in the upper atmosphere could cause depletion of the ozone layer, had first been put forward in 1974. Work by individual research teams to clarify the situation had continued, and fluorocarbon producers had, by the late 1980s, donated some US $23 million to scientific research into the subject. In 1987 the National Aeronautics and Space Administration (NASA) had brought together key scientific groups to examine the available evidence on ozone fluctuations. This group, the Ozone Trends Panel, set out to produce some conclusive evidence on ozone depletion as an international response to research by individual project teams which had pointed to localized incidences of 'holes' in the ozone layer. The evidence was somewhat contradictory, with satellite measurement showing a significant depletion in the ozone layer, whereas ground based measurements indicated no such trend. The Panel's initial studies concluded that there was a small but significant downtrend in the global ozone layer over the previous seventeen years as measured by ground-based instruments, but that the sharper depletion indicated by satellite measurements had been inaccurate.

In September 1987 the Montreal Protocol was signed. This represented the first international agreement to protect the global environment. The Protocol was intended to control the future use and production of CFCs throughout the world. Its initial stipulations were for a 50 per cent cut in CFC consumption (from existing 1986 levels) by 1988, with some short-term exemptions for developing countries.

A key objective of the Protocol is to provide a means of reviewing further scientific, economic and technical evidence that might come to light, which may require the Protocol itself to be revised.

ICI fully supported the Protocol and called for a review of control measures that would take account of the latest scientific research. ICI recognized the desirability of totally phasing out CFCs, but only when industry had successfully developed ozone-benign alternatives capable of replacing CFCs in their many essential uses.

The issue

Sterling was retained by ICI, Europe's biggest CFC producer, to handle an issue which threatened the company's public reputation world-wide. ICI's management recognized the need to take action on the question of CFCs and to look for a safe alternative. However, they also recognized that their total replacement would take time and involve considerable investment. It was crucial to ensure that this fact was understood by both the public and government, and that ICI was shown to be acting in a responsible manner and making every effort to find a safe alternative to CFCs.

ICI had already begun to take steps to reduce its reliance on CFCs and was at the forefront of research into safer alternatives. However, this fact was not generally appreciated and was largely cloaked by the popular outcry against all producers of environmentally-damaging products.

ICI employees and management in particular, were coming under increasing pressure from the media, environmental pressure groups and politicians to respond to concern over the ozone issue. It was recognized that action was necessary to explain the issues to them fully and assist them to handle these enquiries.

The PR objectives

The primary objectives, as defined by Sterling, were:

- To project ICI as an environmentally-sensitive company, committed to protecting the ozone layer by developing 'environmentally-friendly' alternatives to CFCs.
- To explain to government and other key opinion formers that CFCs have many vital uses for which no safe, ozone-benign substitutes currently exist – therefore ICI needs time to develop alternatives before phasing out CFCs.
- To defend and enhance ICI's opportunities to market alternatives to CFCs.

The strategy

It must be appreciated that Sterling was appointed after the issue had escalated to crisis proportions. The consultancy were forced to develop a strategy in the face of a massive consumer backlash, orchestrated by pressure groups such as Friends of the Earth and fuelled by a stream of new scientific findings against CFCs.

Sterling's first strategic priority was to develop a positive position for ICI and to use this to build communications with key audiences. Once agreed, this position would enable ICI to translate negative enquiries into positive opportunities.

The second priority was to research and identify influential and potentially sympathetic audiences, for example:

- ICI constituency MPs and those who were keen supporters of the chemical industry.
- Science, industry and technology journalists, as opposed to the environmental correspondents who were covering the issue.

Research

Amidst the massive media coverage afforded to the issue at the time, it was far from clear just how extensive and deep felt was the concern over the ozone issue. Clearly, it was important to try to establish the real extent of opposition to CFCs, and the depth of understanding of their effect on the ozone layer amongst the public, the media and politicians. In order to gauge this more accurately, research was carried out at two levels:

- A MORI survey of public attitudes to CFCs to track changes in consumer awareness.
- Desk research to determine both knowledge of the issue and perception of ICI among key journalists and MPs.

This revealed that consumer awareness had developed considerably, but that opinion formers and journalists had little knowledge of ICI's position and a poor perception of the company's communications in this context. As a result of the research it was possible to begin to develop an appropriate form of response for ICI.

The preparatory phase

Because of the complexity of the ozone issue in scientific, environmental and business terms, a series of authoritative position papers and a 'Q & A' issue guide for ICI employees were prepared. This was intended to provide ICI staff with the means of responding to questions on the issue of ICI's position with regard to CFCs, and to ensure a consistent and positive message was put across – in effect, to ensure the company was speaking with 'one voice'.

A new 'issue management group' was established, comprising senior ICI and Sterling personnel, which met monthly so that ICI's position could be updated as new scientific findings emerged. A team of ICI business managers and scientists were trained in media technique and the position papers crystallized into a series of sharp, positive messages which stressed:

- ICI's enormous R & D commitment to develop alternatives to CFCs.
- ICI's support for the Montreal Protocol, the international agreement to limit CFC production.
- The vital uses of CFCs – to refrigerate foods and medical supplies and to provide air-conditioning in hospitals, offices and vehicles.

The audiences

Although the ozone issue was of potential interest to the public as a whole, it was clear that certain groups were taking the lead on the issue and warranted special attention. Sterling prioritized a series of key audiences, including:

- government and parliament;
- journalists, particularly those specializing in environmental issues;

- the scientific community;
- ICI employees and customers.

These groups were identified as key opinion formers on the issue, from whom the public as a whole were looking for a lead on the question of the damage to the ozone layer from CFCs.

The programme

Because of the speed at which the communication battle was being lost by ICI, swift action to influence all target audiences was essential, and a programme aimed at the key target groups was initiated:

The media

One-to-one briefings for key national newspaper journalists were held in London. These resulted in the first positive coverage of ICI's efforts to replace CFCs. Following intensive media training, ICI spokesmen were offered to broadcast outlets, again with positive results. Twelve influential science/chemical journalists were flown to Runcorn to see ICI's R&D programme for the first time. This resulted in a five page *New Scientist* feature and wide coverage in the scientific and technical press. Scientific journalists, rather than those directly concerned with environmental issues were targeted, as it was believed they would prove more sympathetic and be prepared to present a more objective and balanced view of the situation. Feature material was also offered to leading regional dailies, again with excellent results.

As the company's spokesmen gained in confidence and ability, more TV and radio appearances followed, both on national and regional programmes. TV crews from several networks also visited ICI's laboratories. The resulting coverage presented ICI with a series of opportunities to demonstrate the efforts it was making to address the CFC problem, and to position itself at the forefront of the battle to combat the damage being caused to the ozone layer.

Parliamentary

Presentations were made to interested groups of MPs and peers in the Palace of Westminster. These attracted great interest and support from targeted MPs and peers. Site visits were arranged to ICI's Runcorn laboratories for MPs, including the then Industry Minister, Robert Atkins. These enabled ICI to demonstrate at first hand how work was progressing on finding a substitute for CFCs. This activity led to positive references to ICI by members of all parties in parliamentary debates, including congratulatory words from the Prime Minister herself. Personal briefings were given to the Secretaries of State for Environment and Trade and Industry, plus their senior civil servants.

The intense level of interest in the issue, created largely by media coverage and pressure group activity, had forced environmental issues to the forefront of the political agenda. Hence, there was considerable interest amongst politicians of all parties in attending briefing sessions and site visits. As a result of this programme of briefings and site visits perceptions amongst politicians, of ICI's position in relation to the ozone issue, changed markedly. From being associated solely with the causes of ozone damage early in the year, ICI was now seen to be at the forefront of international efforts to solve the problem.

Employees

It was recognized at an early stage that internal audiences were a vital target of the programme. In an organization as large as ICI its employees formed a crucial communication channel within their local communities and media. It was also important that managers, and other staff likely to be exposed to media questioning, should be prepared to respond in an appropriate and consistent manner. Internal communication activity fell into three phases:

- Encouraging senior management to be open, responsive and supportive in handling the issue.
- Reassuring employees that ICI was defending its business, protecting jobs and striving to become a major player in the marketing of new, ozone-benign chemicals.
- Ensuring that ICI's work-force understood both the issue and ICI's position.

Sterling contributed to a presentation to ICI's main board which called for the unprecedented announcement of major new plant investment prior to official financial sanction, as a public demonstration of commitment. This announcement proved to be one of the turning points in public and media perception. To keep employees fully informed, newsletters, a video, and regular articles in the various ICI house magazines were produced. The high level of interest in these materials amongst employees was indicative of how important the issue of CFCs was seen to be for the company as a whole.

Customers

The concern about CFCs, being expressed in the media by pressure groups and politicians, was clearly causing ICI's customers considerable disquiet. Some customers were clearly worried that ICI would cease to supply them with CFCs, vital to their production processes, and for which there was currently no obvious short-term alternative. A number of leading retailers were already responding to consumer pressures, and refusing to stock products containing CFCs. ICI, as Europe's leading producer of CFCs, had to respond to these concerns. The aim of the customer communication programme was to:

- Reassure customers in user industries that ICI would continue to supply the product and was leading the race to develop alternatives.
- Keep ICI positioned as a major international supplier committed to developing ozone-benign chemicals.
- Help customers answer questions from their business contacts about the issue.

An extensive programme was set up to achieve these aims. This involved the use of newsletters, trade press coverage, seminars for ICI sales representatives, and a customer video.

In industrial markets ICI's sales representatives bore the brunt of customer anxieties about CFCs. It was crucial that they were fully briefed as to the company's policy, and armed with the facts as to what progress was being made to find a safe alternative to CFCs. However, it was not possible to rely on sales representatives to act as the sole channel of communication with all categories of industrial customers, and hence, trade press and general media coverage had to be relied upon to keep customers appraised of developments, and efforts being made by ICI on the question of CFCs. Many customers were clearly confused about the whole issue of CFCs and their impact on the ozone layer. The production of a video and newsletters explaining the facts clearly and concisely provided a valuable means of educating customers about the issues, while at the same time positioning ICI as a responsible organization acting in the interests of both its customers and the public.

Public speaking

ICI spokesmen were encouraged to take up speaking opportunities at major conferences on the ozone issue, including an international Friends of the Earth/Consumers Association conference in London in November 1988. This reflected the new 'open' stance taken by the company, and positioned ICI as a responsible, environmentally-concerned organization. The willingness of ICI to participate in conferences at which they could face a quite hostile reception, helped overcome any accusations that they might be attempting to avoid the issues and cover up their role as a major producer of CFCs.

The results

At the end of the year's programme, most media coverage of ICI's role in the CFC issue was positive. Desk research indicated high levels of familiarity and favourability towards ICI's position with regard to the CFC issue among all key journalists identified and targeted at the outset of the programme. ICI was positioned in the eyes of journalists, government, and parliamentarians as a company genuinely committed to overcoming the ozone crisis by the application of enormous scientific resources.

Positive coverage was achieved in all target media, including all quality dailies, the *Sunday Times* magazine, technical, scientific and regional press (see Plate 2). Numerous broadcast items including TV news coverage, a 'Newsnight' feature, and a lengthy interview on 'Woman's Hour' presented the story to mass audiences.

The Chairman of ICI was invited to address the Prime Minister's International Conference 'Saving The Ozone Layer', at which ICI's video 'The CFC Challenge' was shown. In Parliament, ICI achieved wide support from MPs and peers of all parties, including some former critics. The effect of the parliamentary programme is best summed up by this December 1988 Hansard extract:

Mr Shersby: Will (the Prime Minister) express the thanks of the House to ICI for its investment of £30 million in two chemical plants to produce ecologically safe substitutes for chlorofluorocarbons?

The Prime Minister: I gladly join him in congratulating ICI on the great initiative it has undertaken to find those solvents.

Among customers ICI is now recognized as an international leader in the race to develop ozone-benign substitutes for CFCs. The potential threat of the loss of trade from customers, worried that ICI might suddenly withdraw from the supply of CFCs was avoided, and existing and potential customers recognized that ICI were likely to be at the forefront of any developments to develop a safe alternative to CFCs.

Budget

The total budget for the programme was £150,000, which included £100,000 consultancy fees.

Case discussion

This case demonstrates how an issue can rapidly escalate into a potentially serious crisis for an organization, particularly once an issue comes under the 'media spotlight'. The CFC issue illustrates just how powerful an influence the media can be on public opinions, once they have chosen to put an issue at the forefront of the news agenda. It also demonstrates the need for organizations to recognize the increased skills of many well-organized pressure groups, in mounting well-orchestrated media relations programmes that aim to mobilize support for their cause.

Although concern over the damage to the environment caused by industry has persisted in one form or another for many years, it is the increased

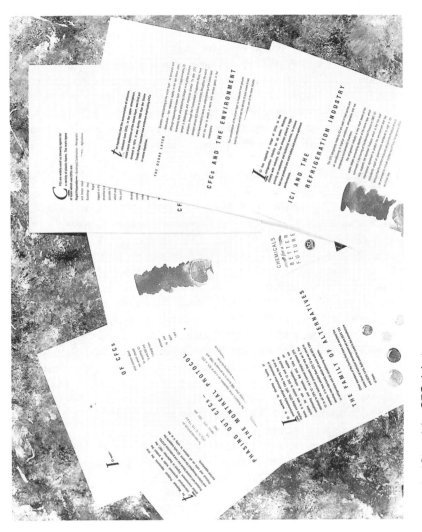

Plate 2 ICI and the CFC debate

scientific knowledge of the damaging effects of pollution and industrial waste and its dissemination through the media, that has provided the stimulus to rising public concern throughout the world.

Despite the fact that ICI, one of the world's largest chemical companies, has largely maintained a good track record in terms of accepting its responsibility to safeguard the environment, the very nature and extent of its business often makes it potentially vulnerable to attacks, whenever concern is raised over the impact of man-made chemicals on the environment. As Europe's leading producer of CFCs, it could not avoid being singled out as a major contributor to the potential damage to the ozone layer, attributed to the use of these chemicals. Although the evidence as to the effects of CFCs was at this time far from conclusive, to simply deny that they were a potential hazard or to plead the case for a lack of a feasible alternative to the use of CFCs would have undoubtedly proved counter-productive.

ICI were faced with a difficult problem. On the one hand, as Europe's major producer of CFCs, they could not afford to cease production and needed to reassure customers of its intention not to withdraw from supply. On the other hand, increasing world-wide concern over the effects of CFCs threatened to damage their reputation and the important goodwill that the company had established over the years throughout the many countries in which it operated.

ICI recognized the need to tackle the problem head-on and not to 'shirk' the issue. It was crucial for the company to be seen to accept its responsibility to avoid contributing further to potential damage to the environment. Although ICI were aware of the potential concerns over the effects of CFCs and had committed considerable resources to the research into safer alternative chemicals, this was clearly not appreciated by the media and the public at large. ICI's problems were not helped by the technical complexity of the issue and the lack of clear understanding of the importance of CFCs by the majority of the media, politicians and the public. There was clearly a need to 'educate' these audiences and to try to put the issues into perspective.

In any organization, and particularly one of the size and diversity of ICI, internal audiences are often important opinion influencers and often form an important channel of communication with the outside world. It was therefore important for ICI to explain the company's position with regard to CFCs to its employees, and to ensure that key spokesmen were armed with the facts necessary to respond to the inevitable pressures they would face from the media, politicians and pressure groups.

Ideally, the management of an organization's response to external issues, requires organizations to identify their potential impact at an early stage, and to take appropriate action before a particular issue escalates to one of crisis proportions. In the case of the CFC issue, although ICI had been monitoring the scientific findings, and were actively participating in research into their effects on the ozone layer, they were unprepared for the speed with which the issue developed into one of widespread public concern. This was undoubtedly fuelled by an upsurge in media coverage of the issue, both in the broadcast and printed media. The majority of this media coverage tended to be of an alarmist nature, and generally failed to portray a more balanced view of the problem, particularly in the popular tabloid press. To a large extent, this reflected the lack of thorough understanding of the problem, which was not helped by the controversial nature of the scientific evidence itself.

As a result, the public relations programme on behalf of ICI became one of 'crisis management'. Although it was crucial for ICI to respond quickly to events, the complexity of the subject, coupled with the limited understanding of the issues by many of the audiences involved, made it more difficult to develop a straightforward and effective communication programme. These problems were exacerbated by the potential conflicting interests of customer audiences and those of audiences concerned only with the environmental effects of CFCs.

The objectives set for the programme sought essentially to address this conflict of interests. The overall aim was to identify a positive position for ICI that encompassed both its commercial obligations to customers and the need to maintain customer goodwill, while at the same time projecting ICI as a company which recognized its obligations to developing environmentally-safer products.

The case illustrates the importance, at the outset of any public relations programme, of clarifying, through research, both the level of understanding of issues among the audiences, as well as identifying those key audiences likely to be most sympathetic to the organization's cause. Given the particular complexity of the CFC issue, and the extensive and sometimes misleading media coverage devoted to it, it was vital for ICI to identify potentially sympathetic and better informed audiences who could be persuaded of the justification of ICI's position with respect to CFCs. These audiences, once persuaded of the ICI case, could act as opinion influencers with wider less well-informed audiences. Research was also necessary to establish how far journalists and the public understood ICI's position with respect to CFCs, or appreciated the efforts ICI were making to identify less harmful alternatives.

The communication programme had to be conducted on two levels. First, it was necessary to develop a communication programme capable of simplifying the complex scientific information into a relatively digestible and easily understood form for the less sophisticated, non-scientific audiences. Second, it was important to present the arguments to the scientific world and better informed audiences, and in particularly, the scientific media. The latter would tend to influence coverage given to the issue in the general media.

The task of reaching the scientific community, as with many other specialist audiences, can often be effectively carried out through relatively few key influential publications. In this case it was possible to target a dozen key science/chemical journalists and yet still reach the majority of the scientific and more technically-minded audiences. The newsworthiness of the issue, coupled with the importance of ICI within the chemical industry, helped ensure a good response from journalists and widespread coverage of the story.

As far as political audiences were concerned, personal presentations and briefings for MPs were crucial to put across the arguments and explain ICI's position at first hand. ICI's importance to the British economy, allied to the high profile that the Prime Minister herself had placed on the environmental issue, helped ensure widespread cross-party interest in attending these briefing sessions.

The communication programme for internal and customer audiences also involved personal presentations by management and sales representatives. However, the size of these audiences required personal presentations to be augmented by the use of internal and external newsletters and specialist trade press. The use, wherever possible, of communication channels over which ICI could exert control, allowed the company to present its case without the risk of any distortion by media sources.

As was suggested in the Forgemasters case, it is important to recognize the interplay between press and the broadcast media in influencing the formation of public opinion on an issue. The press tends to play a more important role during the earlier stages in which issues are still developing and emerging, and when opinion leaders are themselves emerging and looking for more detailed information and analysis of the respective issues. The broadcast media tends to be more important once an issue has actually emerged and established itself in the public's 'news domain', serving to broaden awareness of the issues and provide a 'live' platform for opposing experts to discuss the issues.

The process by which issues emerge into the public domain and eventually become a matter of general public concern and opinion is still far from fully understood. However, both the printed and broadcast media do undoubtedly play an important role in this process. The strength of the press lies in its ability to provide more extensive and detailed coverage of an issue that can be studied and digested by interested parties at their leisure. The broadcast media, although often more limited in the time it devotes to an issue, provides the means of building awareness of the issue more rapidly among mass audiences than perhaps is possible through the printed medium alone. The chief strength of the broadcast media tends to lie in its ability to help crystallize the arguments involved, and in shaping the public's attitudes towards them.

In order to help change perceptions of ICI's position with regard to CFCs and combat some of the misunderstandings surrounding the issue, it was important to exploit opportunities for company spokesmen to address the concerns raised in person. The participation of spokesmen on a number of television and radio programmes provided the chance for them to explain

ICI's position to mass audiences, and to correct many of the misunderstandings that had been spread during earlier coverage of the issue in the media. Because of the crisis nature of the situation, it was particularly important to make use of broadcast media opportunities in order to put across the company's case as quickly as possible, to as wide an audience as possible.

The use of personal communications, involving presentations to specialist audiences, that proved successful with parliamentary audiences, was also employed to address other specialist audiences. Company spokesmen were encouraged to participate in various conferences concerned with environmental issues. This provided the opportunity to explain the company's position to these more specialist audiences and to try to assuage some of their concerns over the future use of CFCs.

In summary, the success of the public relations programme lay in the application of the principles of careful targeting of key audiences and the selection of communication activities based on sound initial research. In handling the communication of the complex and technical issues involved with CFCs, it was crucial to tailor the messages to the specific needs of the different audiences. In particular, the complexities of the subject had to be simplified to allow them to be understood by mass audiences.

By convincing the company of the need to adopt a proactive and open approach to communicating its position with respect to the CFC issue, it was possible to restore public and parliamentary trust in the company's handling of the problem. This openness in its relations with the media, particularly by providing more ready access to company spokesmen, undoubtedly helped to secure a more balanced reporting of the issues. This, in turn, helped the company to secure a media platform from which it could combat some of the earlier more damaging allegations levelled against it.

Perhaps the most important lesson to emerge from this case, is the importance of maintaining a regular monitoring of issues likely to have an impact on any particular organization. Often it may be difficult to predict with accuracy just how rapidly an issue can emerge and escalate into one of serious dimension. However, by instigating a thorough monitoring of all media coverage of issues relevant to the field in which an organization operates, as well as keeping a watching brief on the literature and discussions emerging from relevant pressure groups, or in parliamentary circles, an organization may be better prepared to respond to issues as they begin to emerge.

Student discussion questions and exercises

1. Discuss how far do you feel ICI's position as one of the world's leading chemical companies either helped or exacerbated its problems in combating the CFC issue.

2. Examine the development of any recent issue of general public concern,

identifying both the extent and nature of the coverage afforded to it in the press and broadcast media. Consider what difference, if any, existed in the treatment of the story in the press and broadcast media and try to identify how each type of media contributed to the development of the issue.

3. For any selected organization, construct a list of sources of information that would form the basis for an issues monitoring programme for the organization.

Lilley plc: a crisis in confidence

Anne Dunne

Preview

The 1980s have seen a wave of both large- and small-scale takeovers and mergers of companies throughout the world. Sometimes these have taken place with the full agreement of both the companies involved. However, in many cases the take-over bids have been bitterly opposed by the targeted companies, and have resulted in a drawn out 'battle' for control of the company under attack. The late 1980s have also witnessed quite radical changes in structure, operation, and control of international financial markets, which have had significant implications both for the timing and content of any information that a company releases. Access to potentially sensitive company information has become an increasingly important issue and very rigid rules about the disclosure of information have been imposed by stock exchanges throughout the world. Although companies whose shares are quoted on the Stock Exchange must guard against breaching these rigid codes of practice that surround the disclosure of price-sensitive information, they are often under intense pressure from the media and other audiences to disclose more information about their operations. As a result, the professional communicator, faced with the demand for information from the media, must be constantly aware of the implications of any information released while, at the same time, trying to avoid fuelling potentially damaging speculation that might arise from a refusal to respond to journalists' enquiries. As all quoted companies are only too well aware, rumour and speculation are the 'lifeblood' of the City.

The maintenance of effective communication with the financial media and the City are never more important than when a company is faced with a 'financial crisis'. A financial crisis can take many forms – a take-over bid, the resignation of key company directors, the loss of key contracts, the default by large debtors, to name but a few. Ultimately such crises can threaten the very survival of an organization. A financial crisis often leads to a serious loss of investor confidence in the company which is invariably reflected in a deterioration in the company's share price – a 'barometer' of the City's confidence in that company. Of course, a deterioration in its share price may leave a company vulnerable to a hostile take-over bid. One of the key responsibilities of the public relations function in a quoted company is, therefore, to maintain investor and City confidence in that company and to try to ensure its share price reflects its true worth.

The Lilley Group, a leading Scottish construction company, experienced a serious financial crisis as a result of a disastrous loss of profits, which threatened the collapse of the company. However, the resulting loss of confidence in the company among City audiences, was due, not so much to the decline in its trading position (although obviously a major factor), as to its management's failure to communicate effectively the nature of the company's problems. Almost too late, a crisis team took over the running of the company and began the difficult tasks of restoring both its financial fortunes and rebuilding investor trust and confidence in the company. This case illustrates the value of having a well-rehearsed crisis management plan in place, and the problems that can result when this has been overlooked. Lilley's management committed perhaps the 'cardinal sin' as far as the City is concerned – failing to keep them well informed about its problems. The City dislikes nothing more than shock news, and Lilley almost paid the inevitable price for its failure to communicate. It was only through the efforts of an experienced rescue management team, who fully understood the importance of communication with the City and the financial media, that Lilley was eventually able to emerge from its crisis and begin the road to recovery.

Background

Lilley plc is a large construction group, based in Glasgow. The group's activities cover the full spectrum of construction work, from general building contracting, through house-building and property development, to advanced geotechnical engineering.

Lilley was founded in 1918 as a family building firm and has grown to become a major business force, regarded internationally for its expertise, particularly in the areas of tunnelling and piling. After going public in the mid1960s, the group began to grow by acquisition as well as organically, and bought up other companies whose activities were complementary to Lilley's own. These included an American tunnelling company, Harrison Western.

The crisis

Strong and solid as the group may have appeared to shareholders in 1986, things had begun to go badly wrong for the company in its overseas activities, particularly in the operations of the US tunnelling subsidiary, Harrison Western. In May of that year Lilley had returned an operating profit of over £9 millions. Shares were peaking at 91p. Lilley employed 7,000 people world-wide, with a further estimated 10,000 in related jobs.

The first the outside world knew of any problems was the gradual descent of the share price during the late summer, ahead of the announcement of the half year or interim results due in October. The City, embroiled in the first throes of deregulation, perhaps paid less attention than usual to the problems of this medium-sized Scottish company in the unfashionable construction sector. Alarm bells began to ring, however when Lilley's management announced a week's delay in the publication of the interim results.

A Scottish newspaper, the *Glasgow Herald*, was most persistent in its attempts to elicit comment on the day the delay was announced. The management, however, appeared to be sitting in a marathon board meeting and refused to make any further statement. The *Herald*, keen to flesh out the story, fell back on comments by those who knew the group well enough to make an educated guess at what was happening. An article ran the next morning on the front page under the headline 'FEARS OF SCOT'S BUILDING GROUP COLLAPSE'.

The share price collapsed to 15p and was suspended by the Stock Exchange at Lilley's request. Management's response to the story was to threaten the newspaper with legal action, but public interest was now so great that they were forced to make an immediate statement.

Lilley revealed a dramatic loss of £24m for the half year. A syndicate of banks was prepared to give support to the beleaguered group, but only on the condition that fresh management was found to lead the group out of its troubled position.

Two months later Lewis Robertson, a renowned company 'trouble-shooter' with a string of successful rescues to his credit, was appointed as Lilley's new Chairman, and Joe Barber, released early from his commitments at Christian Salvesen, was appointed as Chief Executive.

They began the task of reconstruction in early December. It soon became apparent that the full extent of the problems had not been revealed by the previous management. The company was facing greater financial difficulties than had been anticipated. Additional problems in a contract in Algeria threatened to bring Lilley once more close to disaster.

The crisis in confidence

In addition to the severe financial problems which had to be resolved, the new management was facing an additional substantial crisis on their own doorstep, a crisis in confidence.

The investor community, clients, suppliers, subcontractors, employees and the local Scottish business community had all lost faith in the group, and were not convinced that Lilley could survive its own problems. At the time the rescue management stepped in, confidence could not have been lower.

Many of the company's long-standing shareholders had sold their stock in the group in the face of what seemed to be an inevitable crash. Faced with little information at the time of the crash, the once staunch investor support for the group evaporated. Speculators replaced the old long-term shareholders, snapping up the shares, gambling on the chance that the group might recover or be taken over. With the share price at one point as low a 15p, it seemed a risk worth taking. Many of these new shareholders were private investors, individuals taking a small stake. Thus the number of shareholders increased dramatically from around 3,000 to 10,000. Most 'City' analysts had yet to be convinced that the group was able to survive.

Clients, too, were reluctant to invest in Lilley. This was felt particularly in the central belt of Scotland, Lilley's homeland, where the problems of the group had remained on the media agenda long after the national and specialist financial press had moved on to newer and bigger stories.

Lilley's two subsidiaries which operated in this area had long been used to regularly securing contracts worth several millions and, typically, having a duration of a year or more. The supply of this type of contract dried up, and the subsidiaries were only able to win smaller packages of work with greatly reduced execution times. Much as the group's established customers hoped for Lilley's survival, they could not afford to place long-term, high value work, with a contractor who might not survive to complete its execution. Suppliers and subcontractors, too, were understandably wary of the giving the company credit.

The employees of the group were perhaps those who had most to feel aggrieved about. Most of the staff, even at quite a senior level, had known nothing of the problems of the company until they read about them in the newspapers. Even after the crisis was common knowledge, the board made little effort to offer explanations or comfort to those whose livelihood depended on the group's survival. Lilley were recognized internationally as a company possessing unique technical skills. Many of the highly qualified staff who made up this skill resource were actively seeking employment elsewhere. Others, pessimistic about their future prospects, were losing motivation. The company's most valuable resource was being eroded.

Thus, in addition to the enormous financial crisis, the rescue management also had urgent and severe communication problems to resolve. Without solid and supportive shareholder base, without good quality contracts to work on, without the confidence of the business community, Lilley had little hope of outliving its problems.

The need for effective communication

All commercial organizations are vulnerable to sudden and unpredictable crises, whether financial difficulties, take-over, sabotage or natural disaster.

Many companies, aware of the value of their reputation, formulate contingency plans or defence strategies against a time when disaster may strike and the support, understanding and empathy of the organization's publics becomes essential for survival.

Lilley, however, had no such defence strategy in place when its financial problems were revealed to an astonished public. Not only had they not prepared for this eventuality, but the subsequent actions of the Lilley board, in failing totally to respond to the natural interest of the press, served to alienate further the media, particularly in Scotland, as well as City analysts. The following comment in *The Times* perhaps summarizes the lack of sensitivity of the board at this time, in its handling of the media:

> Surprisingly, the directors of the group were unprepared to talk to City commentators yesterday, saying they had been advised that the statement provided adequate information.
>
> (Alexandra Jackson, *The Times*, 28 October 1986)

Lilley were fortunate in the appointment of their new Chairman, Lewis Robertson. He had considerable experience of companies in this kind of trouble, and recognized the importance of public relations in engendering confidence in crucial areas.

As he stated at the time: 'Confidence is essentially what the whole thing is about.... The x-factor that has to be embodied and has to be projected, is confidence.'

In recognizing the importance of the role of communications in fostering confidence, he was prepared to put public relations high on the agenda of the rescue team.

Lewis Robertson's presence at Lilley's helm was in itself a boost to confidence in the group, but in order to weather the early, critical months of the rescue, a definite and more positive message about the future had to be drummed home to each of Lilley's audiences. They had to hear that the problems, if not solved, were being brought under much greater control – Lilley were in business, and intended to stay in business. It was imperative that word got round quickly enough to bring the back as near a normal operational position as possible, at least in its UK operations, so that the attention of the rescue management could focus on the problems overseas.

Lilley had not in the past set up effective channels of communication through which to communicate the message of confidence. The channels now had to be established, and within a very short space of time. The full year preliminary results, were due to be announced in early May, and the management expected to announce further heavy losses.

Three key areas were identified where public relations was a major problem:

- Relations with shareholders and the financial community.

- Relations with the business community, particularly in Scotland.
- Relations with its employees.

In addition, it was, of course, necessary to try to restore Lilley's relations with the media and particularly the financial press.

As a result, the rescue management decided to appoint a financial PR consultancy, a Scottish consultancy and an in-house PRO. Despite heavy commitments elsewhere, the Chairman and Chief Executive maintained a personal involvement in the development of PR strategies and the execution of the PR programmes.

Financial PR

In choosing an agency to handle financial PR, Lewis Robertson fell back on a consultancy who had advised him in other company rescues and whose counsel he valued. Streets Communications began their task immediately on the appointment of the rescue team. Their objectives were:

- to establish contact with key financial journalists and City analysts;
- to establish the rescue team in the minds of these opinion formers;
- to win a fair hearing for Lilley;
- to maintain a flow of information about the progress of the rescue.

The strategy

They identified key financial journalists in the national daily and Sunday press, visited them and, where necessary, arranged introductions with the new Lilley management. Many senior journalists, of course, already knew Lewis Robertson of old. They also established an 'A' team of City analysts[1] who might be most influential on Lilley's behalf. These key individuals were kept informed of the progress of the rescue, and at various stages they were contacted to monitor how their opinions of the company's status were changing.

Although the previous management had predicted a return to profits for the second half of the financial year, by early December it was already clear that this was by no means the case.

Aware that the City hates nothing more than a surprise, the new team recognized that although building up confidence in the group was the prime objective, it was vital that clear signals of the continuing difficulties must be given. This dual message, on the one hand of confidence in the group's ability to survive, and on the other, a warning not to place expectations too high in the short term, had to be put across in a very short space of time. The rescue management had joined Lilley on 12 December and the full year results were due on 12 May. Given that for a month before the preliminary announcement the company would be prevented from virtually any comment, and in any event, would have to be sensitive about commenting on their financial position in general, this left a scant four months to cultivate a mood of tolerance and support.

The rules of the Stock Exchange lay down very strict guidelines on the communication of any potentially sensitive information that might affect the share price. Naturally any information relating to its results, particularly given the situation in which Lilley found itself, would have to be very carefully vetted before its release. Whenever there was any question over the possible interpretation of the significance of an item of information, it was first filed with the Stock Exchange.[2]

The first cautionary signal that all was not well with Lilley was the announcement of the intention to sell five of the groups successful UK subsidiaries which were not considered essential to the core construction activities of the group. The second signal came one month before the announcement of the results, when the chairman called an extraordinary general meeting to ask shareholders for an extension of borrowing powers. Although intended to signal to investors and the financial community that they should not expect any 'overnight miracles', neither announcement was expected to cause a fresh wave of panic.

This was as much as could be done to prepare for the results. Streets monitored carefully what the team of key analysts were saying. They were able to confirm, as the announcement of the results approached, that the warnings had been heeded and that a loss for the full year was expected. It was difficult, however, to assess how the size of the loss, at £50 million, would be received.

The news at the interim results stage would not be all bad, however, and considerable progress had been made on some fronts, particularly in the reduction of borrowings. Lewis Robertson was determined that the work that had been done already by the rescue team would not be overshadowed by the enormous losses. The strategy decided upon was to acknowledge the losses, but to place greater emphasis on the reduction in borrowings and the much greater control which was now being exercised over the group's operations.

The share price had been rising steadily since the arrival of the rescue team and this was seen as a barometer of increasing confidence in Lilley by the investor community. On the day of the announcement of the preliminary results, the share price would provide a good indicator of how well Streets had performed their task in preparing the City for the news.

The results had, of course, to be first filed with the Stock Exchange before they could be released to the media or analysts. However, it was important to meet with key analysts and the media as soon as possible after the formal release of the results, to ensure Lilley's new management had the chance to clarify the prospects for the company and answer the questions about the results that might be asked of them. It was decided to hold two conferences, one for press and one for analysts. The analysts, who were seen as the most critical group, were summoned early on the day of the results. Having digested the information contained in the Chairman's statement, they asked a number of difficult and searching questions which were fielded by the Chairman, Chief Executive and Finance Director of Lilley. Once the conference had ended, the analysts rushed to contact their bases to offer advice on Lilley's position. The effect of their advice on the share price would be seen immediately. Within minutes, Lilley's shares dipped by 1p and then rose again, the best indicator possible that the analyst's expectations were on target.

The press, too, were broadly supportive to the new-look group. Coverage in the papers the next day gave full credit to the rescue management for the work they had done in reducing borrowings and in bringing overseas operations under much greater control.

In organizing the two conferences, it was recognized that many journalists would look to analysts of the sector for information on how to interpret the results. Hence, it was important to brief analysts in an attempt to assuage any concerns they still harboured over the future prospects for Lilley.

The announcement of the results for the full year was an important watershed for the new management. Lilley had survived the massive losses, the banks had pledged continuing support. The uncertain time of rescue was over and the process of recovery could begin.

Public relations with the Scottish business community

Throughout this period Lilley had suffered severe difficulties in securing good, profitable work. This was a regional problem, particularly affecting operations in the central belt of Scotland. Elsewhere in the UK and overseas, business had suffered slightly at the time of the crash, but had quickly returned to a position of near normal trading.

However, in the traditional Lilley stamping ground of Scotland, a major market-place for the group, the trading position was quite different. Attention remained focused on the company's problems, and customers were reluctant to place orders with the company's two main Scottish subsidiaries, Melville, Dundas and Whitson and Lilley Construction.

It was vital to restore the company's business in Scotland closer to its normal trading level, in order that the management could turn their attention to the considerable problems overseas that needed to be tackled. Lilley sought the help of a Glasgow-based PR consultancy, Michael Kelly Associates (MKA). Michael Kelly had been a Lord Provost of Glasgow and was well connected in Scottish business circles.

Michael Kelly Associates identified the target areas as the business communities of Glasgow and Edinburgh and the executives of all public authorities in the central belt of Scotland. This would include not only the majority of Lilley's existing or potential Scottish customers, but also the opinion-formers in the community. The consultancy also advised Lilley to make some attempt to court local politicians and, in particular, their own MP who, astonishingly, had never been invited within the doors of the largest employer in his constituency.

MKA had a major task on their hands. They not only had to change public opinion of the Lilley group, but had to engender positive support from the community in the form of substantial new contracts. It was decided that a press campaign alone would not be enough.

In analysing the target publics, MKA recognized that the business communities of Glasgow and Edinburgh were small and close-knit, and operated effective informal channels of communication. By identifying and then canvassing key opinion-formers, a message could be spread quickly throughout the communities by exploiting the existing informal network of contacts.

MKA suggested a programme of informal dinner parties in Glasgow and Edinburgh immediately following the announcement of the full year's results. The parties would each number around ten and would include the Chairman, Chief Executive, Michael Kelly himself and the Managing Director of one of the afflicted Scottish subsidiaries. This ratio in itself would give ample opportunity for the message to be pressed home on a one-to-one basis, but as reinforcement, despite the informality of the evening, at a certain point the Chairman, supported by the Chief Executive, would formally address his guests and spend several minutes explaining the position Lilley was in, asking openly for their support in resolving the problems.

MKA worked with the executives of the two Scottish subsidiaries on the compilation of a target list of influential members of the Scottish business community. Lilley Directors freed dates in their already over-committed diaries to attend the dinners. The take-up of the invitations at such an interesting period in Lilley's history was very good.

It was hoped that by tackling a small but influential number of individuals and convincing them of Lilley's case, they, in turn, would take the message back to their section of the community and persuade others to support the group. In the event, this is exactly what happened. Word spread quickly, and within six months of the campaign's beginning the two subsidiaries found themselves swamped by an embarrassment of tender enquiries. It was almost as if those who had held back work from the group suffered an attack of conscience, and were attempting to compensate for it.

Once the initial objective of restoring the group's order book closer to normal levels had been achieved, the dinners were continued, but on a less frequent basis and as part of an on-going marketing programme. It should be said that, in attracting such a high calibre of guest to an event of this type, special attention was paid to the venue, to the food and wine presented and to the balance of guests. The business community 'grape vine' could carry news of poor hospitality and dull conversation just as quickly as it spread word of

Lilley's survival plans.

Employee communications

It was decided that the best way to tackle the problems of employee communications was from the inside and an in-house campaign was devised. As with the financial PR and business community PR programmes, the need for action was urgent. Staff were continuing to look for jobs elsewhere. Those long-serving staff who had felt a degree of loyalty to their company now felt that loyalty had been misplaced.

The newly-appointed group PRO undertook a 'whistle stop' tour of all the group's UK subsidiaries to canvass opinion on what could be done to improve morale, and to asses what the status of morale was in each location. The story was the same everywhere, it was the sense of being ignored by management and being left out of the cycle of information which rankled far more than the mismanagement of the old Lilley management. Those in locations away from the Glasgow headquarters believed they were neglected because of their distance from head office, but in truth, those actually based in Glasgow were no better informed. There was also some confusion as to what had actually happened to cause the crash and what the situation was now. Above all, the employees of Lilley needed reassurance that the company was now safe from collapse, and that the actions of the rescue team would not result in large-scale redundancies.

The course of action decided upon was to:

- set up an immediate information distribution network which would reach all personnel;
- explain exactly what had happened to cause the financial crisis, what had been done since, and what expectations were for the future;
- produce an in-house journal which would cater for all employees.

The information distribution network was channelled through senior and middle management who, in turn, would ensure that information reached all sites within their care and would be posted on all notice-boards. Every press release issued by Lilley or its agents was remodelled as an internal announcement and copies were faxed to each location simultaneously with the issue of the release.

Senior and middle management were invited to briefing sessions at preliminary and interim results announcement stages, and were in turn encouraged to hold their own briefing sessions.

In order to explain the circumstances of the crash, and what had been done since, a video was commissioned. The programme was made in the form of an investigative documentary, looking at what had gone wrong. Lewis Robertson and Joe Barber featured as talking heads, offering reassurance that much had been done to remedy the situation. This type of treatment, it was felt, would appeal because of the immediacy it conveyed, and it also offered the best format for explaining the quite complex financial and contractual problems which had beset the group.

The video, produced shortly after the preliminary announcement, proved popular and effective with staff who, having been starved of information for some time, were greatly encouraged by such an apparent effort to cater for them. Surprisingly the video was also in demand with outside organizations, despite the fact that it was directed specifically at employees.

The company had for some years produced an in-house newspaper, *Lilley News*. This had mysteriously disappeared in the year before the crisis and there was a general desire in the company to see the paper, or something like it, once more in production. *Lilley News* had been a low budget tabloid, produced with minimum contribution from management by a secretary working together with a freelance journalist. The new management felt the employees deserved better than this.

The tabloid format of the journal was retained but the name was changed to *Lilley Today*. *Lilley News* had relied on contributions from correspondents within the group, but for *Lilley Today*, an effort was made to gather news from the far-flung outposts of group operations. Site visits were limited to the UK due to budget considerations, but an effort was made to feature at least one story on each of the subsidiaries. Contributions from staff were encouraged, but a tough editorial policy maintained uniformly high standards of written English.

By the end of the summer of 1987 staff morale had picked up considerably, staff wastage had returned to normal levels, and recruitment began to prove more easy.

Conclusions

The Lilley Group's financial crisis escalated into a general crisis of confidence in the company largely because of its failure to communicate with its publics. The problems of handling the crisis were exacerbated by the absence of any crisis plans, which placed the group's management under additional pressures in organizing its defences and mobilizing support.

The arrival of a new and experienced crisis management team, headed by Lewis Robertson and Joe Barber, was in itself an important signal to the financial world that Lilley was determined to come to grips with its problems. However, the damage to investor and business confidence in Lilley could not be repaired overnight, particularly as there was little in the way of good news that could be put out by the company, at least in the short term.

The new management recognized that its first priority in trying to restore confidence, was to re-establish more open lines of communication with key audiences. To have effectively 'battened down the hatches' and retreated from an open admission of Lilley's problems would undoubtedly have proved counter-productive. The company adopted a policy of controlled information dissemination, designed to prepare key City audiences for what was bound to be a period of relatively poor results, whilst at the same time seeking to generate a climate of optimism that the company's fortunes would, in due course, be restored.

By targeting specific analysts, who formed the key opinion-influencing group in the City, it was possible to establish a more balanced view of Lilley's position and future prospects. In general, analysts may be prepared to discount temporary setbacks, albeit in Lilley's case, of a very serious nature, if they can be convinced of the longer-term recovery potential of the company. This was the task for the crisis communication programme. It was the lack of communication earlier that caused the damaging shock reaction amongst the financial community threatening, as it did, the survival of the company.

Once the lines of communication had been re-established with the City, it was possible to prepare them for the announcement of what, by any standards, were a fairly disastrous set of results. The fact that the company's share price remained virtually unmoved by the announcement, was largely due to the improved relationship and confidence that had been established with the City during the months following the arrival of the new management team.

Lilley's new management's willingness to talk to the media, particularly in Scotland, helped to put a stop to the damaging speculation over the company's future. The improvement in relations with the media, in turn, played an important part in helping to restore the company's relations with the Scottish business community and with its employees.

The success of the programme designed to restore confidence in Lilley amongst the Scottish business community highlights the importance that key opinion-leaders can play in such situations. Equally, the programme of informal dinner parties, providing the opportunity for face-to-face contact between senior Lilley executives and key members of the business community, illustrates the power that 'word of mouth' communication can exert in influencing opinions. The task of restoring confidence among the business community was undoubtedly helped by the existence of the informal close network of contacts among Scotland's business leaders. The success of this aspect of the programme hinged on the careful targeting of business leaders, and the selection of guests invited to each of the event.

The restoration of employee morale and confidence was critical to Lilley's long-term recovery, particularly given the need to retain existing highly-skilled personnel as well as attract new staff. The breakdown in internal communication had clearly alienated and demoralized many of the company's staff. In turn, this may have had a knock-on effect on confidence in the company within the business community as a whole. In a such a relatively close-knit business community as exists in Central Scotland, and particularly within the construction sector itself, it was inevitable that the discontent among Lilley employees would leak out and be picked up by other firms in the industry. In effect, an informal 'grape vine' existed, through which potentially misleading information about the company could be spread. The failure of the company to keep employees informed about the situation probably fed this 'grape vine' with a source of potentially highly-damaging rumours and misinformation.

The restoration of open lines of communication between senior management and the rest of the company's employees helped to assuage natural worries over job security and began the process of restoring employee confidence in the future prospects for the company. Clearly this was unlikely to happen overnight, given the on-going problems still faced by Lilley. However, the more open communication policy helped to scotch damaging rumours, and the success of this aspect of the public relations programme eventually showed through in lower levels of staff turnover and less problems in the recruitment of skilled personnel.

The overall success of the crisis management programme can be best judged by the fact that Lilley actually managed to survive this business crisis, albeit with its reputation somewhat tarnished. The Group, now with an aggressive, growth-minded management is now prospering, and the new management's commitment to maintaining effective lines of communication will help ensure that it is better prepared to confront whatever future challenges the company is faced with.

Case discussion

This case illustrates, above all else, the importance of preparing for all possible contingencies when planning the on-going communications for an organization. A crisis can take many different forms, ranging from a financial crisis, such as faced the Lilley Group, to disasters such as the recent Piper Alpha oil rig tragedy that befell Occidental, the Boeing airliner crash at Lockerbie, or the discovery of the deliberate poisoning of its baby food products experienced by Heinz in the summer of 1989. In each case, a crisis invariably damages confidence in the organization in question, and may cause permanent damage to its reputation or even threaten its very survival. Although a crisis may arise from a natural or man-made disaster, the organization in question will be judged by the way it handles events and, in particular, the way its handling of the crisis is portrayed in the media. It is often too late to start to build lines of communication once the crisis has happened. The Lilley Group's problems were exacerbated by its failure to maintain regular communication with the financial and business communities, as well as with its employees and the media.

Obviously any organization may be faced at some stage with a potential crisis. However, crises can often take unpredictable or unexpected forms, catching an organization unprepared and thus handicapping its ability to respond quickly. Most large companies, particularly those with a high public profile such as airline operators, oil companies and food manufacturers, have recognized the need to prepare crisis management procedures in advance, and to constantly update these in the light of changing circumstances. The recent wave of hostile take-over bids in the UK, has alerted all publically quoted companies to the need to prepare their defences against such an eventuality. A take-over threat is, in effect, a crisis for the target company. In all crisis situations it is vital that the organization has an appropriate response plan ready to be implemented. The way communication with the public and the media is to be handled must form an essential element of any plan. The media invariably puts organizations experiencing a crisis under a 'spotlight', and they must be prepared to respond and defend themselves against unfair criticism.

A well-rehearsed 'crisis public relations' plan can avoid a crisis becoming a very real disaster. Many organizations now have comprehensive plans covering a variety of scenarios that may affect them. The most important principle of such plans is the need to maintain control over the flow of information during the crisis, and to avoid unfounded rumours and misinformation from spreading. Crisis planning normally involves the preparation in advance of information packs for the media, standard news releases, media distribution lists, background information and photographs, any relevant technical data, and so on. In essence, the aim is to prepare the answers to all the sorts of questions that the media might raise during a crisis. Preparation also often includes rehearsals of procedures for the manning of a crisis press office and the training of the staff that might be called upon to assist during a crisis.

In Lilley's case, clearly, none of these measures had been put in hand, with the result that when the crisis struck, it was ill-prepared to respond.

The case also highlights a number of more general points concerning corporate communications. First, it illustrates the importance in many situations of identifying key opinion-forming groups, rather than adopting a broader based communication strategy. What is often referred to as 'the two-step' flow of communication is often a highly significant factor in seeking to influence opinions about an issue. In the financial world it is the key City analysts and senior financial journalists who set the tone for the coverage of issues, and from whom wider financial audiences take their lead. These can be a relatively small, but very influential, group of individuals, who it is critical for an organization to win over. A second, and allied, point is the importance that 'word-of-mouth' communication often exerts. In many situations an effective 'grape-vine' may exist through which opinions are significantly influenced. It is clearly important to identify key members of such informal networks, and to seek to communicate the facts to them in the hope of influencing the rest of the network. This may be best achieved, where practical, through face-to-face meetings, to put the organization's case in a more direct and forceful manner. Lilley made effective use of such a 'grape-vine' to influence the close-ly-knit business community in Central Scotland. Third, organizations cannot afford to ignore the influence of their employees, who are often those most directly concerned with any crisis situation. Employees are often a key source of information about the company for many in the outside world. They, in effect, form a type of information grape-vine which the media, in particular, often take advantage of to gain an insight into events affecting the company. If employees are kept ill informed of the true facts, rumours and misinforma-tion can be quickly spread.

The handling of a financial crisis poses additional problems for public relations, as the communication of financial news by a publically quoted com-pany is heavily constrained by the rules of the Stock Exchange. All companies quoted on the Stock Exchange have to take special care over what information they release, and to whom it is released. The basic principle is for full and *equal* disclosure of information to all interested parties. When in doubt, the rule is for information to be first filed with the Stock Exchange's Company Announcements Office (CAO), before its release to the media or other par-ties. In Lilley's case, their precarious financial situation meant that particular care had to be taken over precisely what information could be communicated, as well as over the timing of the release of any information.

In summary, the Lilley case supports the adage that 'poor communication simply breeds misinformation'. Companies that fail to communicate effect-ively with their publics cannot expect to retain their trust and confidence.

Student discussion questions and exercises

1. Consider the chief strengths and weaknesses of Lilley's handling of its crisis. In particular, consider if it got its priorities correct, and what other actions might it have taken to handle the situation?
2. Design a crisis management plan for a chosen organization, identifying the type of information that should be prepared in advance, and listing the key target publics for the chosen organization.
3. Examine the media coverage of any recent 'crisis' situation affecting an organization and evaluate how well it appears to have handled the crisis.

Notes

1. These consisted of analysts specializing in the construction sector or who had experience of the Scottish business scene as well as those who had previous direct contact with Lilley.
2. All potentially price-sensitive information must be filed with the Company Announcements Office of the Stock Exchange before its disclosure elsewhere. The aim is to ensure equality of treatment for all interested parties. Information is put out by the CAO through the Stock Exchange's Topic system – a screen-based electronic information service.

The launch of the Ronseal Colour Palette

Diane Thompson

Preview

In today's increasingly competitive business environment, particularly within consumer markets, even the possession of a strong portfolio of brands cannot guarantee an organization's continued success in maintaining its competitive position. The increasing interchangeability of products, the growth of international competition in domestic markets, the increasing availability of high quality own-label brands, and the increased dominance of many consumer markets by powerful retail groups, have all contributed to a markedly changed competitive environment in which the 'corporate brand' rather than the individual brand has often become the dominant influence on customer choice.

The domination of many consumer markets by a relatively small number of major retail groups has led to the strengthening of their bargaining power *vis-à-vis* supplier organizations. One result of this trend is that, as in consumer markets, the corporate brand has often become a key determinant in the choice between alternative suppliers. Although traditional marketing activities continue to play a key role in both creating and sustaining strong brands, public relations activities conducted both at the corporate level, as well as at the trade level, have become an increasingly important weapon in the competitive strategy of many supplier organizations.

In 1986 Sterling Roncraft, despite being the clear leader in the market for woodcare products in the UK, faced a number of problems. The slow growth of the market itself made the targets set by its parent company increasingly difficult to achieve in the face of increasing competition from new entrants, and from an increasing number of own-label products. These problems were exacerbated by the increasing dominance of the DIY multiples, who were pressurizing brand leaders to defend their positions. This case examines how Sterling Roncraft, was able reinforce its position in the market through the relaunch of its existing product range and the development of a new and innovative product – the 'Ronseal Colour Palette'. Crucial to the success of the strategy was the securing of trade acceptance and support for the new products, particularly among the major DIY retailers. The case illustrates how an intensive programme of trade press relations, combined with a carefully planned buyers' conference, was used to raise enthusiasm and interest among key DIY buyers prior to and during the launch period. The combined advertising and public relations campaign helped establish the new product while at the same time providing the platform to reinforce Sterling Roncraft's reputation as the market leader.

Although the major trade and consumer advertising campaign undoubtedly played a significant role in the successful launch of the Ronseal Colour Palette, the public relations programme also played an important complementary role in the overall promotional strategy. As this case illustrates, public relations and advertising should be viewed as complementary communication techniques rather than alternatives, and are best developed as part of an integrated communications strategy.

Background

Sterling Roncraft at the time of preparing this case (1988) was a wholly owned subsidiary of Sterling Drug USA, having been acquired in 1974 when it had a turnover of around £800,000 and employed some twelve people producing a range of Ronseal Varnishes and Colron Wood Dyes. By 1988 the company's turnover had reached some £20 million. It employed 100 people in sales and marketing and its product range consisted of over 200 product lines. The core of the business was still that of the traditional varnishes and wood dyes, which accounted for 65 per cent of total turnover. The company had an excellent record of new product innovation, having successfully launched ten new products during the previous five years. In addition to organic growth, the company had been keen to grow by acquisition and in 1986 had acquired the Isoflex range of products – a range of high technology waterproofing products used to repair leaking roofs.

Sterling Roncraft defined its business mission as:

The Division aims to develop as a broadly-based national manufacturer and distributor of formulated chemical products used for the maintenance, protection and improvement of property.

Its strategy was quite simple, and always consistent, and can be summed up as:

- Top quality/advanced technology products.
- Premium prices.
- Brand leader where possible.
- Supported by heavy investment in advertising and promotion.

Sterling Roncraft had an advertising to sales ratio of 18 per cent, perhaps the highest in the woodcare market, and was the brand leader in virtually every sector in which it operated with, for example, a 63 per cent share of the interior varnishes market, 50 per cent of the external varnishes market, 52 per cent of the wood dyes market and 80 per cent of the wood repair systems market. In terms of the overall market for woodcare products Sterling Roncraft was by far the largest, with 31 per cent of sales by value. Cuprinol, owned by Williams Holdings, was second with around 20 per cent and ICI Dulux a fairly distant third with just 7 per cent. The rest of the market was made up of a multitude of smaller manufacturers, often with only a single product.

The market for woodcare products

The market for woodcare products in the UK was valued at approximately £98 million at the recommended selling price (RSP) and was estimated to be amongst the fastest-growing sectors of the overall DIY market. The market can be segmented into five key areas:

Market	Size (£)	Trend
Interior wood surfaces	30m	slight growth
Cherished old wood	4m	static/slight growth
Decaying exterior wood surfaces	5m	increasing
Sound exterior wood surfaces	14m	increasing
Garden timber treatment	40m	increasing

The main factors responsible for the growth of the market were:

- increased popularity of natural wood as a decorative finish;
- increased consumer awareness of natural wood due to heavy advertising and promotion;
- significant increase in new products on the market.

Distribution in the DIY market

The DIY market is becoming increasingly concentrated with DIY superstores taking an ever-increasing share of the total business. The actual number of DIY outlets has fallen by 40 per cent during the past 25 years. By 1986 DIY superstores still only accounted for 4 per cent of the total number of outlets (560 units), but accounted for 65 per cent of total DIY sales.

Five key multiple chains dominated the sector and accounted for 48 per cent of retail sales:

DIY superstore	Market shares (1986)(%)
B & Q	21.2
TEXAS	12.4
PAYLESS	5.7
DO-IT-ALL	5.2
HOMEBASE	3.9
Total	48.4

The key trends in the DIY market in recent years could be summarized as follows:

- Increasing overall market size – due to rising home ownership, greater leisure time, increased disposable income, and the rising costs of professional labour.
- Growth of DIY multiples.
- Reduction in the number of buying points – due to increased concentration, thus offering manufacturers fewer selling opportunities.
- Move towards own label – some generic products such as timber were, by the 1980s, already almost entirely own-label.
- Growth of female consumers – increasing numbers of single female heads of household prepared to undertake their own basic DIY tasks.

Key issues facing Sterling Roncraft

On the surface Sterling Roncraft seemed, in 1986, to be in a strong position in the woodcare market, having a 63 per cent market share in interior varnishes and excellent distribution in 90 per cent of DIY retail outlets. Its image was also particularly favourable with both the trade and consumers alike – trustworthy, male-biased, the best products and good value for money if just a bit old fashioned.

However, a number of problems had become increasingly apparent:

- The slow growth of the market would make achieving the targets of 15 per cent year on year growth, set by the US parent company, difficult to reach.
- The growing competition from new entrants into the market, particularly from paint manufacturers, attracted by the higher margins in the woodcare market.
- The growing number of own-label products, with research suggesting they would account for 20 per cent of the market in volume terms within two to three years.
- The growing dominance of the DIY multiples and their trend towards a solus preferred brand supplier, would place increasing pressure on brand leaders to defend their position.

In response to these concerns Sterling Roncraft carried out a major market research programme designed to help identify the way forward within the woodcare market.

The main findings can be summarized as:

- Massive confusion amongst consumers about the variety of products on the market.
- Concern amongst consumers about the colouring of wood:
  - the resulting colour of the wood after treatment;
  - confusion over the differences between stains, dyes and varnishes;
  - concern over the level of skill needed to apply products;
  - concern over the inconsistency of colour from tin to tin and between colouring systems.
- The colouring of wood was not seen as particularly fashionable.
- Women were the dominant influence in the choice of colour.
- Ronseal had a very good brand image, but was seen as male-orientated and slightly old-fashioned.

This consumer research was verified by soundings amongst major retailers. In light of the findings a major review was undertaken of the Roncraft product portfolio which revealed the following:

- No clear corporate identity – a variety of products had been launched over the years, each good in its own right, but doing little to remove confusion and aid consumer choice.
- No clear product positioning or communication – with a lack of clear pack design and user instructions.
- Confusing range of colours.

As a result, a comprehensive new marketing and public relations programme was developed. The objectives were:

- To simplify the consumer proposition by redesigning and repositioning the products.
- To aid consumer choice by better designed packs.
- To maintain/improve brand leadership through product innovation.
- To present a more fashionable image for Ronseal.
- To increase female usage of Ronseal products.
- To demonstrate to the trade Ronseal's lead in the woodcare market.

These objectives were to be achieved through two major activities:

- Simplification and redesign of the packaging.
- The introduction of the Ronseal Colour Palette.

The first stage of redesign of the product range was begun in May 1987, using simple colour coding on tins to differentiate between interior and exterior products. The second stage was to focus on the launch of a major new marketing initiative designed to both update the Ronseal image and bring fashion into the woodcare market through the launch of the concept of the Colour Palette.

The Ronseal Colour Palette

The concept of the Ronseal Colour Palette, initially code-named project Pablo, was quite simple – it would offer the consumer a range of natural wood colours consistent across all Ronseal colouring systems. Moreover, consumers would be able to test out the product to determine the final colour and finish of the product on their own wood. Research was used to identify a range of eight colours to be made available:

Mahogany	Antique Oak
Teak	Dark Oak
Antique Pine	Walnut
Pine	Chestnut

To overcome any concerns over the final colour, a colour tester was made available, providing sufficient product to cover approximately one square foot. The colours were available across both interior and exterior woodcare systems, with the name Woodshades being replaced by Interior Ronseal Coloured Satin, and Coloured Gloss and Exterior Satin Wood finishes. In total the launch involved developing eighty-three packs plus the launch of twenty-four colour testers – a major logistical exercise in itself. It was decided that no stocks bearing the old uncoordinated livery would be uplifted, but that any old livery cans still in stock after four weeks would be over-labelled in-store.

The specific objectives set for the Ronseal Colour Palette with respect to the trade were:

- To demonstrate brand leadership.
- To increase the usage of wood colouring products and grow the market.
- To use the Colour Palette vehicle to gain better distribution across several product ranges.
- To maximize display opportunities at point-of-sale.
- To gain increased brand share, overall sales volume and profitability.
- To provide a comprehensive and consistent package in-store to remove confusion amongst consumers once and for all.
- To maximize media coverage for Sterling Roncraft through public relations activities to help improve the company's image.

The promotional campaign

Sterling Roncraft had been a major advertiser in the woodcare market over the years and £3 million was allocated for advertising support in 1988, with £1.5 million specifically allocated to support the launch on the Ronseal Colour Palette.

The advertising campaign, which was carried out by McCann Erickson, consisted of three elements:

- A trade campaign – using seven pages of advertising designed to dominate the trade press in the February issues of all major trade journals.
- A consumer launch campaign – using a full-page colour advertisement in *The Times*, the *Daily Express* and *Daily Mail* in April – total circulation 4 million (see Appendix 7.1 at end of case study). A copy of the *The Times* was mailed with a personal letter to major DIY buyers.
- National Consumer Advertising – a series of three innovative and highly creative double-page spreads (see Plate 3) was taken in all key home interest publications between April and September (see Appendix 7.2). Total circulation provided by the schedule was 32 million.

A range of eye-catching point-of-sale materials was designed for in-store use along with detailed product literature. In addition, a special Ronseal Book of Colouring Wood was produced featuring twelve room settings, illustrating the creative use of wood colours.

The public relations programme

Securing the favourable reaction of the trade was critical to the success of this strategy designed to reinforce Sterling Roncraft's position as an innovative brand leader and reposition the company's products as more fashionable and easy to use. Without the co-operation of the major retail multiples in stocking the new range, the launch of the new product range could not hope to succeed.

Objectives of the public relations programme

The public relations programme was primarily directed at the trade and was intended to generate a high level of awareness and interest in the new products and to reinforce Sterling Roncraft's image as an innovative brand leader in the field of woodcare. The aim was to maximize trade press coverage and to gain positive trade press reaction and support for the new products. The trade press campaign was intended to stimulate a sense of excitement in the industry, conveying the message that the launch of the Colour Palette would herald a 'new era' for the use of wood in home furnishing.

Now you can colour wood around your home without getting butterflies about the final result.

Ronseal offer you 8 natural wood colours. And the beauty is, they're absolutely consistent.

They even remain consistent across all finishes: interior satin and gloss, and exterior satin.

Send for your free book of ideas.

Each can is colour-coded. And the colour on the front of the can is the colour in the can.

If you're not sure try our little Colour Testers. They let you dabble before you commit yourself.

NOW THE COLOUR YOU'RE AFTER IS EASILY CAPTURED.

Which means there's no excuse for not making your wood look lovely. Because now you can pin down the colour you want.

For a free booklet on colouring wood around your home, write to Dept. WH Customer Services, Sterling Roncraft, 15 Churchfield Court, Churchfield, Barnsley, S70 2LJ.

THE RONSEAL COLOUR PALETTE.
The art of colouring wood made simple.

Walnut

Pine

Mahogany

Antique Oak

Antique Pine

Dark Oak

Teak

Chestnut

Plate 3   The Ronseal Colour Palette

The programme

The programme itself was essentially straightforward, involving a major sales conference for key buyers and an intensive trade media relations programme. However, both involved considerable effort in organization and careful timing in order to achieve the maximum initial impact and then to maintain high levels of interest following the initial launch.

The Ronseal Colour Palette was due to be launched to the trade as a whole on 14 March 1988, with the consumer advertising commencing mid-April. It was crucial to sell the product to the major trade multiples in advance, especially in light of the massive logistical exercise involved in organizing the delivery of the new product range throughout the country. The approach chosen was a sales conference for the major multiple buyers at which the new product concept would be presented. It was decided to mount this in Cyprus at the end of November 1987. The attractive venue during the winter months would provide an incentive for buyers to attend and ensure their undivided attention for the presentation of the Colour Palette range. The Buyers Conference involved a presentation by Sterling Roncraft's Marketing Director of the new product concept, which demonstrated the exciting opportunity for the fashionable treatment of wood in the home offered by the Colour Palette. This was followed up by individual presentations, tailor-made for each major account. The reaction from buyers was overwhelmingly positive and enthusiastic. The first major hurdle was thus surmounted – persuading the DIY multiples initially to stock the product.

Trade media relations

In a market where new products had proliferated, it was somewhat problematical how the trade media would respond, despite the fact that the Colour Palette represented a major new development in the field of woodcare. The task for public relations was to try to overcome the natural cynicism amongst trade journalists that the news about the Colour Palette was no more than a further example of product 'puffery'. The respected position of Sterling Roncraft in the industry allied to the inherently revolutionary nature of the new product concept helped ensure a high level of trade press interest.

The approach adopted was to offer a series of personal interviews to journalists from the key trade press, rather than staging a single news conference. It was believed this would increase the chances of securing more extensive editorial coverage of the launch. As far as possible stories were prepared with slightly differing emphases, tailored to the particular interest of each respective publication. A comprehensive press pack was prepared including copies of the glossy brochure, *The Ronseal Book of Colouring Wood*. The response from the trade press was extremely positive and the product received extensive coverage throughout a range of trade publications (see Appendix 7.2 at end of case study for editorial coverage received).

A consumer press launch was held at Searcy's in London on 21 January, at which a number of the interior room settings featuring the use of wood furnishings, coloured with the new product, were displayed. The reaction was, as with the trade press, very positive and the Colour Palette received extensive coverage in the consumer press.

The results

At the time of preparation of this case, it is too early to assess the success of the product with certainty. The acid test will be consumer sales. However, the initial indications are that the Colour Palette has helped stimulate sales of the Ronseal range of products and sales only two and a half months after the launch were up 6 per cent on the previous year on a volume basis.

Undoubtedly the trade relations programme was highly successful in persuading the key multiple DIY retailers as well as a majority of other DIY stockists to support the introduction of the new Ronseal range. The successful launch of the Colour Palette reinforced Sterling Roncraft's leadership in the woodcare market, and demonstrated the company's ability to take the market forward, creating growth for both the trade and itself.

For the consumer, the programme represented a major step forward in simplifying the choice and use of woodcare products, whilst at the same time injecting a new sense of fashion into the colouring and protection of wood.

Case discussion

This case study demonstrates the important contribution that public relations can make to a company's competitive strategy, and particularly to the success of its trade and consumer marketing activities. Virtually all markets in the UK have, in recent years, become ever more dominated, by a relatively small number of major retail groups. As a result, supplier organizations have been forced to recognize the vital importance of developing and maintaining good trade relations with often very powerful distribution channel members.

The situation in the DIY market is very similar to that found in many other consumer markets in the UK, with the market controlled largely by a small number of multiple retailers, and the encroachment of own-label products continuing to threaten the position of supplier organizations. As a result, previous brand leadership is now no longer any guarantee of future success, or even continued support by the trade. Companies must work harder than ever to maintain their relationship with the trade and consumers alike.

The trade press can often be an important channel of communication with both the wholesale and retail trade. If skilfully managed, trade press relations can play an important role in helping to secure trade acceptance of changes in product policy or for new product launches. The problem for most trade press programmes, particularly when associated with a new product launch, is one of trying to overcome the trade press's natural scepticism towards the 'news' of the new product – usually regarding it as merely product 'puffery'.

In an increasingly cluttered media environment, the simple acknowledgement of a new product launch may go unnoticed, or may have limited impact on hardened trade buyers. It requires considerable skill in stimulating media interest in a new product story and in targeting the key trade journals to maximize editorial coverage. Obviously it helps if, as in Sterling Roncraft's case, you are the brand leader and have an innovative new product, but this is no guarantee of extensive or favourable media coverage. In the case of the Colour Palette, key trade journalists were carefully targeted and approached with the offer of an individual personal interview. In each case it was necessary to find slightly differing angles for the story, taking account of the specific readership of each journal. In this way it was possible to secure a high percentage of editorial coverage from those journals approached.

The success in gaining trade press coverage for the Colour Palette launch illustrates the importance of recognizing that the media are essentially looking for exclusive news stories wherever possible. By tailoring stories to the specific interests of the readership of individual publications, organizations are likely to receive far more editorial coverage, than if a single 'blanket' news story is issued.

The proliferation of new products and services in recent years has made it increasingly difficult for supplier companies to generate the level of interest and genuine enthusiasm for new products among experienced and often sceptical buyers and store managers that will secure the necessary shelf-space for them. Products that fail to secure shelf-space in the major retail multiples are usually doomed to failure. Hence, the expense and time involved in organizing the Cyprus conference was, in Sterling Roncraft's case, fully warranted. It provided a relaxed atmosphere, removed from the pressures and interruptions of the normal working environment, in which the Colour Palette concept could be presented to key buyers. Whilst this could not ensure that they would be taken with the concept and agree to support it, it did guarantee an opportunity to gain their undivided attention whilst selling the concept to them.

Trade conferences are often accused of being nothing more than a thinly-veiled attempt to influence buyers' decisions. It would be naïve, however, to believe that experienced trade buyers can be induced to accept anything other than a commercially attractive product, merely as a result of the hospitality provided and a 'slick' sales presentation. However, sales conferences can provide the opportunity, in a very crowded market-place, to gain their attention and to present the full benefits of an offered new product. An attractive location can assist in encouraging often very busy executives to find time to participate. The first step for any public relations practitioner responsible for organizing a trade conference must be careful research to establish the commitments of the targeted key buyers. Clearly, it is vital to select a date for a conference which does not clash with the existing commitments of the majority of the target audience. While this may appear obvious, it is a basic step that a number of sales conference organizers fail to carry out, only to find that the planned conference has to be cancelled or at least rearranged for lack of support. Once the date and venue have been agreed, the practitioner's role is to ensure the careful preparation of the event to give the best chance of the presentation being well received.

As this case illustrates, although advertising usually receives the largest share of the promotional budget and attracts the greater attention, particularly in consumer markets, public relations can play an important complementary role in supporting an organization's other promotional activities. Those organizations that develop their communications activities as an integrated strategy will tend to see the best results. Public relations can often help to secure the important third party endorsement for an organization's claims that can give added credibility to its advertising. Equally, by helping to maintain an organization's reputation, public relations enhances the source credibility of the advertising message. In this sense, public relations can help to create an environment in which advertising can work more effectively. In addition to supporting advertising, public relations also fulfils a vital role in its own right. If an organization is not well known, or the nature of its business is misunderstood, then its chances of success in today's often highly competitive markets will be severely reduced. Similarly, even established companies may require to educate their markets about new products or changes in their operating policies. They cannot assume that their past reputation alone will guarantee them acceptance and support. Public relations provides the means by which organizations can maintain and update their relations with either customer audiences or other relevant groups on whom their future success may depend.

One of the most important contributions that public relations can make to any company's marketing activities, is to provide management with an understanding of how the company and its products are perceived, or how emerging issues may affect its future marketing activities. In this sense, public relations becomes the 'voice of the consumer' within the company, helping to ensure the relevance of its communications with its markets.

Student discussion questions and exercises

1. Consider what other ways public relations might have been able to assist Sterling Roncraft in reinforcing its market leadership and supporting the launch of the Colour Palette.
2. Compile a mailing list for the distribution of news of a new product launch

in the DIY market to the trade press and complete the same exercise for a new alcoholic drink to be sold in free trade and off-license premises.

3. Prepare a proposal and provisional costing for a sales conference aimed at key buyers from the DIY sector, intended as the vehicle to unveil the launch of a complete new range of hand tools by a major UK supplier. This should identify suitable locations, accommodation costs, travel and sales presentation costs.

Appendix 7.1 Roncraft Colour Palette: media plan

	April				May					June				July				Aug.					Sept.			
	4	11	18	25	2	9	16	23	30	6	13	20	27	4	11	18	25	1	8	15	22	29	5	12	19	26
National press																										
Daily Mail		X																								
Daily Express			19																							
Times		X																								
Double-page spread, colour (magazines)																										
You magazine			X B					X S	X M				X	B							X S					
Observer magazine				X	X B	X M						X		M								X M				
Sunday Times magazine							X S																			
Sunday Telegraph																X B										
Sunday Express		X								X S		X M		M				X S								
Good Housekeeping						12 B									14 M								8 M			
Country Homes					4 B					8 S																
Country Living		14 B								8														15 M		
House & Garden			21 B									24 M			14 M										23 B	
Homes & Garden						12 B					16 S								11 S							
Ideal Home			22 B									24 S				22 M					26 B					
World of Interiors				29	B																26 S					
Prima						12 M										22 S				19 M						
Options								27 M			16 S			M												
Family Circle											16 S		X S 30	M									X B			
Living					05B									M							25 B					

Note:
B = Butterflies
S = Snooker
M = Mushrooms

Appendix 7.2 The Ronseal Colour Palette – editorials published and forecast

Published

Evening Standard	10 February
ITV Oracle	8–12 February
Hardware Trade Journal	12 February
W.P.W. Home Decor	February 1988
Superstore Management	February 1988
D.I.Y. Superstore	February 1988
Woman's Weekly	5 March
Bella	7–13 March
The Kitchen Magazine	April/May 1988
D.I.Y. Today	April 1988
Ms London	21 March
Hardware Trade Journal	25 March
Marketing Week	1 April
Best	3–9 April
Practical Householder	April 1988
D.I.Y. Today	May 1988
Texas Homecare	Spring 1988
Daily Mail	1988
Do It Yourself Home Interiors	
Shropshire Star	2 April
Hardware Trade Journal	22 April
Best	17–23 April
What's New in Interiors	April 1988
Hardware & Garden Review	April 1988
Wedding & Home	Early Summer 1988
Essentials	May 1988
Ideal Home	May 1988
Setting Up a New Home	
Hardware Today	May 1988
Do It Yourself	June 1988
W.P.W. Home Decor	May 1988
Marketing	19 May
Evening Standard	25 May
Shropshire Star	28 May
Bella	11 June
Ideal Home	June 1988
Practical Householder	July 1988
Creating A Home	July 1988
D.I.Y. Today	July 1988

Forecast

Successful D.I.Y.	Issue 8 (end July)
Traditional Kitchens	July 1988
Living	August 1988
Annabel	November 1988
Practical Householder	August 1988
Ideal Home Book of Improving Your Home (N.H.I.C. Supplement)	October 1988
Ideal Home Decorating Supplement	July 1988
Ideal Home Decorating Supplement	August 1988
Texas Homecare	September 1988
Do It Yourself	August 1988
Property Review	July 1988
Cosmopolitan	August 1988
The Country Diary Book of Decorating	October 1988
Traditional Woodworking	Summer 1988
Best	18 June
Pickfords Magazine	July 1988
Bella	20 June
Annabel	July 1988

Volex Accessories Designer Range

Bill Daring

Preview

A perennial question that has been the subject of considerable, and often acrimonious, debate amongst public relations and marketing professionals is the relationship between marketing and public relations. Opinions have tended to polarize between those who refuse to countenance that marketing and public relations are in any way connected, and those who maintain that public relations is merely part of marketing or marketing communications.

The controversy surrounding the relationship between public relations and marketing stems largely from a failure to recognize that the marketing function is only one aspect of a corporation's activities, albeit a vital one. In today's society, and increasingly competitive markets, companies must recognize that their success in marketing their products or services (and in fact their very survival) may largely depend on maintaining the trust and goodwill of many disparate groups. This task is one that public relations, not marketing, is best equipped to carry out. Without the support of public relations, marketing strategies, no matter how potentially effective, may be insufficient to guarantee a company's competitive success.

The relationship between public relations and marketing is perhaps best understood in terms of an organization's overall communications strategy. Whether this strategy employs advertising, direct marketing, merchandising, literature and brochures, editorial, or a combination of these and other techniques, it is likely to be more effective when developed as part of an integrated communications programme.

Viewed in this way, marketing and public relations become complementary and mutually supportive elements of a single and more focused communication activity. As a result, organizations can gain synergistic benefits from a communications strategy that exploits the inherent strengths of the two disciplines.

The following case illustrates the roled played by public relations in supporting the launch of a new product by Volex Accessories. It shows how a public relations programme can form part of an integrated overall marketing strategy. The programme described shows something of the problems of securing trade and consumer press coverage in an increasingly crowded media market, and highlights some of the chief differences in handling media relations with trade publications and the consumer press. The case also illustrates the importance of building into communications programmes, wherever possible, appropriate methods of evaluating the contribution made by public relations. This can help management to evaluate the specific results of the various communication techniques employed and thus to plan its future communications strategy more effectively. However, as the case study illustrates evaluating the effects of public relations alone is often difficult to achieve with any certainty. This is particularly so in the context of a marketing campaign, when other marketing activities that form part of the overall campaign may exacerbate the problems of isolating those responses that can be attributed specifically to the public relations activities taking place. As the Volex case shows, however, some relatively straightforward methods can be used to at least gauge the initial response to media coverage, if not the direct impact of the public relations activities on the final level of sales.

Background

In the design-conscious world of today, even products as straightforward as plugs, sockets and switches are marketed with as much flair and imagination as the latest Georgio Armani suit. This is especially true of wiring accessories designed to match the interior decor of the modern home or commercial premises. The consumer can now chose from an exciting range of products manufactured in attractive finishes whether it be brass or textured plastic.

One company that has strengthened its product range in recent years by moving away from purely functional white moulded fittings, and 'switching on' to stylish colour co-ordinated accessories, is Volex Accessories. Based in Hindley Green, near Warrington, Lancashire, the company is part of the larger Volex Group plc, one of the leading electrical wiring accessory manufacturers in the UK – employing nearly 1,000 people.

As a supplier of a wide range of products for the domestic, building and contracting markets, Volex Accessories has established a reputation for quality, safety and innovation, especially among the major national distributors. The division is the holder of the coveted Association of Short-circuit Testing Authorities (ASTA) Diamond Mark of Approval on its major installation products and was also the first UK company to be awarded the BS 5750 (part 2) Certificate for electrical wiring accessories.

The product

With innovation as a core Volex philosophy, it was only natural for the company to respond to the changing demands within the wiring accessories market with an exciting new range of plugs, sockets and switches, named the Designer Range. Available in either Chamois (a light cream colour) or Burnt Oak (a dark russet brown), the fittings came with a solid brass trim, slim flush plates which concealed screws, and large dolly switches. The range was aimed at the more discerning customer who wanted accessories to fit in with a variety of interior colour schemes.

To orchestrate the Designer Range launch in 1987, Volex Accessories appointed Burgess Daring Public Relations. The brief was to design a public relations programme to launch the product to the company's existing customers, potential customers, and the trade.

Objectives

The communications objectives of the first phase of the launch were as follows:

- To create awareness of the Designer Range amongst retailers and encourage stocking of the range.
- To develop a set of promotional materials to support the range.
- To create awareness amongst trade customers in the trade media and at the point-of-sale to help motivate purchase.
- To assess the purchase motivations and attitudes of customers and consumers in general in the post-launch period.

The Designer Range was to be prepacked and distributed to key accounts – the major DIY superstores and department stores – by Pact International, and to lighting specialists and other independent retailers by Wellco Electric. The first phase of the launch was scheduled to start in May 1987.

Phase two of the launch followed in October, with a launch to the trade and professional market under the Volex brand name. The objective of the trade launch was to inform the electrical industry that a major new product was on the market, whilst at the same time positioning Volex Accessories as a supplier of quality products with a reputation for safety and reliability. The target publics were identified as electrical contractors, architects, interior designers, building contractors, property developers and local government specifiers. Again, this launch was to be supported by promotional literature.

The public relations programme was incorporated into a fully integrated marketing communications campaign, which included advertising, direct mail and extensive product literature.

The account team working on the Designer Range public relations programme consisted of an Account Director, an Account Executive, and two PR co-ordinators. The Account Director also co-ordinated the work of an Advertising Account Executive, who liaised with the client on the advertising campaign for the Designer Range launch. The account team reported to Volex's Marketing Manager, liaising with him to ensure the accuracy of all material released to the press, and the completion of activities on schedule.

Integrated strategy

The programme's strategy consisted primarily of a comprehensive media relations programme involving the following elements:

- a press pack;
- media liaison including personal visits;
- news releases (dispatched on Volex Accessories press information paper);
- feature articles;
- quality photography and press visits.

The key aim was to gain product editorial in the relevant trade, consumer and national press. The prepacked products, under the names of Wellco and Pact, were expected to hit all potential retail stockists by June 1987. The public relations programme was intended to support this phase of the launch through trade press relations, with press material targeted at the trade publications such as *Electrical and Electronic Trader, Electrical Retailing, DIY Superstore, Hardware Today* and *Housewares*.

The press pack contained full product and price information, technical specifications and good quality photographs in both colour and monochrome. This was presented to editors in May for inclusion in June issues. Editorial coverage was seen as vital to support the efforts to sell in to the trade.

It was also seen as important to gain coverage in the consumer press in order to put across the aesthetic appeal of the Designer Range, and to reassure consumers of their acceptance in the market. The press pack was targeted at key consumer opinion-formers amongst the women's interest and home DIY publications. Targeted publications included *Good Housekeeping, Ideal Home, Do It Yourself, Woman* and *Practical Housekeeping*.

Early on in the planning of the programme, it was recognized that there was little chance of attracting the editors of the target publications to a press launch. Increasingly, publications today are operating on lower staffing levels and are inundated with requests to attend new product launches. Instead, Burgess Daring recommended a series of visits to the main publishing houses armed with an unusual press pack and product samples.

The press pack consisted of a single gang socket and switch mounted in a presentation folder with a press release, technical information, full colour brochure, line drawings, colour photographs and a list of national stockists. This was presented on a one-to-one basis and proved highly successful. The pack contained everything required for a new product write-up. The novelty element of this approach allowed the Designer Range to be actually demon-

Plate 4   Volex Accessories 'Designer Range' press pack

strated to journalists, and remained as a permanent reminder of the product
– so increasing the chances of editorial coverage. A cut-down version of the
pack was mailed out to those publications not visited by Burgess Daring (the
press pack used is shown in Plate 4).

Phase two of the campaign to launch the Designer Range to the trade market was able to build on the earlier awareness of the product, created by the
success of phase one of the programme. The aim was to reinforce awareness
through coverage in the more specialist building trade press, such as *The
Builder*, *What's New in Building*, *Design* and in the electrical trade press, such
as *Electrical Contractor* and *Electrical Wholesaling*. A similar press pack to that
used in phase one was mailed to the target publications, except that the information was angled towards commercial as well as domestic applications. Key
journalists were personally contacted and offered products for review and/or
photography. This phase of the programme was completed by October 1987.

Developing the press relations

Cultivating good media relations is a central part of most public relations programmes, and the Designer Range launch was no exception. Continual liaison
with editors and journalists of key journals enabled Burgess Daring to gauge
the reaction to the product and improve the opportunity for forthcoming edi-

torial coverage, in particular the possibility of submitting a feature article on the product.

The identification of feature article opportunities was a key element of the next stage of the programme. Throughout the launch period Burgess Daring were collating scheduled feature lists from all the relevant publications in order to explore the possible openings for a more in-depth study of the new product, and how designer switches and sockets had become an integral part of the design conscious world of today. The articles were written by the consultancy, but outlined by senior Volex personnel, such as the Marketing and Sales Director. The offer of such feature articles was well received by several important building and electrical press publications, and gave Volex a vehicle for not only promoting their new product, but also positioning themselves as an authoratitive 'voice' in the industry. By supplying good quality photography with the editorial copy, it was possible to ensure that the features looked impressive on the page, inviting the reader to stop and read the information before him.

It was important to recognize that, with features of this kind, the editorial has to be written to suit the style of the publications. For example, *Electrical Contracting News* is aimed at electrical contractors and has a very solid tabloid house style – something akin to the *Daily Mirror*. On the other hand, *Building* or *Interior Design* has a more up-market readership profile, and requires a less 'punchy' writing style. In all cases the publication's readership had to be borne in mind to ensure the information supplied was relevant.

Factory visits can prove an effective method of gaining editorial coverage, and were used in this case to good effect. Ray Maloney of *Electrical Contracting News* and Jonathon David of *Electrical Design* were both given guided factory tours and visited the production line to see for themselves the manufacture of the Designer Range. After the factory tour interviews were arranged with senior Volex personnel, to allow them to question them on production techniques, safety tests, BS 5750, marketing strategies and views on the industry as a whole.

The results

Measuring the results of a public relations programme is not always easy, particularly in trying to determine the extent to which target audiences become aware or are influenced by editorial coverage. In this case did electrical contractors become aware of the Designer Range through seeing the advertising or by reading the editorial coverage? In practice it is almost impossible to answer the question with any certainty. The overall marketing and public relations strategy has to be viewed as an integrated whole. One element could not necessarily be removed in preference to the other. One useful measure of the success of media relations activity can be the number of reader enquiries generated through the trade press. Most of the trade press offer a reader enquiry service, with product reviews accompanied by a product enquiry number, which can be circled for further information on a reply paid card. In the case of the Designer Range, an analysis of these figures reveals 958 trade enquiries were passed on to Volex's sales team between May 1988 and April 1989. All of these were classed as good leads and came mainly from people in business – that is, potential customers.

In terms of coverage gained, a space equivalent analysis, showing how much the coverage would have cost if the space had been bought through advertising, revealed some interesting figures.The total amount of space would have cost the equivalent of £59,633 at rate card costs. The total cost of the public relations programme was £36,797. Hence, had Volex paid for the space obtained it would have cost an additional £22,837, before advertising production costs. Naturally such calculations must be treated with a degree of caution, not the least because variations in available rate card discounts can dramatically effect the calculation. Also, it can be misleading to compare the impact of editorial with paid advertising space, as the former tends to carry greater credibility and is hence worth more column inch for column inch.

An analysis of the cost per column inch achieved over the life of the programme is shown in Figure 3, with cost per column inch reflecting the success in gaining editorial coverage. The cost per thousand of potential exposure is shown in Figure 4. This averaged just over £1 per thousand throughout the campaign. The cost per response gained is shown in Figure 5. The average value of order per response was £2,500.

The results of the programme both in terms of media coverage and customer response, were overall highly satisfactory. The decision to approach editors and journalists in targeted publications on a one-to-one basis, rather than via a press conference or by use of blanket releases, laid the foundation for the success of the programme and prepared the ground for the subsequent success in securing acceptance of feature articles. On reflection, phase two of the launch was more successful than phase one, highlighting the intense pressures on editorial space in consumer and women's interest press. In the consumer and women's press the Designer Range of plugs and sockets had to compete for coverage with a whole range of products with more instant appeal.

It is important to be honest with the client about the appeal of the product, particularly as they are often naturally excited about their new product and fail to appreciate how it will be viewed by a possibly jaundiced editor inundated with new product information releases. Careful media targeting is the key to a successful media relations campaign. This basic ground rule was well illustrated in phase two of the programme. When it came to hitting the trade press and getting the message across to the electrical wholesaler, contractor, builder and specifier, the programme was a complete success.

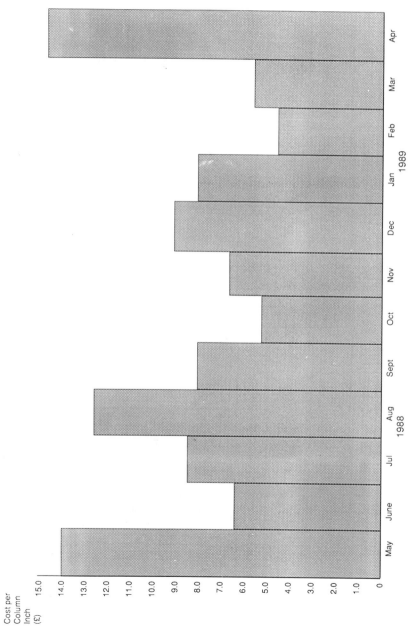

Figure 3 Volex Accessories, cost per column inch

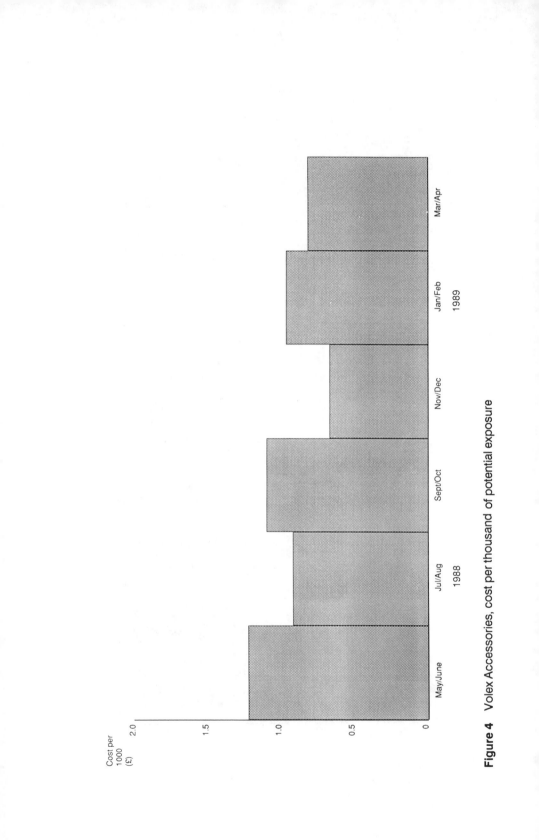

Figure 4 Volex Accessories, cost per thousand of potential exposure

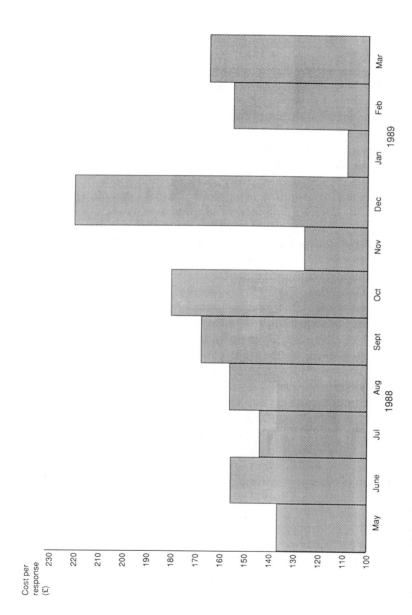

Figure 5 Volex Accessories, cost per response
Note: Average value of order per response was £2,500.

The next stage

The Designer Range programme concept was extended into a complimentary Designer Range which included shaving sockets, TV points, 45A kitchen switches and telephone sockets, all in the same designer colours and trim. The public relations programme to support the launch of the extended range concentrated on the different applications for the range whether it be office, hotel, luxury home or even stately home. In each the applications were developed into case-study articles aimed particularly at the interior design and new building press. The success of the earlier launch programme laid the way for the more ready acceptance of news of the extended Designer Range, and illustrates the value of time spent cultivating relations with the media.

Case discussion

This case illustrates the valuable contribution an effective public relations campaign can make to an organization's marketing operations. It helps to show that rather than being treated as entirely separate disciplines, public relations and marketing should be viewed as essentially complementary activities, albeit using different techniques and working in different ways towards a common goal.

In particular, the case highlights the basic ground rules of good media relations work – careful and realistic targeting of publications; the provision of clear and relevant information; the use of the appropriate house styles for the targeted publications; forward planning that takes account of publication deadlines and identifies opportunities for the placement of material; building respect and good relations with key journalists and editors and, where appropriate, the use of creative or novel techniques to capture attention. However obvious these may seem, no excuse is needed for restating them, as they are critical to the success of every media relations programme.

A number of other valuable lessons can be drawn from the case. First, the importance of investing in high quality photography, particularly for new product information. It must be remembered that gaining editorial coverage is only half the battle, it is attracting the attention of the readers that is the ultimate aim. An eye-catching and good quality photograph, in addition to being more acceptable to publishers, can help capture the readers' attention and induce them read the accompanying copy.

One of the basic ground rules of good media relations, to which less experienced readers should take particular note, is the value of forward research to identify which topics the targeted publications are planning to cover as special features in the coming months. These can be obtained from most publications in advance. This is often a vital step in developing a successful media relations campaign, as the planning of features usually involves quite long lead times and it is therefore, important to approach editors with relevant material at an early stage.

An further important lesson to be drawn from this case concerns the client–consultant relationship, particularly with regard to a marketing support project. In assessing the part that public relations can play in a new product launch and advising a client on his communications strategy, honesty and objectivity are essential. In recent years new products have proliferated, often competing for the same limited editorial space in the more popular consumer magazines and journals. There is little point raising client expectations over the likely coverage that can be achieved, especially in the national press and consumer magazines, if the product simply does not have the inherent news appeal that will make it stand out from other products competing for the same editorial space. Realistic and objective advice, however painful for the client to accept in the short term, will help gain their respect and trust for the consultancy in the longer term. Raising false expectations of what can be achieved will invariably lead to disappointment and discontent on the part of the client and to the eventual breakup of the relationship.

The problem of evaluating the impact of public relations is a perennial issue. The problem of isolating the specific effects of public relations activities from other factors affecting target audiences and measuring them accurately is one that has preoccupied practitioners for many years. These problems are exacerbated when the public relations programme is part of a larger marketing programme employing other promotional activities. Although there is no obvious solution to this problem, it is sometimes possible to build into a public relations programme mechanisms that at least allow some elements of the programme to be evaluated. In the Volex campaign, for example, reader enquiry services or response cards were used as a means of measuring those responses that were attributable specifically to the media relations activities.

This case also highlights the controversy that often surrounds the question of whether some types of activities carried out by public relations practitioners in support of marketing campaigns really warrant being called 'public relations'. Many might argue that they are often simply another form of marketing promotion. Obviously, in many cases this is a very 'grey' area. However, this type of argument is somewhat futile as the chief concern in such circumstances is not whether a particular type of activity should be designated public relations or marketing, but whether it can assist in developing a more effective and coherent communications strategy. This debate often arises more out of the internal rivalry over the allocation and control of budgets rather than out of any profound concern over the fundamental nature and title of the techniques employed.

Gaining independent endorsement of a new product or service in the form of press editorial can be an important factor in the success of the launch. This is particularly so when dealing with the launch of a very innovative or more expensive product or service which may involve the purchaser in a higher degree of perceived risk. There is little doubt that gaining editorial coverage is the responsibility of public relations and, in this sense, public relations provides support for the other more traditional marketing tactics such as sales promotions, personal selling and advertising.

Student discussion questions and exercises

1. Consider what are the key factors that distinguish public relations from marketing and in what circumstances is it important to distinguish between the two functions?
2. For a chosen category of publications, for example women's consumer press or photography magazines, find out on what topics they will be running special features in future months and what lead times they are working to in preparing these?
3. Examine the recent issues of one category of publications – photography, cooking, homes, DIY, and so on – identify any new product editorials and feature articles, and try to identify what public relations techniques were probably used to gain the coverage.

The Shell (UK) Livewire scheme

David Budge

Preview

The 'Livewire' scheme, initiated in 1982, with the support of Shell UK Ltd, represents part of the company's wide-ranging commitment to its community activities. The nation-wide scheme was initially designed to encourage young people to consider self-employment at a time when the economic climate made it difficult for young people to find more traditional opportunities for employment.

Given the somewhat chequered history of government-sponsored initiatives, intended to alleviate the problems of youth unemployment in the UK, it was important to project a positive image for the Livewire scheme, both to encourage young people to participate in it and to recruit the additional local industrial sponsors and voluntary advisers necessary for its successful implementation. This case examines the public relations programme carried out on behalf of Livewire and illustrates, in particular, how an effective national and regional campaign was developed that has succeeded in positioning Livewire as 'The Definitive Youth Enterprise Scheme' in the UK.

The case highlights the crucial importance to any major public relations project of thorough planning and meticulous attention to detail. Livewire involves the co-ordination of local news events on a massive scale, both to raise awareness of the scheme among young people and to publicize the Livewire competition. The latter involves a series of county and regional competitions to find the young entrepreneurs with the best new business ideas and culminates in a national final in London. As this case illustrates, the management of such an event requires practitioners to be not only excellent communicators, but also to possess first class organizational and logistical skills. The co-ordination of any major event, such as the Livewire competition, can always be prone to both minor and major 'disasters', and requires every aspect of the timing and organization of the event to be carefully orchestrated and rehearsed to avoid unforeseen problems detracting from its impact.

The task of raising awareness and interest in a scheme such as Livewire among a potentially apathetic audience, often revolves around engineering opportunities for a lead to be given by the audience's 'peer group'. In this case the programme enlisted the help of successful young entrepreneurs to demonstrate the possibilities that self-employment could hold for even relatively inexperienced young business people.

The task of communicating news about the scheme to what has traditionally been a particularly difficult 'market' to reach through more conventional media channels, has been eased by the appearance, in recent years, of a number of publications targeted specifically at the younger reader. The media relations programme for Livewire has been able to successfully exploit opportunities for feature coverage within many of these publications. However, the case also illustrates the innovative development of the scheme's own dedicated newspaper, *Link*, which not only served as a means of communicating with the 'enterprise network' as a whole, but also served to reinforce the position of Livewire as the pre-eminent scheme for young enterprising people.

Background

Livewire is a scheme supported by Shell UK Ltd which, when initiated in 1982, was designed to encourage and help young people between the ages of sixteen and twenty-five to consider self-employment as an alternative option in an economic climate where traditional full-time employment was, and still continues to be, more difficult to find.

The basis of the scheme is that each young person who comes forward with a reasonable idea for a business project will be allocated an individual adviser who will assist, encourage and support the youngster over a period of several months or longer, until the idea reaches the 'start-up' stage. The advisers are voluntary, being recruited from all areas of the public and private sectors. They are selected for their business experience and ability to relate to young people.

There is a secondary element to the scheme, in the form of a competition where Livewire entrants are encouraged to submit their business plans to adjudicating panels. The best plans are awarded grants for equipment and services and there is an overall Livewire UK winner, announced in June each year.

Livewire is co-ordinated by Project North East, one of Britain's best-known enterprise agencies.[1] They are employed by Shell UK to organize and administer a network of support groups, which in turn are responsible for running Livewire in specific areas of the UK via local co-ordinators and adviser networks.

The Glasgow-based consultancy, PR Consultants Scotland, were retained to carry out publicity and public relations in general for Livewire. The consultancy had been involved with the scheme since its beginnings as a pilot scheme in the Strathclyde Region of Scotland in 1982, and were in fact responsible for developing the scheme's 'corporate identity'.

Objectives

The Livewire scheme represents part of Shell UK's wide ranging commitment to its community activities. It was originally intended to contribute to the nation-wide movement to foster a sense of enterprise amongst the young in the face of the economic problems of the late 1970s and 1980s, which had severely affected traditional employment opportunities. The success of the scheme clearly depended on stimulating interest amongst the young sections of the population eligible to participate, and in attracting the necessary support for the scheme in terms of local advisers, volunteer counsellors, sponsorship, and so on.

PR Consultants Scotland were given the brief of developing a programme to generate and sustain the interest and support for the Livewire programme on a nation-wide basis. The key aim was to position Livewire as 'The Definitive Youth Enterprise Scheme in the UK'. This case study specifically covers the public relations programme carried out on behalf of Livewire between September 1987 and June 1988. The objectives set for the launch of the 1987 Livewire scheme were:

- To develop an awareness of the scheme amongst young people within the appropriate age group (16–25 years) in order to maximize the number of entries.
- to overcome an important credibility barrier by conveying the message to young people that self-employment is a realistic option, whatever their age, experience or background.
- To develop an awareness of Livewire amongst other relevant groups in order to attract support for the scheme in terms of local sponsorship, volunteer advisers, and so on.
- To equip local Livewire support groups with the basic public relations skills required to exploit local publicity opportunities.

With Livewire being a nation-wide scheme, it was essential that, in addition to national publicity generated through, for example, national newspapers and magazines, regional and local publicity was also generated.

The programme

The public relations programme had to take account of the need to stimulate initial interest in the programme during the launch phase, and then to sustain the interest during the life-span of the programme, climaxing with the national Livewire final, held in London at the end of June. The programme thus divided into three broad phases:

- The launch publicity for the scheme.
- The on-going publicity and media relations.
- The public relations for the Livewire competition at regional and national levels.

In addition, given the intention to exploit both national and local publicity opportunities, it was necessary to assist local groups to carry out basic media relations activities themselves.

Media skills training

In order to equip Livewire co-ordinators with the basic media relations skills necessary to exploit the local media opportunities, PR Consultants Scotland designed and conducted two intensive media skills training days in London and in Newcastle upon Tyne. These provided participants with a basic grounding in the structure and workings of the media, writing news releases, exploiting photo opportunities, negotiating features, and so on.

The launch

The launch date for the 1987 scheme was 22 September and comprised a series of simultaneous regional launches around the UK. Eight regional launches were held in the major population centres of London, Birmingham, Manchester, Bristol, Cardiff, Newcastle upon Tyne, Glasgow and Belfast. In order to maximize the awareness of the launch of the scheme, local county and regional co-ordinators were encouraged to repeat the launch concept on a local basis.

The adopted format involved holding the launch, wherever possible, on the premises of a young entrepreneur who, by example, would demonstrate the potential for young people. In addition, local celebrities or established entrepreneurs were invited along to provide endorsement for the scheme. PR Consultants Scotland handled the public relations activity for all eight of the regional launches. This included media relations, identification of suitable venues, celebrity appearances and photography, as well as the logistics and catering associated with each event.

The cumulative impact of these launches generated considerable media coverage around the country, and ensured that the 1987 Livewire scheme got off to a flying start.

On-going public relations activity

Recruitment to the Livewire scheme was open from September to the end of January. Hence it was necessary to sustain awareness and interest in the

scheme to encourage potential entrants to come forward. It was also important to help sustain the enthusiasm and commitment of those young people
who had initially responded to the launch. To this end it was important to
ensure on-going media coverage, both nationally and at the local level. The
strategy adopted was for the consultancy to pursue editorial coverage through
the negotiation of feature articles in national publications, whilst at the same
time assisting local co-ordinators to secure local media coverage by the supply
of 'prompt' draft releases and publicity ideas that could be actioned locally.

Major features were negotiated, for example, in *Cosmopolitan*, *Living*, *19*,
and the *Today* newspaper. This required considerable effort and forward planning, particularly in the case of consumer magazines such as *Cosmopolitan*,
where the long lead-times involved for features necessitated an initial approach and negotiations over the feature some six months in advance of its
appearance.

The considerable effort involved, both directly in securing national coverage, and in supporting the media relations activity of local co-ordinators, was
fully justified by the resulting sustained media coverage devoted to the
scheme. The combination of both local and national media coverage proved
mutually supportive and served to build up a momentum of interest and
awareness of the Livewire scheme amongst all target groups.

The Livewire Link *newspaper*

A key aim of the programme was to position Livewire as the definitive youth
enterprise scheme in the UK. In the knowledge that there was no publication
devoted specifically to the topic of enterprise in the UK, it was agreed with the
client to produce a regular newspaper specifically devoted to theme of youth
enterprise. Entitled *The Link*, the newspaper was initially conceived primarily
as a vehicle for communicating with Livewire co-ordinators (see Plate 6).
However, it was quickly recognized that *The Link* provided the means of communicating with the wider Youth Enterprise movement as a whole, carrying
news of general interest to individuals and organizations involved or interested in the movement – enterprise agencies, careers officers, youth and community workers, youth enterprise specialists, volunteers, sponsoring
organizations and government agencies. *The Link* offered the opportunity for
Livewire to become the authoritative source of information on issues of interest to the Youth Enterprise movement, as well as providing the means of dis-
seminating news throughout the Livewire network. The concept and design
for the newspaper was developed by the consultancy, with the co-ordination
of news relating to both Livewire and the enterprise movement in general
being carried out at the Livewire headquarters in Newcastle. Livewire co-ordinators throughout the country regularly submit local news stories to the
Newcastle HQ, where the newspaper is edited and subsequently produced by

Plate 5 *The Link* newspaper

the consultancy. Some 10,000–15,000 copies of each issue of *The Link* are distributed nationally. Naturally, *The Link* also provides an excellent means of publicizing the Livewire scheme and competition, as well as publicizing the results of the area, regional and national finals.

The Livewire competition

The competitive element of Livewire is manifest in a series of finals at county, regional and national and UK levels. Competition entrants submit their business plans, which are then judged by appointed expert panels in terms of such factors as the viability of the idea, the potential for growth, and the ability of the entrant to realistically carry out the plan. Winners at county and regional level can eventually progress to the national and UK finals. Shell UK donated £50,000 in awards for finalists, and this sum is matched by other regional sponsors offering substantial cash awards for finalists.

PR Consultants Scotland were directly responsible for publicity for the national finals in Wales, Northern Ireland and Scotland. This consisted of an extensive media relations programme and, in the case of the Scottish final, the complete orchestration of the event (see Appendix 9.1 the text of the press release issued at the time of the Scottish final).

The UK final

The UK final presentation itself, held in London on 28 June 1988, was a major event, with twenty Livewire finalists from all over the UK competing for the title of Britain's Top Young Entrepreneur (see Appendix 9.2 the text of the press release issued at the time of the UK final). The consultancy was again responsible for the complete stage management of the event, which was held at the Mermaid Theatre in Blackfriars. The awards were presented by Victor Kiam of Remington fame, one of the world's best-known entrepreneurs.

The management of such an event requires meticulous attention to detail, to ensure the smooth running of the event. The ceremony involved the arrangement of an audio-visual presentation, on-stage graphics and lighting, with the whole event being carefully scripted and rehearsed. Furthermore, a major media relations programme was mounted in advance, during and following the event.

The media relations programme amounted to a massive task in co-ordinating the release of news material both on a national and local level. The local media for each of the twenty finalists were contacted in advance of the event, with the Livewire story built around their representative in the final. This resulted in widespread advance publicity for the event.

The national media were contacted and invited to attend the event. Particular attention was paid to picture desks, news agencies and the broadcast media. A complicating factor was that the winners were not decided until 10.00 p.m. the night before the ceremony, judging having taken place in London during the day. However, before 8.00 a.m. the following morning, colour slides of the winners had been dispatched by Red Star to local television stations and London picture desks had been telephoned with details.

The resulting editorial coverage was impressive and included items on TV-am (six minutes), BBC Breakfast Time, Capital Radio, LBC, BBC External Services and Radio One Newsbeat. The story was widely covered in the national daily newspapers, including items in the *Daily Telegraph*, the *Guardian*, *The Times*, *Daily Express*, *Daily Mail* and *Today*, as well as a whole range of regional dailies and regional television and radio. Close liaison with the Press Association, conducted during the weeks prior to the final, ensured widespread coverage throughout the UK.

Following the final, news releases covering all the main winners were again prepared on a localized basis and despatched to the respective local media.

Bearing in mind that there are over 1,200 local weekly newspapers in the UK, albeit only a proportion of them were contacted directly, something of the sheer logistics of conducting the media relations campaign for Livewire can be gauged. In order to maximize media coverage for Livewire in general, and the final in particular, it was necessary to localize each news release to a very fine degree to take account of the specific local news interest. This meant, in effect, that often over sixty versions of a single release were produced, each with a slightly different and local angle on a story.

Consultancy commitment

It is important to acknowledge the invaluable assistance and commitment of the many co-ordinators involved in making the scheme a success. Also the quality of the relationship between the consultancy and the client had an important influence on how the creative input reflected the strategic objectives. As far as the consultancy's staff commitment was concerned, the account team varied in size over the course of the year. During the peak periods of the launch and national final a team of six was fully occupied on the programme. At other times between three and four of the consultancy's staff were working on aspects of the programme at any one time.

The results

The effectiveness of the public relations programme can be measured in a number of ways:

- First, in terms of media coverage, which was extensive, and which, according to research, generated 33 per cent of all entries to the Livewire scheme. As well as attracting direct entry into the scheme, editorial coverage succeeded in attracting interest from potential local sponsors and willing advisers keen to join the network.

Editorial coverage also played a valuable role in helping to convince young people that self-employment in general is not simply a pipedream, and with the assistance of schemes such as Livewire it could become a reality.

During the 1987–8 scheme, a total of over 620 editorial items were secured, including 595 press, 23 radio, and 10 television items.

- Second, in terms of recruitment of entries to the Livewire scheme – over 4,500 young people were attracted to the scheme to explore the option of working for themselves.

  Everyone who entered the scheme had the benefit of professional advice and guidance which the Livewire organizers believe will greatly assist them in deciding on their future careers.

- Third, the publicity generated has attracted widespread international interest and enquires have come from as far afield as Canada and Australia, and Livewire schemes have in fact already been established in Eire and Western Australia, based on the UK model.

The future

The outstanding success of Livewire has met with the enthusiastic approval of Shell UK Ltd, and they agreed to continue their support for at least three more years. Advance planning for the 1988–9 Livewire scheme began shortly after the completion of the 1987–8 UK final competition event. The lessons learnt from prior campaigns has allowed the approach adopted to be continually refined and modified to enhance its impact on Britain's young people.

Case discussion

The public relations programme for the Livewire scheme illustrates the importance of thorough planning and meticulous attention to detail in co-ordinating such a large-scale national and locally-based campaign. The success of the programme hinged on attracting young people to enter the scheme, as well as attracting support from companies, individuals and voluntary agencies. The message strategy for the programme had to overcome the natural reluctance of young people, who largely lacked business experience, to believe they could successfully start up in business for themselves. The approach taken recognized that merely raising awareness of the scheme and the competition prize money would not necessarily be sufficient. It was crucial to try to assuage the natural worries of young people, regarding the credibility of the self-employment option.

The approach adopted was essentially one of providing 'peer group' endorsement for the scheme by staging the launch events on the premises of successful young entrepreneurs. It was equally important to demonstrate the high degree of expert advice and support available to Livewire entrants. It should also be borne in mind that Livewire was taking place against a background of relatively high unemployment and deprivation of traditional employment opportunities for young people in many parts of the UK. A variety of government-funded schemes such as The Youth Opportunities Programme (YOP's) and The Youth Training Scheme (YTS) had been introduced during the 1980s, in response to the problems of unemployment amongst school leavers. In the main these had acquired a poor reputation and generally were seen as a 'last resort' option by young people seeking a career. It was important that Livewire distanced itself from such schemes, and presented a positive message of the realistic and exciting opportunities that Livewire offered for enterprising individuals. The fact that the scheme was sponsored by major private sector companies was an important factor in giving it credibility and encouraging entry.

The case provides some useful lessons for the management of a major grass roots media relations programme. The sheer volume and diversity of media opportunities, both in the local press and broadcast media, made for a massive logistical exercise in maintaining a nation-wide high profile for the scheme. Whilst news stories of national significance are of interest to the regional and local media, it is the local news angle of these that is of principal interest to these groups. The success of the local media relations activity stemmed from the careful fine tuning of each story to localize it to a very fine degree. This amounted to far more than merely researching the distribution list for news releases; it necessitated the customizing of stories to identify the specific local news angle that would maximize the chance of gaining local editorial coverage.

Managing a nation-wide local media relations programme involves a vast amount of background research to identify the structure of the local media in any area, the individual journalists and editors to be targeted, and the specific bias and interest adopted by different local publications. Armed with this information, it was then necessary to produce multiple versions of the same basic news release, tailored to the interest of each area. This often involved over sixty different versions of any one release being written. Clearly this involved an immense amount of work, and the partial solution to the problem of maintaining on-going media relations was to devolve some of the responsibility to local co-ordinators. This was made possible by first, organizing basic media relations training for co-ordinators, and second, by PR Consultants Scotland acting to issue basic draft 'prompt' releases that could be adapted by local co-ordinators to the interest and needs of their local media. Picture stories formed an important part of the media relations programme, and it was therefore important to ensure that high quality photography was available to editors, or that they were made aware of photo-opportunities. The overall success of the local media relations programme can thus be attributed both to its careful and detailed planning, and to the effective management of a network of local news co-ordinators.

At the national level, the story of the launch of Livewire and the competition final undoubtedly had natural news appeal. However, to sustain media interest over the course of the year was more difficult and required the proactive negotiation of feature stories with a variety of publications. A key lesson to be learnt is the need for considerable advance planning in seeking feature coverage, particularly in the case of consumer magazines, such as *Cosmopolitan*, where lead times for the planning of features can amount to six months or more. In the case of *Cosmopolitan*, negotiations to secure a four-page colour feature took place over a six-month period prior to the appearance of the article. The lead times for different publications and for the broadcast media can vary considerably, and must be understood if the maximum coverage is to be achieved.

The creation of the Livewire newspaper played an important part in establishing the primacy of Livewire in the Youth Enterprise movement. It allowed Livewire to assume the role of an authoritative source of information on all matters relating to the movement. It also fulfilled an important role in helping to maintain communication between the dispersed network of Livewire co-ordinators, facilitating the dissemination of information and giving an added sense of cohesion to the network.

The Livewire scheme involves the staging of numerous 'events' at national and area levels which, in themselves, provide the platform for much of the media relations activity, and require a great deal of careful forward planning. The selection of venues, the orchestration of the event itself, the co-ordination of timetables for any speakers, and the management of the publicity for each event, are time-consuming and sometimes complex matters. That these all passed off relatively smoothly and received extensive media coverage was a result of the consultancy's thorough attention to detail and careful forward planning. However, as with any complex programme of events, particularly one that is repeated from year-to-year, there are always lessons to be learnt from the previous year's experience. An important part of the planning for Livewire, carried out by PR Consultants Scotland, is a thorough review of the previous year's campaign to identify the cause of any problems experienced, and to identify ways to improve on the success of the programme. As Livewire illustrates, it is important for any on-going programme to constantly look for new ways in which the interest of the media can be maintained. In the case of Livewire, it is vital not only to stimulate interest amongst a new set of young people, and also possibly new advisers and sponsors each year, but also to find ways of maintaining the freshness of the story and combat the possible tendency of the media to view the story simply as 'old news'.

Student discussion questions and exercises

1. Consider to what extent the British government's promotion of the 'Enterprise Culture' during the 1980s proved a positive or negative influence on the Livewire scheme. If asked to counsel the client on how Livewire should be positioned in relation to government-sponsored schemes, what would be your advice?
2. Compile a local media distribution list for your county or region to be used for the distribution of news releases for Livewire or a similar programme. Identify the particular emphasis that you would try to build into the story for specific publications.
3. Select six consumer magazines and contact them to ascertain the lead times for feature articles and their planned schedule of features for the coming twelve months.

Note

1. Enterprise agencies are organizations, often involving collaboration between the private and public sector, whose role is the regeneration of local economies through the promotion of new business start-ups and enterprise amongst the young and unemployed in particular.

Appendix 9.1 Body copy of the press release for the Livewire 1988 Scottish final

---

DESIGNS ON SUCCESS

Scotland's top young entrepreneur is a 25-year-old graphic designer from Kirkcaldy.

Brigid Doherty is the winner of the 1988 Livewire Scotland Award, set up by Shell UK Ltd to encourage young people to create their own work.

Her business called 'Bridg-it Graphics' provides a complete graphic design and printing service.

As a result of increased business activity, Brigid is about to move to new and larger premises in Kirkcaldy as well as employing a full-time designer.

At a presentation ceremony held in Glasgow today (Wednesday, 1 June 1988) she received the Livewire Scotland trophy and a cheque for £1,000. The presentation was made by Mr Tom Farmer, Chairman and Chief Executive of Kwik-Fit Holdings plc.

Brigid's entry was judged best overall by a panel of experts out of a total of 364 entries from throughout Scotland.

Now she will go on to represent Scotland in the Livewire UK final on 28 June 1988 in London, where she will compete with young entrepreneurs from all over the UK for the Livewire UK title and a top prize of £3,000.

The basis of Livewire is that every young person between 16 and 25 who comes forward with a reasonable idea for their own business is allocated an individual adviser who will assist and encourage development of viable projects until a 'start-up' position is reached.

Also representing Scotland in the Livewire UK final as a special category winner will be 21-year-old Ellen Arnison from Aberdeen who runs 'Orchard Lingerie'. She won the £500 award in the best start-up business category.

Livewire originated in the Strathclyde Region of Scotland in 1982 and was supported throughout the UK by Shell, Livewire has grown to become the UK's definitive youth enterprise scheme.

1 June 1988

Issued on behalf of Livewire by David Wallace/David Budge, PR Consultants Scotland. Telephone 041–333–0557.

Appendix 9.2 Body copy of the press release for the Livewire 1988 UK final

RUSTY SPRING LEADS TO UK AWARD

The UK's top young entrepreneur is 25-year-old Nick Munro from Chester, who was inspired to set up in business after finding a rusty old spring in the attic.

Going on to develop a range of designer tableware has won Nick the top Livewire UK award which is sponsored by Shell UK Ltd to encourage young people to become self-employed.

He received a Livewire gold medal and £3,000 from world-famous businessman, Victor Kiam, at a presentation ceremony in London on Tuesday, 28 June 1988.

Nick was judged the most promising young entrepreneur from 4,500 original entrants to the Livewire scheme.

Based in Chester, Nick started his company in July 1987 providing a range of stylish tableware under the name of 'Trinkets'. He was awarded the Design Centre selection in late 1987 and is currently selling his products in Harrods, Selfridges and The Design Centre Shop.

The idea started when Nick discovered that a rusty old spring found in the attic made a perfect egg cup holder.

Other major awards included £1,000 and a Livewire silver medal to 25-year-old Alison Wood from Darley near Harrogate, who was voted the Most Promising Established Business. Her business 'Alison Elizabeth Originals' produces hand-knitted garments and hand-knitting kits.

There were two joint winners in the Most Promising Start-Up Business category winning a silver medal and £1,000 each.

They were 24-year-old Jenna Shaw, a designer of fashion accessories from Newtownabbey, Belfast, and Ellen Arnison, aged 21 from Aberdeen, who supplies mail-order lingerie for the woman with the fuller bust.

Originally set up in 1982 by Shell UK, Livewire is now widely recognised as Britain's definitive youth enterprise scheme.

As well as allocating a personal adviser to every entrant, Livewire offers a total of over £100,000 in regional and national awards, allocated throughout England, Northern Ireland, Scotland and Wales.

Livewire will be re-launched throughout the UK in September 1988.

1 July 1988

Issued on behalf of Livewire by David Wallace/David Budge, PR Consultants Scotland. Telephone 041–333–0557.

British Telecom: the payphones story

Avril Macdonald

Preview

Few organizations in the UK are perhaps better known, or evoke more violently opposing views among the media and public than British Telecom. British Telecom was the first company returned to private ownership as part of the Conservative Government's programme of privatization of the UK's nationalized industries. However, because of the obvious public concern over its near monopoly of the telephone services in the UK, a regulatory body, OFTEL, was established to safeguard the interests of all telephone users and ensure BT could not abuse its near monopoly position.

Since privatization BT has been under virtually constant 'fire' from both OFTEL and the media for its failure to achieve its promised improvements in the quality of the telephone services. As a result of this dissatisfaction with its services, its announcements of apparently large profits have also naturally been criticized heavily. BT's severe 'image problem' has stemmed largely from a failure by the public to fully appreciate the nature of its business or the huge investment that the company is required to make to maintain and upgrade its services.

The payphones service has, perhaps, attracted more criticism than any other part of its services. Even prior to privatization, BT recognized the need to invest heavily in improving the payphones service and had begun a nationwide campaign of improvements to this service. However, many of the problems of payphones being out of order were due to vandalism, a fact that the public and media failed to acknowledge, placing the blame squarely on the company's failure to attend to the faulty equipment. Despite significant progress being made with its programme of improvements, BT continued to come under attack both in the media and from OFTEL.

BT realized that in order to improve its public image, it must not only effect the promised improvements to the payphones service, but it must be seen to have done so. This would require a major programme to educate the public both as to the real cause of problems and the progress BT was making in rectifying the situation. This case examines the public relations programme carried out by the West of Scotland Division of BT, in particular, to restore public confidence in the payphones service and improve BT's image both with the media and the public. It illustrates the important principle, that public relations cannot hope to effect a change in public opinion unless they have a positive and credible message to communicate.

Background

British Telecom operates the largest in-house public relations teams in the UK and 1988 saw the company take massive steps towards the most effective organization of some 150 people working in this capacity.

Two events, one after the other, resulted in BT being described in 1987 by the *Financial Times* as 'Britain's most hated company'. First, privatization in 1984, followed by industrial action, thrust BT into the glare of the media in a way it had never before experienced. Privatization, and the publicity campaign which encouraged private and institutional investors to become shareholders, presented the company as one poised to provide the latest in telecommunications to all UK customers. It was also the first nationally-owned utility to be privatized.

Until this time BT had few image problems, probably largely due to public apathy. However, industrial action in January and February 1987 made sure that public attention was focused on the company and its activities, and BT did not fare well.

Household name

Although BT is a household name in the UK as a national telephone company, the full extent of its business is not really recognized. While its principal business is to provide domestic and business customers with telephones and a local, national and international telephone network, it is also involved in an extraordinarily diverse range of other activities in the world of communications. These broadly include information transfer, data transmission and entertainment.

It employs 245,000 staff and has almost 23 million telephone customers. More than 70 million calls are handled daily and an ever-growing number of products and services, ranging from telex, Prestel, high-speed data transmission and radio-paging to facsimile, electronic mail and cellular mobile radio are being marketed to both the domestic and business sectors.

With privatization came liberalization and, for the first time, BT faced competition in the provision of a network telephone service. Years of underinvestment were finally being recognized, as the company's new status impelled its managers to tackle the resultant problems. Too late it was realized that the company had been thrust under a spotlight and found to be wanting. As far as the public were concerned, BT was perceived as an inefficient profit-mad organization.

In fact, sweeping changes *were* being effected, for BT had been a huge bureaucracy operating many outdated practices, but change could not happen overnight. However, following privatization and the ensuing publicity campaign, the public expected BT to change instantly, and when it failed to do so the consequences were predictable. BT became the media's 'whipping boy'. Staff morale dropped and the share price began to slide as, day-after-day, damning stories appeared.

In order to change and improve the service it offered to customers, BT had to implement policies that would be unpopular, although carried out with the agreement of OFTEL, the independent industry watch-dog body for telecommunications. Some of the improvements that were taking place included: tariff rebalancing, network modernization, training of staff for directory enquiries, negotiations with trade unions over demarcation, improvements in the quality of service offered to customers and efforts to help customers understand the changes that were taking place.

BT staff at the grass roots level could not understand the contradiction between what they knew was taking place to improve the service to customers and the company's worsening reputation.

This situation presented a complex set of public relations problems for BT. Senior management in BT recognized the importance, not only of actual improvement in operations, but also of good public relations. They recognized that BT's image would only improve with an increased understanding of the company's efforts by its customers.

The structure of public relations at BT

BT faced major issues on a national level as well as at regional and local levels. At the national level it had to adjust to its newly-privatized status, which placed its financial performance under the spotlight of the City analysts. Turnover for the financial year 1986-7 was in the order of £9,424 million. Whilst undoubtedly a large sum, investment was running at £15 million a week.

Although profit levels were respectable and on target for a company of its size, this fact was not given full recognition by the financial press. However, it was the tabloid press in particular that seized on the expectations of major improvements in customer service levels raised at the time of privatization, and the company's subsequent failure to match them overnight, running stories vigorously attacking BT's performance.

Many of the problems stemmed from outdated management practices and the lack of investment, which had resulted in an ageing network and methods of dealing with customers' sales and bills enquiries that fell far short of the excellent service expected. BT's world lead in telecommunications technology was virtually unrecognized by the customers.

Modernization

Privatization had allowed BT to invest in a massive programme of modernization which was under way in every part of Britain. By the year 2000 the entire network will operate using digital exchanges, with all the extra facilities this will allow, such as bill itemization. The imminent introduction of a new computer CSS (customer service system) is intended to provide a single point of contact for all customers rather than transferring them from person to person.

In a concerted effort to improve customer service, BT had committed itself to a management process known as 'Total Quality Management'. This process had been successfully adopted from American management practice by the Japanese in the 1950s to help them work towards rapid economic growth. BT's involvement would see increased training throughout the company at all levels over a period calculated to take between five and seven years.

A large team was needed at headquarters, and consisted of corporate PR advisers, the HQ press office, government relations and sponsorship advisers, as well as a large organization involved with world-wide advertising and exhibitions.

The single biggest revenue earning part of BT is its UK Telecom operation, and in order to promote the company's improving service and products, a group known as the Customer Communications Unit was set up to develop the marketing strategy and handle advertising, promotional and PR campaigns.

Gaining commitment

BT operates nationally and internationally. Within the UK, in 1987, it was divided into twenty-eight operating districts. The importance of public relations was recognized when these districts were created. Each district appointed a public relations manager and a team to carry out media relations and internal communications – usually functioning within a marketing department and working alongside colleagues working on advertising and exhibitions.

At that time the West of Scotland District public relations operation had a Public Relations Manager, an Internal Communications Manager and one PR assistant. Public relations was seen as an important way of keeping the staff informed about developments – both as a courtesy and as a way of gaining commitment to projects through improved communications and, subsequently, morale. Increasing importance was attached to the regular staff newspaper designed to inform BT employees about issues concerning them.

The media relations activities carried out by the district were designed to to inform carefully targeted sectors of the public about the company's activities.

Together these groups work on integrated campaigns with both internal and external communications objectives, covering a range of issues unequalled in the UK for their complexity.

Whilst it is impossible within the scope of a case study to cover fully the range of work carried out on behalf of BT by the West of Scotland public relations function, and by the other twenty-seven districts and the HQ PR function, the following case study illustrates one particularly successful project in which all parts of the company played significant parts.

The payphones issue

One of the first projects undertaken in my capacity as PR Manager in the West of Scotland was the production, in early 1987, of a video to be used in customer awareness sessions on the Total Quality Management programme. It aimed to offer BT staff in the West of Scotland District the opportunity to see a video in which customers gave their views on the company in a series of street interviews which took place in towns and cities throughout the west of Scotland. When asked to single out any particular area for criticism, most interviewees chose payphones.

As far as the public were concerned, payphones never worked, they were dirty, there were never enough of them and they were in the wrong place. Many of these problems were due to vandalism in the attempt to remove cash. However, customers perceived the failure as BT's, and blamed the company for failing to provide a reliable service. Unknown to these customers, a modernization programme had been underway since 1979, when Glasgow payphone engineers designed and launched a new telephone box, forerunner to the now familiar smoked perspex box.

The replacement of the old pay-on-answer telephones with stronger, more attractive, and better-designed models, and the removal of the old red payphone boxes, had been gradually improving the service for some time. With the increased pace of improvements that were beginning to meet targets, there was a positive news story to be told about the company.

The public relations programme

Following on from the vox pop interviews, the West of Scotland public relations unit devised a medium-term programme designed to raise public awareness of the work being done to improve the service, in order to improve the image of the company and position it as one committed to improving its service to customers.

Before deciding on what form the major events of the programme should

141

take, discussions were held with payphone staff, talking through the major issues, exploring their work schedule, and focusing on problem areas. In the course of these discussions it became clear that the West of Scotland payphones division had one major objective. They planned to renew all public telephones by March 1987 and replace old red boxes by mid-1990. They were improving the gathering of information on all boxes as a result of better systems and improved technology, and card phone were also being introduced. Their information showed, for example, that West of Scotland District spent £500,000 each year on repairs to vandalized telephones and telephone boxes. Vandalism was costing the company vast sums of money each year and causing payphones not to work. However, the public in the west of Scotland were unaware that any of this activity was taking place, and to judge from the street interviews,was unaware of the extent to which vandalism caused communities to be without a public telephone service. In addition, the mounting media criticism was having a depressing effect on staff, particularly in the payphones division.

It was necessary, therefore, to set up an event which would appeal to the media, and at the same time allow BT's side of the story to be told. The perfect opportunity would occur in July when the last pay-on-answer telephone would be replaced with an electronic model.

it was decided to arrange for the presentation of an old red box to Glasgow's People's Palace Museum in the exotic setting of the Winter Gardens to mark the milestone. A press release and background information detailing the story behind the improved service was prepared.

The result

The story was well received and proved highly successful in providing the platform for BT to demonstrate the nature of its big drive to improve its service to customers. The story was carried by all Scotland's national newspapers and interviews were set up with the BBC and Independent Television, as well as with local and national radio.

Scottish daily newspaper crime reporters followed up with stories on the organized crime involved in theft from payphones, thereby positioning BT as a company acting responsibly in the community, both to stop crime and improve payphone serviceability. The success of the programme illustrates the fact that public relations can only be really successful when it has a positive story to tell, and in this case the payphones division provided just such a story.

Whilst the presentation of the phonebox to the People's Palace marked the highpoint of the campaign, a series of other activities were also carried out between March and July 1987:

March

● A newsletter issued by the payphones group to community relations police.

Objective: To help police, with whom BT worked on anti-vandalism initiatives, understand how their co-operation was vital in the fight against crime, while BT installed modified and crime-resistant telephones.
Result: Increased police awareness and a gradual increase in the number of convictions in court from 73 in 1986–7 to 109 in 1987–8.

● The launch of an on-going editorial and advertising features campaign in local newspapers.

Objective: To help customers in larger towns understand the benefits of new card phones, and to explain how their installation would help improve the payphones service as a result of the cash target being removed.
Result: Increased customer familiarity with the concept, breaking down the traditional reluctance to accept a new service – some 50,000 readers being reached.

April

● A new scheme of installing particularly badly vandalized phoneboxes at police stations and community centres was introduced.

Objective: To demonstrate to police and communities that BT is committed to reducing vandalism by siting payphones where there is less opportunity for vandalism to occur.
Result: Eighteen phone boxes were provided or resited and as a result continued to work and offer the public a service in a protected environment.

July

● The presentation of an old red phone box to the People's Palace, Glasgow (see Plate 6).

Objective: To position BT as a company committed to the improvement of the service and to provide, through an attractive picture opportunity and newsworthy background story, the basic ingredients of a good news story.
Result: Extensive media coverage, raising awareness of BT's progress towards completing its promised programme improvements to the payphones service.

August

● The launch of 'Protect Your Payphone Poster Competition' for schools.

Plate 6 The presentation of a red telephone box to the People's Palace, Glasgow, in July 1987

Objective: To involve children in the concept of safeguarding the public payphone service from vandalism.

Result: The competition was successfully launched to all children in the Strathclyde Region.

The second phase of the payphone issue

In September 1987, against the backdrop of the work being carried out in the districts, and HQ support in the form of a general anti-vandalism campaign aimed particularly at children, the Office of Telecommunications (OFTEL) published a report showing that only 76 per cent of public payphones worked at any one time. The report was widely publicized and clearly placed the payphones division once more under the critical media spotlight.

In response, Mike Bett, BT's UK Managing Director, promised to improve the service by raising the percentage of working payphones from 76 per cent to 90 per cent by March 1988. This commitment obviously put the payphones division on trial.

The programme

The resulting increased attention focused on the payphones issue required both a stepping up of the modernization programme, and also an increased role for public relations.

In the West of Scotland District more staff and money were devoted to the payphones group, and the PR team working at HQ in Corporate Communications devised a programme that built on district initiatives and the under-recognized strengths of the organization.

Operationally, BT payphone engineers worked tremendously hard to achieve the target. Follow-up research in January, February, and March 1988, showed that major improvements had been completed and the first target met.

In February Mike Abbott of the Customer Communications Unit, now in charge of the payphones public relations programme, introduced a number of measures aimed at addressing the issues:

- Regular quarterly meetings to update progress and review the issues.

- Recruitment of PR consultants, the Quentin Bell Organization (QBO), to carry out a national public relations campaign.

- Presentations by district PR Managers on their local initiatives.

The public relations programme was managed centrally to make it both more efficient and effective.

The huge public relations programme was carried out at both national and local levels, with each of BT's districts carrying out locally-devised media campaigns in their communities, while HQ colleagues gathered information, produced press releases and organized the on-going medium-term campaign.

The results

The success of the payphones group in meeting its target was acknowledged in a news release in April 1988 headed, 'Professor Carlesburg congratulates BT for achieving call box targets'. The story detailed the company's success in beating its own objective to make 92.3 per cent of all call boxes work by the end of March. It demonstrated that BT's promised improvements in the payphone service had now been achieved, and received approval from Professor Carlesburg of OFTEL, which had published the earlier damning report.

In April the HQ press office issued a further release entitled, 'BT promises further payphone improvements'. This heralded the move to make still further improvements in BT's service to its payphone customers, and a subsequent corporate advertising campaign was devised for national television, to ensure that as many of the company's customers as possible were aware of the achievement.

The mammoth public relations campaign continued with corporate television advertising in the autumn, after research showed that customer's perceptions about the improvement in the service lagged behind the reality.

In June the company organized a conference in conjunction with TVS entitled 'Combating Vandalism', which followed on from their successful joint children's poster competition in December. More than 150 police and community figures interested in the subject attended, and the event positioned BT as a company seriously concerned about the issue and also forged an exchange of ideas with other organizations such as British Rail and London Transport, who suffered similar problems.

QBO continued the media relations campaign, and produced a useful press pack containing a variety of feature articles on the payphone service which the districts could use.

The story so far

British Telecom promised further improvements and they too have been achieved. In April 1989 BT were able to announce that they had increased serviceability to 96 per cent nationally. West of Scotland District achieved 97.2 per cent. This achievement was released to the press and most newspapers commented on it. More importantly it was possible to publish the results of a survey carried out by QBO, that showed that the public are now far more aware of the improvements in the service than before. A national advertising campaign promised that although nineteen out of twenty boxes are now working at all times, 'we're still working on the other one'.

Summary

This continuing campaign demonstrates how a combination of actual improved service, together with a public relations campaign which seeks to educate and inform customers, can work well. Without the dedication of all those who worked so hard to achieve and maintain improvements, there would be no public relations programme. However, without the public relations programme customer perceptions would be very different:

- There would be greater resistance to the introduction of cardphones.
- There would be general acceptance of BT as being responsible for all damage to payphones.
- There would be less awareness of the importance of vandalism to payphone serviceability.
- There would be less awareness of the target which payphones provide for criminals.
- There would be less awareness of the massive improvements which have taken place in the service, and on which BT plans to improve further.

The payphones campaign is, of course, only one of a wide range of public relations activities being carried out, but is one that illustrates how public relations can play an important role in providing increased understanding of a company's activities to a huge community. It also shows how it is important for a company such as BT, with a very high public profile, to recognize the importance of honest communications with its public, and the importance of maintaining careful monitoring of the perceptions of customers, and the public in general, about the company.

BT Chairman, Ian Vallance, recognized the vital importance of public relations for the company at a top management seminar at which he commented:

> It's reputation that's the key word, because public relations is about reputation. There are two things that are needed if we are to turn around our reputation. The first is delivery. Its the reality of the quality of service that we produce, and the value for money that we offer – that's the reality; but the second thing is the perception of that reality; and that's where public relations comes in.

Case discussion

This case helps to illustrate something of the problems that any high-profile organization can encounter in communicating with its public and in managing its reputation. It also highlights some of the fundamental maxims of effective public relations practice.

British Telecom is one of the best known companies within the UK, the vast majority of the population make use of its services, and a relatively large number of people now own shares in the company since its privatization. However, as this case shows, familiarity does not necessarily lead to more favourable attitudes towards a company. Many people still believe that BT is essentially operating a public utility. This has merely exacerbated the problems faced by the company in the post-privatization period in trying to establish its reputation as an efficient, well-managed company, and a leader in the field of telecommunications. Perhaps BT's biggest problem has been the task of trying to shake off the somewhat tarnished image associated with its days as a nationalized industry. Privatization placed the company under intense public and media scrutiny, and faced the company with the major challenge of trying to communicate the nature of its business to an array of different publics who tended, in the main, to harbour some degree of hostility towards it. As a result, public relations had, and continues to have, a major role in re-educating the public, as well as the business community, about the company and the true nature of its operations. This task is not helped by the highly complex technical nature of the telecommunications industry.

By the very nature of its business, BT is involved with vast numbers of customers – domestic subscribers, business users, as well as payphone users. These customers' day-to-day experiences of BT's services are clearly a very powerful influence on their perceptions of the company. BT's problems highlight an important lesson for all public relations programmes, namely, that public relations activity on its own cannot change audience perceptions of an organization unless it has a positive and credible message to communicate. As Ian Vallance, BT Chairman, acknowledged, it was improvements in delivery that had to be the number one priority. However, the case also illustrates that even when an organization has taken action to correct failings in its service, there still often remains the task of convincing audiences of this fact and of changing their attitudes towards the organization.

As the case illustrates, public perceptions of an organization, once well established, can be very difficult to change. BT, despite its efforts to improve its services in general, and to combat the particular problem of payphone vandalism, has continued to suffer from its old image as a huge and largely inefficient nationalized industry. Any failure to meet the exacting standards set for the service have attracted a barrage of criticism, and any good news regarding the improvements taking place have tended to be discounted as nothing more than what the paying public should expect. Clearly, as this case shows, any high profile organization such as BT must work hard to cultivate and win over the media, who can prove a very powerful enemy or an equally valuable ally in the battle to create a positive image for the respective organization.

As far as the critics of BT were concerned, the payphones issue became something of a *cause célèbre*, with the media often acting as both 'judge and jury'. Given the hostility that existed towards BT, it was clear that perceptions of it would only change slowly. The payphones service, as perhaps the most visible symbol of the company's public service, naturally became a prime target of public criticism of the company. The fact that the problems with payphones not working were, more often than not, due to vandalism, went largely unacknowledged. Instead, the blame was squarely placed on BT's shoulders. It was vital, therefore, for BT to recognize the 'symbolic value' of solving the payphones problem. However, achieving the targets for improvements in the payphone service alone could not change perceptions overnight. But once the planned programme of improvements was completed, the public relations staff at least had a positive message that they could begin to communicate and build on.

It is important to recognize that the payphones issue threatened BT's relationship with audiences other than just its customers (and the media). The payphones issue was also an important 'test' of BT's real ability to shake off its old public utility image and reposition itself as an efficient, customer-centred, and socially responsible organization. As a publically-quoted company, BT needed to maintain the confidence of its new shareholders and the City in general (whilst at the same time avoiding falling foul of the regulatory body – OFTEL). In this sense the payphone issue placed BT on 'trial'. For City audiences it was an indicator of the company's ability to deliver its promised improvements in efficiency. While for government audiences, and those critical of privatization, it was a test of BT's ability to act responsibly and to maintain a vital public service.

BT, therefore, faced something of a dilemma; on one hand it needed to maintain investor confidence in its performance and ability to generate a satisfactory level of profits. On the other hand improved financial performance only served to stoke-up crticisms of its failing to fully achieve the promised improvements in its services. BT's public relations staff are therefore, constantly faced with the delicate task of balancing the image projected of the company, in order to maintain the goodwill of these different audiences.

In terms of the practical aspects of a public relations programme, the payphones case illustrates the benefits of a carefully co-ordinated public relations programme conducted at both local and national levels. In BT's case, the sheer size of its operations, particularly with its payphones service, made it necessary to address the problem on a regional and local basis, as well as at the national level. This allowed the programme to be adapted to local situations and allowed its district public relations staff to exploit news opportunities within their local and regional media. This resulted in 'grass roots' coverage of local news items to be generated that could also, where appropriate, be worked up into national media stories. The payphones campaign succeeded in generating a string of locally-based stories that cumulatively worked towards raising public awareness of BT's efforts to improve the service. This local media relations activity, when combined with that carried out on a national level, gradually worked to bring about a change in the tone of the coverage afforded to the company.

The centrally co-ordinated anti-vandalism campaign helped to reinforce the local groundswell of positive news coming out from the company. The targeting of children in particular, through an anti-vandalism poster competition, proved a useful means of raising awareness of the need for public support to prevent damage to payphone boxes.

As the case also illustrates, internal communication programmes can often form a vital part of any public relations programme. During the payphones campaign, BT's public relations staff identified the importance of both internal and external communications, recognizing that the promised improvements in the service, necessary for the public relations effort to be credible, depended on the efforts and commitment of the payphones division's staff. The repeated attacks by the media on the service depressed morale and threatened the success of the programme. Public relations was, therefore, used internally to help keep the staff informed of developments and bolster morale, whilst activities at the district and national level sought to correct the misperceptions amongst the media and public. In an organization the size of BT, internal employee communication must always assume a high priority, helping to maintain staff morale and foster good industrial relations. However, it is also important to recognize that employees can also act as important opinion formers about a company, both through their daily working contact with the public and through their position in their respective communities.

In summary, the success of BT's campaign illustrates many of the key principles found in any effective public relations programme. Its success depended on careful planning, targeting and attention to detail during its implementation. The starting point was careful research of public attitudes and opinions towards BT, which was maintained throughout the campaign to monitor results. The campaign employed sound media relations techniques, producing well-written and informative materials and, wherever possible, adopting a proactive approach to the generation of news stories for distribution both at the national and local level. Particular attention was paid to maintaining channels of communication with the police and local community leaders, this being critical to the campaign to combat vandalism.

Finally, the importance of independent and authorative opinion, in this case in the form of OFTEL's recognition of the achievements of BT with respect to the payphone service, should not be overlooked. Independent expert reports or statements, as was shown in the Forgemasters case, can be a very potent weapon in the hands of public relations, providing indisputable support for the claims of the organization.

Student discussion questions and exercises

1. Consider what other PR techniques BT could have employed in seeking to combat the problem of customer perceptions of the payphones service.
2. Examine and compare the internal staff newspapers or magazines of several public sector or private sector organizations. Try to evaluate how effective they are as a means of internal communications and what role they play in the public relations activity of the respective organizations.
3. For one of the recently privatized companies (British Gas, TSB, British Steel, and so on) analyse the coverage it has received in recent months in the national press (at a national and local level) in terms of:

   - The extent and content of the coverage.
   - The issues involved and the overall positive or negative tone of the articles.
   - The differences in the treatment of issues by various publications.
   - Consider how far it is possible to identify a proactive role played by public relations in gaining the coverage for any particular issue involving your selected company.

Handling the deregulation issue: a public relations programme on behalf of the Scottish Bus Group

John Morton

Preview

This case examines the Scottish Bus Group's (SBG) campaign to correct the widespread misperceptions, among the media and the general public, of its role in the traffic chaos that affected the city of Glasgow, following the first phase of the deregulation of the city's bus services in 1986. It illustrates some of the key principles involved in conducting an effective media relations programme.

The largely false and misleading accusations made against the SBG by its rival, Strathclyde Buses, were given credibility by enlisting the support of the Chairman of the local authority transportation committee as a spokesman. As this case illustrates, 'source credibility' can be a crucial factor when developing a media relations programme.

As with many issues nowadays, the media played a critical part in influencing the opinions of both the local authorities and the travelling public on the question of the deregulation of the buses. SBG realized it was vital to try to correct the false perceptions of its role in the bus controversy, largely created by earlier media coverage of the accusations made against them. The sustained media relations campaign carried out was designed to confront the company's critics with the true facts and to challenge their false allegations. Ultimately this was able successfully to reposition the SBG as a company actively trying to solve the traffic problems caused by deregulation, and concerned to improve the service offered to the travelling public. This case illustrates how, through skilful presentation of information and open honest communication with the media, it is possible to develop a successful campaign that can work to change the perceptions of a particular target audience.

Background

In October 1986 TMA Communications were appointed by the Scottish Bus Group to provide public relations support for its position following the deregulation of bus services in Scotland. Until 31 August 1986 Strathclyde Buses had a monopoly on all city-centre services in Glasgow. On this date the Scottish Bus Group, comprising the Clydeside, Central, Kelvin and Western bus companies, introduced services into the city-centre, as part of a four-phase deregulation plan introduced by Strathclyde Region.

Strathclyde Buses immediately accused the Scottish Bus Group (SBG) of 'muscling in' and 'overloading the system'. Many false allegations and misrepresentations were made in the press by Strathclyde Buses. The culmination of this unfair press occurred after city-centre traffic was brought to a standstill on 11 October, with the blame being levelled at the SBG. On this day Glasgow city centre witnessed a two-mile traffic jam as more than 400 buses an hour crawled through the main city-centre streets.

The criticisms of deregulation of bus services were not peculiar to Glasgow alone. The question of the deregulation of bus services, introduced by the Conservative Government as part of its policy to promote competition, was the subject of considerable controversy throughout the UK. It was the government's intention that deregulation would lead to a better and more efficient service for commuters, and that increased competition would act to restrain the prices charged by bus operators. However, the initial response to deregulation from commuters, other road users and local authorities in those cities and towns where it had been implemented was somewhat mixed. The principal criticisms included: claims of unfair competition amongst bus operators; confusion over the timetabling of new services; and, particularly, the excessive congestion being caused to local city traffic systems as a result of the virtually uncontrolled expansion of services. In most cases deregulation was accompanied by fierce competition both between the new rival private bus operators as well as between the private operators and the remaining local authority controlled services. This was particularly the case on the potentially more profitable urban and city-centre services.

Immediately following the introduction of the first phase of the planned deregulation in Glasgow, the Strathclyde Bus Company expanded its service outwith the city-centre at the same time as it was attacking the SBG for introducing its services into the city-centre. Strathclyde Bus Company used the Convener of Transport on the council, Councillor Waugh, as a spokesperson to make allegations about the SBG. His position on the council gave him the credibility that Strathclyde Bus Company needed. The allegations he made were, however, essentially false.

The Scottish Bus Group were accused of introducing 450 minibuses into the city-centre when, in fact, they introduced only 35. This alleged overcrowding was cited as the reason for the traffic chaos in Glasgow on 11 October. SBG, in their defence, alleged that the problem on this date was actually caused by a combination of factors – an abnormally high incidence of roadworks and street closures, a CND march, excessive illegal parking and the breakdown of buses.

Although the first phase of the deregulation was introduced on 31 August 1986, the Strathclyde Regional Authority still retained certain powers to control bus operators in the region and, ultimately, could appeal to the Traffic Commissioner to impose new rules on all bus operators. The Traffic Commissioner could order bus operators to redivert services, reduce their services or even take action to cancel their registration. Hence the criticisms that were being levelled against SBG, if allowed to go unanswered, could have led to new regulations being introduced that would threaten the viability of their operations, or even force them out of business altogether. It was therefore vital to correct the misleading coverage afforded to the issue within the press, and to counter, in particular, the accusations levelled against SBG which were causing the public (particularly, those commuters worse effected by the traffic chaos) and local MPs, to 'point the finger of blame' at SBG for the traffic problems that had occurred.

The programme objectives

In response to the criticisms and concern over the situation regarding the newly-deregulated bus services, the SBG presented to the police, Local Authority, Passenger Transport Executive and other bus operators, an eight-point plan which included the establishment of a working party to examine the future control of bus services in the city. However, Strathclyde Buses refused to participate in such a working party. As a result, the SBG were forced to accept that they must launch a campaign to win over the travelling public, Regional Authority and other key audiences to understanding their position, and to defend themselves from the attacks being made on them by Strathclyde Buses and their supporters.

TMA Communications were appointed to work on behalf of SBG and identified the following primary objectives for the programme:

- To clarify the position of the SBG in relation to the traffic problems in the city-centre on 11 October.
- To overcome the false allegations made against the SBG by Councillor Waugh on behalf of the Strathclyde Bus Company.
- To generate a sympathetic view towards the SBG from the media and consequently from the fare-paying public.
- To gain support for the SBG in the political arena where questions were being tabled following the traffic stoppage on 11 October.
- To adopt and maintain a proactive stance on behalf of the SBG throughout the period of deregulation.

The publics

In developing the programme it was recognized that a number of key audiences had to be addressed:

- Strathclyde Region Executives, who held the power to impose new controls over bus operators or refer the issue to the Traffic Commissioner.
- The Transport Convener and Head of the Transport Committee, Councillor Malcolm Waugh.
- The Passenger Transport Executive who were directly responsible for the control of transportation systems in the region.
- Local MPs who naturally had a vested interest in the issue.
- The travelling public throughout the region, particularly both bus users and those using private road transport within the region.
- Transport-users' pressure groups.
- The police.
- All bus service operators within the region.
- The media, particularly the regional press and broadcast media.

The media were seen as particularly crucial as the key channel through which the issues were being debated. The earlier coverage of the deregulation issue had been largely critical of the SBG, and had been based on largely inaccurate and misleading information supplied by Councillor Waugh and Strathclyde Buses. It was crucial for the SBG to try to correct the misperceptions of the situation, generated through the media's treatment of the issues.

The strategy

The main facet of the strategy was to engineer a 'platform' from which the SBG could counter the misleading allegations made against them in the media. This would then provide the basis from which the SBG could be repositioned as a responsible company, prepared to co-operate with other bus operators as well as the Regional Authority, in resolving the question of how best to develop the region's bus services following the full-scale deregulation. The imminent introduction of full-scale deregulation at the end of October meant that timing was critical, and swift action had to be taken to avoid the regional authorities taking action to impose new controls that could prove highly detrimental to the SBG.

In offering its eight-point plan to solve the problems, the SBG had, in fact, already taken the first steps to demonstrate its willingness to work with all interested parties in reaching a solution to the problem. However, this had not received widespread coverage in the media, and had been rejected by Strathclyde Buses and other bus operators, who had refused to participate in the proposed working party to examine the problem.

The programme

The press conference

The first and, perhaps, most important element of the programme implemented by TMA, was to organize a major press conference to which the national and regional press were invited, as well as the television and radio. District and regional councillors, in particular, Councillor Waugh, the Transport Convener, as well as the Passenger Transport Executive and the police were also invited. This was intended to provide the all-important launch pad, from which the SBG could begin to change perceptions of its role, in what the media had named the 'Bus Wars'.

The press conference was held at Buchanan Street Bus Station on 19 October. A comprehensive slide presentation was prepared to highlight the key issues in the controversy. It was organized so as to make sure of the attendance of Councillor Waugh, thus positioning him in the 'lion's den' to confront him with the various false allegations that he had been making on behalf of the Strathclyde Bus Company.

News releases were also sent to all regional and national media, highlighting the initiatives taken by the SBG to solve the problem and end the lack of co-operation among bus operators in the region.

Although the press conference did not change perceptions of the problem overnight, it succeeded in challenging the 'facts' contained in the earlier coverage of the issue, and opened the way for the SBG to begin to improve its image with the media and other audiences. During the two weeks following the press conference, with the date for full deregulation approaching, the issue continued to occupy a prominent position on the local news agenda. Spokesmen from the SBG continued to take part in a number of local television and radio interviews, including: BBC Scotland – 'Reporting Scotland', ITV Scotland – 'Scotland Today', Radio Clyde and Radio Scotland. Several of these programmes took the form of round-table discussions, involving representatives of the various protagonists in the controversy. These provided the SBG with the opportunity to reinforce its willingness to co-operate in finding an amicable solution to the problem, as well as allowing it to counter the misleading allegations made against them.

Parliamentary audiences

A number of Scottish MPs had already joined in the debate over the deregulation issue. In general, they had been highly critical of the situation that had developed, seizing on the problems that had resulted as an opportunity to launch a further attack on the Conservative Government's policies in Scotland.

Their stance on the issue tended to be essentially critical of the private sector bus operators. This was undoubtedly largely as a result of the misleading coverage the issue had received in the media. In order to encourage Scottish MPs to support the SBG's position, it was essential to try to correct their misperceptions of the issue. TMA arranged to distribute information to all Scottish MPs, explaining the action the SBG had taken and the attempts they were making to reconcile the situation. As the issue developed, MPs were sent further updated information to ensure that they were aware of the SBG's position and willingness to co-operate with the regional authority.

Building support

In order to gain support for the SBG, it was vital to demonstrate both their willingness to co-operate with other bus operators and the regional authorities in solving the problems and the intransigence of the Strathclyde Buses. It was equally important for the SBG to gain the initiative, and counter the adverse criticisms being made by Strathclyde Buses and their spokesman, Councillor Waugh. To highlight the Strathclyde Buses's lack of response to their initiatives, it was essential for the SBG to take every opportunity to challenge them strongly.

Constant monitoring of the situation was required in order to allow the SBG to rapidly respond to any new developments. This involved both the issuing of frequent news releases, together with engineering interviews for an SBG spokesman with the broadcast media as new aspects of the issue emerged. Regular meetings were also arranged with the various authorities, in order to convince them of the SBG's willingness to co-operate in reaching an amicable solution to the problem that would benefit both the travelling public and all bus operators with a vested interest in the outcome.

The SBG's proposal

In developing its eight-point plan to improve traffic management within the city, the SBG had set up a street monitoring system using inspectors and video cameras to provide statistical evidence to support its proposals. The SBG proposal was in two parts. The first part involved an eight-point plan to improve traffic management in the city. This contained proposals, for example, for improvements in the phasing of traffic lights, action on car parking, the introduction of bus-only lanes, additional 'yellow-box' junctions, and contingency plans in the event of emergencies. The second part of the proposal concerned suggestions for the rerouting of a number of bus services in the city-centre, away from particularly sensitive areas that had been subject to the worst congestion.

Naturally the proposal required the rival bus operators to reach a compromise, and accept the need for some rationalization of services. It was this crucial aspect of the proposal that proved the particular 'sticking point', as rival operators were reluctant to give up their right to compete for all city-centre routes. Without the agreement of the rival bus operators, the regional authority would be faced with no alternative other than to impose a solution on them that might benefit none of them. It was therefore vital to the success of the strategy that this proposal was widely publicized, to demonstrate that the delay in reaching a solution was due almost entirely to the intransigence of other bus operators, as well as the unwillingness of the Traffic Convener to respond to the proposal.

The results

When full deregulation actually came into effect on 26 October, the much-heralded traffic chaos failed to materialize. The traffic problems that had resulted during the previous two weeks, following the first phase of deregulation, seemed to have convinced commuters to opt for alternative modes of travel, and many turned to the use of taxis or private transport. Although there was a notable increase in traditional seventy-seat bus and minibus traffic, the police, well prepared for the day, had extra patrols out in the city ensuring that the traffic was kept moving.

Although it had not been possible to convince the rival bus operators, and particularly Strathclyde Buses, to agree to a compromise solution to the problem, the campaign had succeeded in gaining a more sympathetic hearing for the SBG's position. The media, in particular, had accepted their genuine efforts to reconcile the problem of city-centre traffic, and their initiative to find a solution to the problem had received widespread coverage. From being previously held as responsible for the traffic problems, the SBG were, as a result of the campaign, seen as acting responsibly in an effort to improve the lot of the travelling public.

Although Strathclyde Region's Traffic Convener, Councillor Waugh, appealed to the Traffic Commissioner to intervene and impose cuts on the number of bus services in the city, this plea was rejected. The Traffic Commissioner expressed the view that he wished to see a mutually-agreed solution to the problem between the bus operators and the regional authority. The campaign on behalf of the SBG undoubtedly played a significant part in gaining this ruling.

A number of the measures included in the SBG's eight-point plan were eventually adopted by the authorities, including the introduction of bus lanes and measures to address the problems of illegal parking and to improve the flow of traffic.

Conclusion

This case is an example of how, by effective presentation and communication of the true facts, a reversal of opinion was achieved and misrepresentations were overcome.

Case discussion

This case study serves to illustrate three particularly important features common to virtually all public relations programmes. First, the power of the media in mobilizing public opinion on issues; second, the importance of source credibility in changing opinions; and third, the importance of consistent and effective presentation of information when attempting to change perceptions of an issue.

The Scottish Bus Group faced the problems of establishing its right to operate bus services in Glasgow and of combating the threat of damaging restrictions being imposed on private bus operators by the authorities. To achieve these aims it was important to try to create a sympathetic climate towards private bus operators among members of the regional authority, the police, and the travelling public. This could not be achieved without winning over the local media who had largely adopted a hostile attitude to private bus companies.

Although much of the criticism in the media of the SBG and other private operators was based on false and misleading information, the fact that much of this was supplied by Councillor Waugh on behalf of Strathclyde Buses gave it credibility in the eyes of the media and the public.

The SBG faced a difficult task in correcting the misperceptions of its position largely created by the media reporting of the issue. In this it was not helped by the bitter rivalry between private operators who largely refused to co-operate and presented a united front against Strathclyde Buses. This, itself, added to the impression of an industry concerned only for its own profits, possessing little regard for the interests of the travelling public.

The criticism of deregulation made by Councillor Waugh and Strathclyde Buses was almost entirely based on the traffic problems that had afflicted the city on 11 October. Although traffic congestion continued to be a problem, there was no evidence that it was significantly worse than might be expected in any major city, such as Glasgow, during peak periods. The police, alerted to the potential problems, were in fact able to take measures to ensure the smoother flow of traffic during peak periods. However, despite the fact that the severe problems of 11 October appeared to be an extreme and isolated incident, the media continued to treat this incident as a foretaste of what might be expected after full deregulation. The SBG had to counter this impression and try to convince both the media and public that this was in fact an isolated incident.

The case illustrates the importance to the media of presenting them with 'hard evidence' on which to base their reporting of an issue. The media deal essentially in facts, and are more concerned with immediate news rather than predictions and forecasts. The SBG could not deny that the traffic chaos on 11 October was largely caused as a result of the unprecedented influx of buses into the city-centre. It is hardly surprising, therefore, that this created a vision of worse to come once full deregulation took place. The task for the SBG was to try to persuade the media and public to recognize this incident for what it was – a largely isolated incident that had not recurred subsequently, and was unlikely to do so if all the bus operators could be persuaded to act responsibly.

Having experienced an unfavourable 'vision of the future', media and public opinion could not be easily changed by simple statements of intent. The SBG had to demonstrate it possessed concrete plans to avoid further disruption to the city's traffic and was actively seeking agreement to have them implemented. This was difficult to achieve without the co-operation of other bus operators. It was only by the consistent and effective presentation of its case through the media, as well as through face-to-face meetings with the various authorities, that it was able to gradually change perceptions about the company.

This case illustrates how the success of so many public relations programmes hinge on the credibility of the organization in question; perhaps the most important factor determining how audiences and the media in particular respond to the various messages it puts out. Credability with the media can only be achieved through a consistent policy of frank and open communication. The willingness of SBG spokesmen to accept that they, along with other bus operators, were at least partially to blame for the traffic problems in the city, and to discuss frankly how the problems might be solved, proved important in building credibility for the SBG. Ultimately this worked to change perceptions of them, and helped in securing support for their proposed solution the bus deregulation issue in Glasgow.

Student discussion questions and exercises

1. Consider what factors contribute to the credibility of an organization with the media or the public in general. Discuss how the task of maintaining or building credibility for an organization may differ for public and private sector organizations.
2. Consider the strengths and weaknesses of the press and broadcast media as communication channels in a programme, such as that carried out for the Scottish Bus Group, designed to build credibility for the organization, and campaign on behalf of a particular issue.
3. Draw up a list of priorities in both selecting and preparing a spokesperson

to appear on behalf of an organization. Consider whether these would differ if one was preparing them for an appearance in the broadcast media as opposed to a press conference.

The international public relations programme on behalf of the Government of Brunei Darussalam

Alan Mole

Preview

In the course of the last decade, public relations has assumed an increasingly important role in the conduct of international relations and diplomacy. Perhaps the most striking example has been the development of international relations between the two superpowers, the USA and the Soviet Union. Mikhail Gorbachev, the Soviet Premier, has both initiated and championed the development of a new policy of openness in the Soviet Union's relations with the West.

Under Premier Gorbachev, the terms *glasnost* and *perestroika* have entered the international vocabulary, as references to a new sense of openness and restructuring within the Soviet Union. The term *glasnost* has, in particular, been used by the international media to refer not only to the Soviet Union's relations with the West, but also to East–West relations in general.

Diplomacy has traditionally been conducted between the politicians and diplomats of respective countries. However, in recent years a new form of 'public diplomacy' has emerged as an increasingly important force for change in the relations between countries. Public diplomacy seeks, largely through international media relations, to influence the course of foreign policy and relations by influencing the attitudes of the general public in the respective countries. In this way a climate for change can be created, and pressure brought to bear on political leaders to adjust their position with respect to their foreign policies.

The recent course of East–West relations provides perhaps the best example of the use of public relations in an international context to improve mutual understanding between countries, and thereby their respective diplomatic and commercial relations. This trend towards the use of 'public diplomacy' as a tool in promoting international relations between countries is undoubtedly one that is likely to assume even greater importance in coming years.

This case, which examines the development of international relations on behalf of the Government of Brunei Darassalam, illustrates the use of an international communications programme to raise awareness and understanding of a country as a means of improving its relations with both overseas governments and the international business community. It illustrates how an effective international media relations campaign was developed using a relatively small number of national and international publications, a fact that points to the growing concentration of the international business media. The case also illustrates the value of an international consultancy network in implementing a communications programme across a number of countries.

Introduction

Following a competitive pitch in November 1987, Shandwick was appointed by the Government of Brunei Darussalam to conduct an international public relations programme. The government was concerned about the lack of awareness of the country, which had only regained full independence in 1984, and distressed at the lack of objective and balanced media coverage of Brunei.

Background

History

The Sultanate of Brunei was a powerful state in the early sixteenth-century, with control over the whole of the island of Borneo. By the nineteenth-century its power had been considerably reduced to more or less its present limits, and by the end of the nineteenth-century the Sultan of Brunei had entered into a treaty with Great Britain which placed the country under its protection. In 1979 a treaty was signed which led to Brunei becoming a fully sovereign and independent state at the end of 1983.

Area and population

Brunei is situated on the north-west coast of Borneo, and is bounded on all sides by Sarawak territory which splits the state into two separate parts. The total area of the country is some 2,226 square miles and it has a population of some 222,000 (estimated in 1985). The country is divided into four principal districts: Brunei/Muara, Belait, Tutong and Temburong. The capital Bandar Seri Begawan has a population of some 64,000 (1981 census) and is situated nine miles from the mouth of the Brunei river. Approximately 50 per cent of the population speak Malay and 26 per cent Chinese.

Government

The Sultan is His Majesty Sir Muda Hassanal Bolkiah Mu'izzadin Waddaulah. He succeeded his father in 1967, following his father's abdication, and was crowned on 1 August 1968. The Sultan promulgated a Constitution in 1959, although parts of it have not been fully in force since 1962, and supreme political powers are vested in the Sultan. Brunei is a member of the United Nations, the Commonwealth and ASEAN (Association of South East Asian Nations).

The economy

The economy of Brunei is primarily based on its oil industry, which employs more than 70 per cent of the entire working population. Other minor industries are rubber, pepper, sawn timber, gravel and animal hides. Local industries include boat-building, cloth-weaving and the manufacture of brass and silverwear. Crude oil accounts for 56 per cent of the value of total exports and re-exports, and the second major export is liquified natural gas, which contributes 40 per cent and petroleum products 3 per cent.

In 1985 exports totalled Br. $6,140m and imports Br. $1,155m (1988 £1 =Br. $3.56). In 1985 Singapore supplied 24 per cent of all imports, the USA 15 per cent and Japan 20 per cent. Also Japan took 68 per cent of all exports. Trade between Brunei and the United Kingdom has favoured the UK, with exports from Brunei to the UK rising from £27m in 1983, to a peak of £72m in 1986 before settling back to a more normal level of £34m in 1987. Imports to Brunei from the UK have risen steadily from £106m in 1983, to £204m in 1987 (with a notable 'hiccup' in 1985).

Communications

Communications in Brunei are relatively good with some 1,223km of roadways linking the main towns in the country. Brunei operates its own Royal Brunei Airline (RBA) and Singapore Airlines also provide a daily service linking Brunei with Singapore. RBA also operates services to Bangkok, Kuala Lumpur, Hong Kong and other major capitals. British Airways provides a weekly service between Brunei and the UK.

Radio Brunei is operated by the department of Radio and Television, broadcasting in Malay, Chinese, Iban, Dusan and English. In 1984 there were an estimated 52,000 radios and 31,000 television sets in Brunei homes.

Education and religion

The official religion of the country is Islam. In 1982, 63 per cent of the population was Moslem, 14 per cent Buddhist and 10 per cent Christian. There is a reasonably well-developed education system with free schooling at the primary and secondary levels. In 1986 there were some 243 schools of all types with 64,000 pupils. Scholarships for tertiary education overseas are also available for the most able students, and in 1985 the University of Brunei Darussalam opened for the first time.

Research and analysis

The first step taken by Shandwick was to launch a detailed communications audit to assess the perceptions of Brunei in the printed and electronic media, and the resulting perceptions amongst politicians, business people and opinion leaders, and the general public. This was conducted by the six offices in each of the key target areas of ASEAN (comprising Indonesia, Malaysia, the Philippines, Singapore, Thailand and Brunei), Australia, Hong Kong, Japan, the Middle East, the United Kingdom and the United States. This involved interviews with representatives of the key target audiences in each target area, together with a detailed appraisal of the news coverage afforded to Brunei over the years. The research data clearly revealed that knowledge of Brunei overseas was very limited and that up-to-date information was not readily available. There was almost no balanced reporting of Brunei, and press coverage tended to to focus solely on the head of state, His Majesty the Sultan, rather than on the country itself. This coverage was often trivial and sensational, based on the growing number of inaccurate stories which had been allowed to circulate uncorrected in the international media.

Objectives and planning

As a result of the findings of the communication audit, the objectives became clear:

- to establish accurate sources of information on Brunei;
- to raise awareness of the country's development and progress;
- to counteract certain specific inaccuracies and misconceptions about the country.

The basis of Shandwick's action plan for the programme was the establishment of Brunei Darussalam Information Desks – through Shandwick's world-wide network in all ASEAN capitals and in Bahrain, Hong Kong, London, Sydney, Tokyo and Washington. These desks, which were established in January 1988, have been controlled and co-ordinated from a central information office established in Brunei and manned by a staff of five. Each of the separate offices were given an individual budget allocation, and made proposals for an overall action plan based on their local knowledge, and they, of course, also implemented the programme initiated in Brunei. Each office monitors the local media coverage of Brunei and transmits this to the Brunei office on a daily basis.

The first task of the Brunei office was to prepare a comprehensive Press Information Pack on all aspects of Brunei and its development. Given the international nature of the target audience, it was necessary to produce copies of this information pack in a number of languages, and to date over 2,500 copies of the information pack in English, Arabic, Japanese and Thai have been distributed to selected media throughout the world. The information desks have worked closely with their local Brunei diplomatic missions and have assisted the government on a range of local activities. For example, supporting journalists in their coverage of the Sultan's visit to the Middle East and Thailand, and the Royal Brunei Airlines with its inaugural flight to Dubai. In addition, a set of 'model questions and answers' on Brunei were prepared for use by the information desks, Brunei missions overseas and by officials in Brunei itself. This first·stage of the action plan was intended to address the immediate problem of establishing authorative and accurate sources of information on Brunei on a world-wide basis, whilst at the same time raising awareness of the shortcomings of earlier media coverage of the country.

Once the international network of information desks had been established, they provided an effective local conduit for the further dissemination of up-dated information on Brunei, as well as a point of reference for those seeking specific and accurate information about the country.

Shandwick was then able to address the longer-term elements of the action plan. The longer-term aim was to improve the awareness and knowledge of Brunei amongst the media, business communities, politicians and general public on a world-wide basis, and in the specific targeted areas in particular. The principal elements of this phase of the plan included:

- the publication of the first comprehensive and up-to-date reference book on Brunei for foreigners, with a first edition print run of 10,000 copies;
- a programme of 'advertorials' in sixteen newspapers and magazines across the world – this was to account for not more than one-third of the budget;
- the production of a video introducing Brunei to foreigners, based on the first filmed interview with the Sultan by Lord Chalfont;
- the arrangement of fact-finding visits to Brunei by UK parliamentarians, by senior individual journalists, and by selected groups of reporters from each of the countries with an information desk.

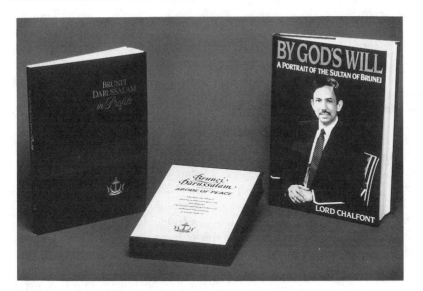

Plate 7 Books about Brunei

Note: from left to right
  Brunei Darussalam – in Profile
  Brunei Durassalam – Abode of Peace
  By God's Will – A portrait of the Sultan of Brunei

Implementation

While the information desks began to issue the press packs, handle routine enquiries and plan the media visits and local activities, the Brunei office researched and produced the reference book, *Brunei Darussalam in Profile*, a 164-page full colour book which was designed and printed by Shandwick in London. This was published in three editions – limp bound for general distribution, hard covers for use by government officials, and a limited edition bound in Brunei woven cloth, for presentation to VIPs (see Plate 7).

The advertorial programme, launched in August 1988, was developed specifically to create awareness about Brunei – its government, its economy and its culture, and to promote the publication of the reference book. The advertorials bore the same title as the book and carried a coupon for the book and details of the nearest information desk.

Major national publications in all relevant countries carried the advertorial, along with international publications such as *Newsweek* and the *International Herald Tribune*. It was translated into Arabic, Japanese and Bahasa (for Indonesia) and reached a circulation in excess of six million and an estimated readership of fifteen million, through sixteen publications distributed in some twenty-five countries. As a result, some 11,000 coupons have been returned requesting copies of the *In Profile* book, requiring a second edition of a further 11,000 copies to be printed. The advertorials, designed by Shandwick, appeared in four-page broadsheet and eight-page A4 format, and reprints have been used by information desks as a further source of information. Early in 1989 the advertorial also appeared in *Muhibah* – the in-flight magazine of Royal Brunei Airlines.

In addition to the advertorials, Shandwick was instrumental in helping to facilitate the first ever *Financial Times Survey of Brunei* in August 1988.

The filming for the twenty-five-minute video also began in August 1988, for which His Majesty the Sultan agreed to give his first television interview to Lord Chalfont. The first screening of this video was on television in Brunei on National Day 23 February 1989. Copies were also made available to the fourteen Brunei diplomatic missions and the eleven information desks, and will be used as a general introduction to modern Brunei for foreigners.

Meanwhile the Brunei office began a programme of visits to the country. In July 1988 British parliamentarians were invited to spend four days in Brunei, coinciding with His Majesty's birthday celebrations, to acquaint themselves with recent developments and plans for the future. The first press visitor was Mr Peregrine Worsthorne, editor of the *Sunday Telegraph*, who was granted the first ever personal interview with His Majesty the Sultan, in which His Majesty took the opportunity to state publically his position with regard to the controversy surrounding the House of Fraser acquisition. Two more journalists, Susan Crosland of the *Sunday Times* and Mr John Andrews of *The Economist*, have since visited Brunei, and senior journalists from Japan's largest daily, *Nihon Keizai Shimbun*, were due to visit in April 1989. In addition, the information desks were asked to select a small group of journalists from their country or region to be invited to visit Brunei. So far, press trips from ASEAN, Hong Kong and Australia have taken place, and groups from the USA and the Middle East were arranged for April and March 1989.

Measurement and evaluation

The measurement and evaluation of the impact of the programme and the progress in achieving the set objectives within the allocated budget, were carried out continuously during the project. The information desks submit monthly activity reports, and the Brunei office, which is in daily contact with the government, holds a monthly review meeting at which current issues are considered and progress assessed. The office also presents a regular evaluation of media monitoring from around the world and submits reports on progress in each area of the project, such as press visits and the advertorial programme.

The coupon response alone provided an indication of the success of the advertorial programme, while coverage received as a result of the press visits was very encouraging, pointing to a new emphasis on the country rather than its ruler and reflecting changes in the perceptions of many of the journalists who visited Brunei. A significant addition to the programme came as a result of the realization that not enough was known of His Majesty the Sultan, and this was the primary cause of much of the sensational coverage. Shandwick enlisted Lord Chalfont, an established journalist and author (and a non-executive director of Shandwick) to write a biography that would go behind the clichés and gossip and attempt a serious analysis of His Majesty the Sultan, as a head of state. The book, published by Weidenfeld & Nicholson in May 1989, will be distributed throughout the Commonwealth countries and the USA. A specific leaflet about the video interview has been produced as an insert for the book, to merchandise the video to the widest possible audience.

The only real modifications to the planned programme were in terms of the timing of some activities rather than to the budget or fundamental elements of the programme, although the book by Lord Chalfont was an addition to the original programme.

At the end of 1988, after the first full year of the project, an annual review covering all aspects of the programme was carried out and presented to the client, together with examples of the work produced and the progress achieved.

The future

At the time of writing this case, there is still a considerable amount of work to be done. Although the programme to date has led to a significant improvement in both the extent of media coverage afforded to Brunei and in the accuracy of the coverage received, the influence this has had on final target audiences has yet to be fully evaluated. However, judged by the coupon response to the advertorials, it would be reasonable to expect levels of awareness and understanding about Brunei to have increased significantly. Clearly, the information desks proved a highly successful innovation, and will continue to provide a means of regularly updating information on Brunei within the key areas of economic and political interest to Brunei.

Case discussion

The case illustrates a number of important lessons of relevance to those conducting either international communication programmes or communication programmes in general. The fundamental problems faced by Brunei, of both a lack of awareness of the country and widespread misperceptions about the state of its development, stemmed from its failure to establish and maintain effective channels of communication and to manage the flow of information on a regular basis. These problems were exacerbated by the secrecy that surrounded the life of the Sultan, who, as one of the reportedly wealthiest men in the world, naturally attracted many journalists to write often speculative and sensational news stories. The Sultan's alleged involvement in the House of Fraser acquisition is perhaps a prime example of such stories. As a result, most of the media coverage of Brunei was confined almost exclusively to items on His Majesty the Sultan.

An important first step in this situation, and one that is necessary before commencing any major communication programme intended to change audience perceptions, was the completion of a detailed communication audit. This analysis both of the existing sources of information and the perception of Brunei derived from them by key audiences, provided the basis for the development of the subsequent public relations programme. It was important to establish whether the existing low level of awareness and misperceptions about Brunei stemmed primarily from a lack of up-to-date information, or whether the nature of the media coverage of Brunei reflected inadequacies in the actual content of the information issued, as well as a degree of bias amongst journalists in their interpretation of the information.

In this case both these problems were found to exist, thus making the task for the consultancy more complex. It is important to recognize that in conducting a communications audit, the aim is to evaluate the perceptions of the final target audiences and the sources of influence on their perceptions, not simply to examine the extent and nature of media coverage.

In Brunei's case, although the problem of lack of awareness was a worldwide one, in order to keep the programme to one of manageable size and remain within the allocated budget, it was necessary to target the key publics in those areas of the world of particular economic and political importance to the country.

A requirement for any international communications programme is for the communication to be translated into the respective languages of the targeted countries. Whilst this may be seem obvious, particular attention has often to be paid to local idiomatic usage and in some counties to the local dialects. Whilst English is undoubtedly the predominant language in today's international business world, a failure to communicate in the native tongue of overseas countries can both alienate audiences and lead to misinterpretation of the message by local translators and the local media.

A detailed knowledge of the local media, in terms of its particular influence and readership profiles, the news interests of specific publications, the copy deadlines of different publications or broadcast programmes, as well as the format in which material should be supplied, is obviously essential to the success of any international media relations programme. By delegating local media relations activity to its various overseas offices, Shandwick was able to overcome the potential problems of managing an international media relations campaign, whilst still retaining central control over the essential content of the communication. This also helped ensure that appropriate local media opportunities were exploited to the full.

A specific objective of the programme was to establish accurate sources of information on Brunei, which could not be achieved simply through a programme of international media relations. It was impossible to predict either when, or from what sources, the need for information might arise, hence it was necessary to establish permanent sources of accurate information, and to provide for these to be constantly updated. Both the establishment of the information desks and the production of the *In Profile* publication addressed the need for both a permanent as well as an ongoing source of further information.

The production of the *In Profile* book also provided the means of exerting greater control over both the quantity and quality of the information conveyed to target audiences than could be achieved through a media relations programme. The book offered the means of providing a comprehensive source of reference on Brunei to meet the differing interests of the various target publics – covering the potential need for economic, political or general information on the country.

The inclusion of a coupon to request copies of the book in the paid advertorials, provided a means of reinforcing the message contained in the advertorials, and increasing the depth of information that could be supplied to interested parties. By monitoring the coupon responses, it was possible to gain a measure of the level and distribution of interest that the programme had generated. This highlights one important lesson for communication programmes in general, namely, the need, wherever possible, to build methods of measurement and evaluation into elements of the programme.

The use of paid advertorials in selected publications recognized the limitations of relying entirely on media relations activity to generate the required level and depth of coverage for Brunei. Advertorials enabled both the content of the message and the timing of its transmission to be precisely controlled, something that would have been impossible to guarantee with a media relations programme, no matter how newsworthy the issue or well conducted the campaign. In particular, it was also important to co-ordinate the international media coverage, to ensure that the coverage in the selected international and local publications reinforced one another, and contributed to raising the overall awareness and interest in Brunei. Although the use of paid advertorials is a more expensive communications technique than a programme based solely on media relations, the far greater degree of control over both the content and timing of the communication may, as in this case, warrant the expenditure.

Of particular significance to those involved in international communication is the fact that the advertorial programme was able to reach a potential audience of some fifteen million readers in twenty-five countries, through the use of only sixteen major publications. This points to the increasing internationalization of the media, particularly in the fields of business and current affairs. In recent years dramatic technological changes have taken place in the speed and nature of news and information transmission, and in the production technology used by the media organizations. These changes, coupled with the concentration of ownership of media organizations, have radically changed the options open for international communications programmes. Although there will continue to be a need to localize international communications programmes for the dissemination of information in particular countries, the ability to conduct international or global communication programmes, particularly within the business context, are certainly now a reality.

This case also illustrates how a potential communications problem can be turned into an advantage. The initial analysis had highlighted the concentration by the media on the personality of His Majesty the Sultan, at the expense of the coverage of the country of Brunei itself. However, it was possible to exploit this widespread media interest in the Sultan, as a means of initially stimulating the interest of journalists in Brunei itself. By persuading the Sultan to agree to giving some individual interviews, and by the use of the video-interview with Lord Chalfont and the commissioned biography, the programme was able to respond to, and build on an item of proven news interest to the international media, and to the general public in many countries throughout the world.

Student discussion questions and exercises

1. Consider what similarities and differences would exist between conducting an international communications programme on behalf of a entire country, such as Brunei, and an international communications programme on behalf of an individual company or organization.
2. Compile a list of the key media for an organization wishing to communicate with the business community and political leaders in the European Economic Community (EEC).
3. Identify the principal obstacles faced by an organization in trying to implement an international communications programme from the United Kingdom, and consider how valid it is to use the term 'global communication'.

Case thirteen

The Barbican Centre: public relations for a major arts and conference centre

Sam Black

Preview

This case study examines the planning, construction and inauguration of the Barbican centre in the City of London near St Paul's Cathedral. It illustrates the contribution that a public relations counsellor is able to make to a complex and protracted project, particularly when, as in the case of the Barbican, there are many vested interests which have to be carefully managed in order to retain their confidence and support for the project throughout its duration.

The case emphasizes the need for public relations to be seen as a function of management, and not merely an 'add-on' activity intended to achieve publicity or media attention. Not only should there be a public relations input at the early stage of the planning of any corporate strategy, but it should continue to receive consideration throughout the planning and implementation of any viable corporate strategy whether it be in the public or private sector.

It was necessary to sustain the interest in the Barbican Centre during its long period of construction, not only within the UK, but also among the vitally important international conference organisers. As the case highlights, major conferences are often booked several years in advance, and hence it was vital to raise awareness of the Barbican's facilities well in advance of their completion, in order to ensure that the Centre had a chance to win its share of the important international conference trade business on its completion. This was effected through a sustained programme of media relations and organized site visits, which together ensured that the Barbican Centre received international publicity throughout the period of its construction. The careful management of the release of information and the arranging of many celebrity visits to the site, helped to retain a sense of 'freshness' to the story and thus retained the media's interest.

The case also illustrates the important role that public relations can make to internal relations within an organization, as well as between those bodies with a vested interest in a project. In the Barbican's case, it was important to maintain the confidence and support of the officials of the City of London Corporation, in order to ensure that any necessary changes to the original

173

plans would receive their approval.

The Barbican project also serves to illustrate that public relations is not always only concerned with the more obvious forms of communications activity. A practitioner can often be called upon to provide skilled advice and counsel to client organizations, and to facilitate the presentation of the arguments involved with an issue. In this sense, public relations fulfils an important general management function and helps to ensure that an organization's senior management is armed with the relevant information with which to take important decisions.

Background

Due to the bombing of London during the Second World War, a very large area of the City of London had been completely flattened and its residents widely dispersed. At the initiative of Duncan Sandys in 1956, when he was Minister of Development, the City approved an ambitious housing scheme which would provide flats for over 5,000 families in a mixed development of high rise and conventional building. When the Corporation announced this large-scale building project they stated that in the centre of the housing units they would build a large arts centre for the benefit of residents and people working in London.

The housing development progressed slowly due to strikes and construction problems, but by 1969 the majority of the flats had been completed and occupied. However, there was no sign of the arts centre, merely a large expanse of open ground where the centre should have been. Although the City was under pressure to redeem their promise to provide an arts centre, there was considerable disquiet amongst members of the Corporation of the City of London as to the financial viability of the scheme. Their concern was perhaps understandable, as the whole Barbican scheme was financed by the Corporation, and estimates for the cost of the centre's completion by 1974 were placed at some £24 million (the final cost was to be £153 million).

A novel aspect of the scheme was the plan for a podium construction, with connected walk-ways within the site linking to adjacent office areas, thus making the residential areas into a pedestrian precinct free from noise and traffic.

About this time, 1970, a number of features were published pointing to the remarkable growth in the demand for conference facilities and pointing to the lack of custom-built accommodation in London. Several City councillors suggested that the proposed Barbican Arts Centre might also be used for meetings and conferences, bringing in revenue to offset the running costs of the centre. It was decided that research should be carried out to evaluate the potential for conference trade at the proposed centre.

Research

As public relations adviser to the London Chamber of Commerce since 1966, I was acutely aware of the shortage of conference facilities in Central London. I was commissioned by the Corporation of the City of London to carry out a feasibility study into the practicality of using the proposed centre for conferences as well as the arts. A questionnaire was sent out to the 10,000 members of the Chamber enquiring if they experienced problems in securing suitable accommodation for meetings and conferences and whether they would be likely to take advantage of such facilities if available at the Barbican. A near 20 per cent response was received and the answer to both of these vital questions was positive. There was a clear indication that the business community would use the facilities if provided.

Armed with these findings it was necessary to examine with the architect, whether suitable facilities could be incorporated into the scheme. In evaluating how the initial scheme could be adapted to provide suitable conference facilities, it was important to appreciate the needs of the professional conference organizer, to ensure that the facilities would meet the highest standards required of the modern international conference trade. Some additions were necessary to the plans, notably the addition of simultaneous translation booths in the large concert hall and facilities for the reception of delegates in the main foyer. Given the findings of the survey, and having ascertained that there were no insuperable construction problems, it was possible to recommend the feasibility of proceeding with the development of the arts centre but incorporating facilities for conferences and meetings of varying sizes.

The Corporation accepted the recommendation and I was appointed as a consultant to assist Mr Henry Wrong, who had been appointed Administrator of the Centre. We formed a small team to take the plans forward and bring them into reality. During the next few years the future of the project was still under threat, as delays and escalating costs began to cause a number of Councillors to have second thoughts. Frequent meetings were held with Corporation committees to report on progress, explain problems and, at times, persuade them not to abandon support for the project. By 1977 the point was reached when it would have been as costly to abandon the scheme as to proceed, and the persisting uncertainties regarding the commitment of the Corporation to the project were at last removed.

The consultancy role

Once the decision to proceed with the project had been taken, my role moved into the next phase; on one hand, working with the architect to ensure the building would be suitable for its intended dual function, while on the other hand beginning the task of advance publicity for the Centre and establishing an on-going dialogue with the media and potential users.

Although the completion date was still some years ahead, it was important to recognize that if the centre was to become a successful international conference venue, it was necessary to begin at this stage to generate interest amongst international conference organizers and larger organizations, who often work on a planning horizon that extends a number of years ahead.

The first step was to change the name of the centre from the 'Barbican Arts Centre' to the 'Barbican Arts and Conference Centre' – a small, but nevertheless significant, first step in establishing an identity for the Centre. It was clear that throughout the construction period there were a number of audiences with whom it was necessary to establish and maintain communication. In planning the action that needed to be taken, seven key audiences were identified:

- The Corporation of the City of London and its committees.
- The permanent officers of the Corporation.
- The residents of the Barbican.
- Potential users of the centre's facilities.
- The London Symphony Orchestra and the Royal Shakespeare Company, who were designated as the resident companies in the Concert Hall and Theatre respectively.
- The architect partnership responsible for the building.
- The media – national, local and trade – both in the United Kingdom and overseas.

Throughout the early years an important part of the task was maintaining a close watch over the actual planning and design of the building, and resisting, where necessary, some of the architect's unacceptable proposals. It was vital that, when completed, the Centre's facilities would match up to the high expectations that the advanced publicity promised to potential users

The time-scale problem

The prolonged time-scale of this major project naturally caused significant problems in maintaining the interest and attention of the media. The opening was originally scheduled for 1976, but this became steadily unrealistic, and the Centre did not, in fact, hold its first events until late 1981. This in effect meant that media and public interest had to be maintained over a period of some ten years.

At an early stage a *Barbican Newsletter* was started and published several times a year. This included information about the progress with the project, interviews with the many celebrities who started to visit the site, and provided a platform for the description of the many facilities the Centre would offer. This newsletter was circulated on a world-wide basis as well as to a large audience in the UK. The newsletter proved to be a valuable channel for maintaining awareness and interest in the project during the extended development period, as well as often helping to stimulate further media coverage of issues first raised in the newsletter.

Henry Wrong began visiting many international conferences, meeting with major conference organizers, and helping to promote the Barbican Centre. As a result, a number of major advance bookings were signed up, including the World Petroleum Congress and the meeting of the American Bar Association. In order to assist in promoting the Barbican's facilities an attractive four-colour brochure was produced, illustrating the planned facilities for the Barbican. This was followed by a second brochure when photographs became available.

The growth of UK conference facilities

In the early 1970s, other large conference centres were being built in the UK. The Wembley Conference Centre (opened 1977), the Brighton Centre and the National Exhibition and Conference Centre in Birmingham were under construction, and the new Harrogate Centre was in the final planning stage. At the suggestion of the British Tourist Authority (BTA), a group was formed with the grandiose title, the British Conference and Exhibition Centres Export Council (BCECEC). I was appointed the first secretary, and so became involved with all the new centres while continuing to be actively concerned with the Barbican.

The primary aim of BCECEC was to secure overseas publicity and to help tap the lucrative international conference market. To this end an annual brochure was produced and a certain amount of joint advertising was undertaken for 'the Big Five'. Additionally, overseas receptions were held in Brussels and Geneva and BCECEC shared BTA stands at all appropriate trade fairs. This publicity activity was invaluable in stimulating enquiries for bookings at the Barbican and other UK conference and exhibition centres.

A secondary, but valuable benefit of the formation of BCECEC was the opportunity for the sharing of experiences and ideas at regular quarterly meetings held at the various centres as work progressed. It was considered that the five centres were sufficiently different to avoid undue competition, and the sharing of information at these meetings undoubtedly added to the final design of the centres. BCECEC continues in operation but the Big Five have become a membership of twelve, as new centres have continued to open in many parts of Britain. The development of what amounted to a generic publicity programme for the UK conference trade illustrates the mutual benefits and cost savings that can result from the pooling of resources to tackle what has now become a very lucrative international market.

Maximizing the Barbican's potential

A principal aim of the public relations work was to help ensure that the Barbican's potential as an exhibition and conference centre was fully exploited. From the earliest stages I had urged the need for the conference facilities at the Barbican to be supplemented by exhibition halls. The main problem was where such facilities could be housed, as virtually every inch of the complex was spoken for. In addition to the main Concert Hall and Barbican Theatre, the building had to house the Guildhall School of Music and Drama, an Art Gallery, a Sculpture Court, the new City Lending Library, a cinema, restaurants and all the supporting infrastructure.

A suggestion to use the area around the main concert hall was rejected by the Greater London Council. Finally, however, it was decided to take over some large empty warehouses adjacent to the Centre and convert them into two large self-contained exhibition halls. These provided much needed exhibition space for many medium- and small-sized events and were to prove very popular. Securing the approval of the Corporation sub-committee for the exhibition project was just one of numerous occasions at which it was necessary to reassure the Corporation of the future success of the project, and to persuade them to accept necessary amendments to the scheme. A key task for any adviser, and one which was important to the Barbican project, is to secure the confidence and respect of his client, without which it is impossible to push through any necessary changes to a project that may be opposed by some factions.

An important aspect of the work was to assist Henry Wrong in the preparation of the innumerable reports for the Corporation covering first the progress with the construction phase of the project, and latterly, the proposals for the administration and organization of the Centre after commissioning. It was important that these reports presented a clear and rational case for any proposed amendments to the plans, however small, and that the facts were presented in a way that members of the Corporation would find easy to digest.

At this time the City of London employed a large public relations consultancy to handle most of its public relations work. However, it was agreed in negotiation with the executives of the Corporation, that the Barbican Centre's public relations should be handled separately. This involved not only the publicity for the Centre's arts and conference facilities, but also relations with the local business community and local residents.

Relations with the local residents

The residents in the 5,000 flats at the Barbican had two main grievances – they were still awaiting the promised facilities of the arts centre, and meanwhile they had to experience all the noise, dust and general inconvenience caused by the construction process. Those residents most severely affected were given rent reductions and regular meetings were staged to keep all residents informed of the progress with the development and provide them with the opportunity to ask questions. This helped to reduce the level of animosity felt towards the Council, and provided a 'safety tap' for any particular grievances felt by residents. Residents were ultimately offered the opportunity to purchase their flats at discount prices under the government policy of selling houses and flats to sitting tenants – which helped compensate them for the inconvenience they had to suffer during the long development period. It was clearly important to try to avoid serious complaint from residents that could have proved detrimental to the scheme and could have militated against maintaining the support of the majority of the Corporation for the project.

Relations with the Corporation

As the Barbican was financed by the Corporation, it was administratively under the control of the City's Town Clerk's department. It soon became obvious that the somewhat bureaucratic and cumbersome administration of local government was unsuited to the requirements of dealing with a rapidly developing project of the magnitude of the Barbican. It agreed that a well-qualified engineer be appointed to supervise the construction and Henry Wrong – as a senior officer of the Corporation – was increasingly allowed to act under powers of delegation from the Corporation. Given all the often unavoidable construction hold-ups, it was vital to avoid further delays due to the inherently slow workings of the local government decision-making machinery. In order to obtain a degree of necessary independence of action, it was important to secure and maintain the confidence and trust of the Corporation executives. The Corporation were kept regularly informed of all significant developments and presented, when necessary, with a clear and well-argued case for any required changes to the plans. As a result, the Corporation presented very few serious obstacles to the progress of the project.

An example of the good working relationship that was developed with the Corporation is illustrated by the Frobisher Crescent episode. Although the plans for the Centre provided for large meeting spaces, VIP rooms, a press office and administration offices, the lack of small- and medium-sized meeting rooms, important for conferences use, was an issue of some concern. There was no provision in the architect's plans for such facilities. However, it was discovered that phase V of the Barbican housing development had not been fully completed, and an area now known as Frobisher Crescent was lying idle. The Corporation was asked to release this for conversion into meeting rooms and it agreed to do so with little opposition, accepting the argument of the need for this additional form of conference facilities. In effect, the area was far larger than was needed, and two floors were leased for use by the City University Business School. Through close consultation with the architects it was possible to influence the design of these rooms, to ensure they were planned to be very 'user-orientated'.

Media relations and overseas contacts

A key problem that had to be addressed was how to maintain the interest of the media in the Barbican Centre over what amounted to a ten-year development period. The sheer size and ambitious nature of the project helped ensure a certain minimum degree of interest, particularly at the time of key events, such as the announcement of the inauguration of the scheme and the actual official opening itself. However, it was necessary to develop a programme of on-going media relations, seeking continually to identify new angles on the story in order to feed the media with potentially interesting new stories that would help keep the Barbican story 'alive'.

In addition to building awareness and interest in the Barbican amongst the public, it was also necessary for the media relations programme to address the issue of relations with the local residents and stimulating interest amongst international conference organizers. These considerations dictated that the media relations programme had to be broken down into a number of separate yet complementary campaigns, targeted in each case at the relevant audiences, and using the appropriate media channels. The media relations programme intended to help publicize the Barbican was structured around a number of key events that formed a natural part of the development programme: the inauguration of the scheme, the laying of the foundation stone, the completion of specific stages in the development, and ultimately the opening ceremony. In addition, it was possible as the project progressed, to 'engineer' a number of publicity events that served both to show the Centre's facilities to influential audiences, whilst providing the basis for additional news stories.

The Eighth Public Relations World Congress

In May 1979 the Eighth Public Relations World Congress was held in London and the Lord Mayor invited the 1,000 participants from over fifty-six countries to visit the Barbican to see the project, then nearing completion. The reception, which was attended by the Lord Mayor, Lady Mayoress and the Sheriffs in full ceremonial robes, was naturally a highly newsworthy event and greatly impressed the many overseas participants. The event and photographs were widely reported in the UK and overseas media, putting the Barbican Centre at one stroke on the international agenda.

It was important to conduct this media relations campaign on an international level, particularly in light of the need to stimulate interest in the Centre amongst the international conference trade. By 1979 the construction of the Barbican had advanced sufficiently to allow visitors to be shown around the facilities. Numerous visitors were received from both the UK and overseas and provisional conference bookings were being taken. The constant stream of international visitors to the project over the years, provided the basis for many international news stories, and every opportunity was taken to encourage celebrity visits which, in turn, were used as the basis for further news items and photo-opportunities. The success of the media relations campaign in maintaining the Barbican Centre on the international news agenda throughout its long construction period illustrates the value of adopting a proactive approach to handling public relations.

Despite all the efforts to facilitate the ease of use of the Centre, the UK media, in particular, orchestrated a campaign suggesting that the Centre was a confusing and difficult building for the public to use. Although journalists were repeatedly invited to view the facilities and the efforts taken to assist the public to readily find their way around the building, the tone of most of the articles written tended to be essentially critical of the building's complex design. Although somewhat irritating, this campaign did in practice help to publicize the Centre, and bring visitors to see it for themselves.

Obviously it is not always ease to influence the media once they have identified what they perceive as a controversial and newsworthy angle on a story. The criticisms of the complex design of the Barbican persisted, in one form or another, throughout the construction phase of the project, as well as after its opening. However, every effort was made to address these criticisms and journalists were constantly invited to visit the Centre to see the facilities for themselves and ask relevant questions. No issue involving design can hope to please everyone, or even the majority. Accepting this fact, it was possible to take advantage of the media debate to raise further interest in visiting the Centre amongst both the public and the business community.

The 'voice of the user'

Perhaps one of the most important contributions that an independent adviser is able to make to a project is that of acting as the 'voice of the user'. In the case of the Barbican this was an important role, ensuring the arguments for particular facilities or design features that would help ensure the Centre would be very 'user friendly' were heard and acted upon. In a building of the size and complexity of the Barbican, intended for multi-purpose usage, it was important to consider the needs of all potential users. A number of features were incorporated into the Centre's final design and into its administration procedures that facilitated its ease of use. Two examples are worthy of mention. It was agreed at an early stage that all internal signposting must be both very bold and comprehensive and that the various floors should be designated as 'levels'. Both these suggestions proved successful in helping users to navigate around the building. The idea was also put forward and adopted of the

Plate 8   The opening of the Barbican Centre by Her Majesty the Queen on 3 March 1982

'Yellow Line'. Visitors approaching the Centre from Moorgate Underground station are able to follow a bold yellow line right across the podium direct to the Centre's entrance on level seven. Both these ideas were relatively simple in concept, but made a significant improvement to the 'user friendliness' of the Centre.

The opening

As the opening day approached, the Corporation appointed a number of full-time staff, including a Conference Director and supporting staff, a Press Officer, and a Head of Publicity. The Grand Opening of the Barbican Centre was performed by Her Majesty the Queen on 3 March 1982. This Royal event was naturally a grand affair and received world-wide media coverage, helping to firmly launch the Barbican Centre to an international audience (see Plate 8).

Evaluation

The success of the project must be judged by whether the objectives were achieved. Undoubtedly they were, as the Barbican Centre very quickly established itself as a centre of excellence for the arts. The acoustics of the Concert Hall have been widely praised (see Plate 9) and the Barbican Theatre provided the Royal Shakespeare Company with a theatre worthy of their talents.

In terms of the role of public relations, it is possible to identify a number of important contributions that were made to the ultimate success of the project.

- The initial feasibility study and report provided the basis for counselling the Corporation as to the viability of the project and thus averted the threat of cancellation.
- Throughout the prolonged development period all parties with a vested interest in the project were kept informed of developments – helping to retain their support and confidence in the eventual success of the project.
- Relations with the residents, who suffered the inconvenience of a major construction project on their doorsteps, were handled sympathetically thereby avoiding any major ill-feeling.
- Effective relations were maintained with the Corporation, ensuring their support and willingness to grant the degree of relative autonomy to Henry Wrong that was essential for the completion of the project on time.
- A carefully orchestrated media relations and publicity campaign was successfully carried out over the many years of the Centre's construction, which helped keep the story 'alive'.
- By adopting the role of the 'voice of the user', it was possible to advise on necessary changes or improvements to the plans for the Centre that helped

Plate 9   The Prince and Princess of Wales attending the Royal Concert in aid of the Musicians' Benevolent Fund at the Barbican Centre on 20 November 1982

ensure that the facilities met with the expectations of an arts-going public and the professional conference organizers.

My role in the project ranged far wider than what might be seen as the norm for a public relations adviser. However, the complex nature of the project, involving many vested interests, sometimes with conflicting aims, demanded very delicate handling. An independent counsellor is able to bring a degree of objectivity to often contentious issues and assist in presenting the relevant facts clearly to decision-makers. Much of the work on the Barbican project was, in fact, concerned with the counselling of how issues and arguments should be presented to respective parties, as well as assisting in their actual presentation.

With many differing parties being involved either directly or indirectly in the project, it was vital to establish effective communication channels from the outset, in order that each were aware of, and understood, the aims and concerns of the others. Regular reports covering all issues concerning the progress of the project were circulated to all the key parties – Corporation officials and committee members, architects, builders, administration staff and local community leaders. In addition, extracts of these reports were incorporated into news releases sent to the media for wider distribution. Where appropriate, face-to-face meetings were arranged between representatives of the different interested parties to discuss particular problems or issues of concern. Without these efforts to maintain the understanding and co-operation of the various parties involved, the project would have undoubtedly have taken even longer to complete and may, in fact, have 'never seen the light of day'.

This case seeks to illustrate that the public relations practitioner can, at times, be called upon to assist with projects that extend beyond the conventional remit of public relations. However, he can make an invaluable contribution to the management of many types of projects, bringing to them clarity of thought, objectivity and, perhaps of most value, an awareness of the importance of effective communication between the parties involved. Effective communication in its many forms is essentially a function of good management.

Case discussion

A number of valuable lessons emerge from this case study, not the least being the importance of recognizing that in all forms of management effective communication skills should never be underestimated. Counselling of management is an increasingly important part of the work of public relations professionals. The limited recognition it has received in past years is undoubtedly due to the fact that its results are not immediately evident. However, without a clear understanding of the relevant issues, the attitudes and opinions of interested parties, and the likely implication of alternative courses of action, management is not fully equipped to take important decisions.

The public relations professional can play a valuable role as an independent and objective commentator on the issues concerning a particular situation, and thus may be able to present a more rational view of the issues of concern to the interested parties, as well as of the implications of the issues for the organization involved.

One important role that public relations professionals can fulfil is that of 'the voice of the user or consumer' within the organization – helping management to understand their needs, expectations and beliefs about the services, products or facilities offered. In the case of the Barbican Centre it was necessary for the architects, builders and, of course, the Corporation, to appreciate the requirements of the conference organizer. The various changes and additions to the original plans that resulted from the advice given, helped to ensure that the Barbican Centre, when completed, offered the type of facilities to enable it to become a leading international conference centre.

The problem of developing advance publicity for the Barbican Centre's conference facilities was exacerbated by two particular factors – the need to maintain interest over the prolonged construction period and the need to address both UK and international audiences. The main aim was obviously to stimulate awareness and interest in the Centre and inform potential users of its facilities. However, it was also necessary to address the issue of relations with the local residents as well as the adverse criticisms of the Centre's design. In addition to these considerations, the problem of how best to position the Centre, given its intended dual purpose usage, had to be confronted. The solution was to develop a series of separate, yet mutually supportive, media relations programmes. In each case news items were tailored to the interests of the specific media relevant to these different target audiences.

The media relations activities could not hope to maintain a constantly high level of media coverage, rather they followed a steadily rising wave-like pattern, with peaks and troughs each year over the life of the project. As the opening date approached, the pressure to accelerate the frequency of media exposure naturally increased. This was achieved by adopting a proactive approach. News stories were constructed around the visits of celebrities, whose presence provided many opportunities for picture stories. In order to reach the international news media, international press agencies were regularly contacted with news of progress. The business community and, in particular, international conference trade organizers, were also targeted through the relevant trade press.

The case also illustrates how it is sometimes possible to turn adverse media comment into an advantage. The controversy surrounding the Centre's design became the basis of sustained press comment. This allowed the issue of the Barbican to be maintained on the media's news agenda, through the letters columns, feature articles and by arranging press receptions at various stages of the Centre's construction.

A particular aspect of public relations work of relevance to this case is that of assisting with the presentation of issues or arguments to appropriate bodies. Clear and well-argued business presentations and reports can significantly affect the outcome of crucial decisions. This important aspect of public relations work often fails to receive the credit it deserves. Throughout the construction period of the Barbican it was important to persuade the Corporation to support the many changes that were seen as necessary to the Centre's design and facilities. The many vested interests involved had to be persuaded that the proposed changes, often involving significant additional expenditure, were crucial to the ultimate success of the Centre as both an arts and conference venue. This involved the preparation of numerous reports and face-to-face presentations which often had to be given to a largely non-expert audience. The issues and arguments had therefore to be presented in a clear and easily-understood form. The fact that most of the important proposed changes were accepted is a testament to the effectiveness of this aspect of the work.

The case also illustrates the importance of understanding the lead times involved in the organization of large events, conferences and exhibitions. It was intended that the Barbican Centre should compete for a share of the lucrative international conference market. In many cases international conferences, particularly those that are staged on a regular basis, are booked many years in advance to allow the extensive organization involved in mounting them to be carried out smoothly. This meant that the advance publicity for the Barbican's conference and exhibition facilities had to commence at a very early stage in its development, in some cases even before the full details of the facilities had been finalized. Had the publicizing of the conference facilities been delayed, it would undoubtedly have reduced the chances of the Centre attracting some of the major conference events due to take place around the time of its planned completion.

Student discussion questions and exercises

1. Compare and contrast the problems of developing public relations for the Barbican with those experienced in supporting a new product launch.
2. Select a conference or arts centre, leisure complex or other venue which has opened in recent years or is due to open, and with which you are familiar. Prepare a schedule of public relations activities and key target publics, designed to raise awareness and stimulate interest in the venue.
3. Consider how you might prepare a mailing list for the distribution of details of the conference and exhibition facilities available at either the Barbican or a similar centre. (The aim being to reach potential exhibitors themselves rather than conference/exhibition organizers).

Accidents do happen: designing an emergency response plan for Unocal UK Ltd

John Macdonald

Preview

In recent years crisis management programmes have been put in place by an increasing number of larger organizations, in an attempt to mitigate the potential damage that could result should a crisis strike the organization. A 'crisis' can take any number of forms, and can arise from many different situations. In ICI's case, the potential crisis arose not as a direct result of any particular failing on the part of the company, but, nevertheless threatened its reputation for 'good citizenship' and could have resulted in considerable damage to its business world-wide. British Rail were recently faced with handling the tragic Kings Cross fire and its aftermath, Occidental suffered the loss of the Piper Alpha platform in the North Sea, and the Exxon Corporation experienced a disastrous oil spillage in Prince William Sound, Alaska, when the Exxon Valdez ran aground. These examples of physical crises arising from disasters can often have very tragic consequences for both the employees of the organizations involved as well as, in many cases, the members of the public caught up in them. A crisis can sometimes have a quite dramatic effect on the reputation and image of the organization involved, often causing the organization serious, if not irreparable, damage. In Exxon's case, the 'clean-up' operation following the oil spillage has, to date, cost the company some US $1.3 billion. However, the longer-term damage to its reputation throughout the world has yet to be calculated.

Organizations operating in hazardous industries, such as the offshore oil industry, invariably have extensive emergency plans to cope with operational emergencies. However, they may overlook the importance of developing and testing an emergency/crisis media response plan. The failure to adequately prepare for the media attention that will invariably accompany a serious emergency can cause the organization involved serious problems, both in coping with the likely pressure of media attention, as well as in responding to the weight of inquiries from other interested parties. The failure to handle these inquiries effectively can lead to misinformation and speculation which can cause serious damage to the organization's reputation.

This case examines the development of an emergency media response programme for Unocal UK Ltd, operators of the Heather Alpha oil platform in the North Sea and a subsidiary of the Union Oil Corporation of Los Angeles. It illustrates the importance of meticulous attention to detail in preparing an emergency response team to face a possible crisis, as well as the need to establish clear procedures and guidelines for all eventualities. It may be impossible to fully prepare an organization for the trauma that may accompany a serious incident, especially when involving offshore oil installations. However, a carefully planned and rehearsed emergency response plan can at least ensure that the organization is able to maintain control over the flow of information during an emergency, and avoid damaging misinformation and speculation taking place.

Background

The offshore oil industry in the North Sea has an excellent safety record. However, accidents do happen in what is a hazardous industry. Accidents can range from relatively minor injuries which can be treated at the offshore location, to others which require evacuation of the casualties to shore facilities. In exceptional circumstances a major incident can occur, resulting in death, serious injuries or complete evacuation of the offshore installation.

In recent years there have been a number of such serious incidents in the North Sea involving fires or explosions on various producing platforms, and, of course, there have also been many instances of accidents involving both diving operations and helicopters. The Piper Alpha disaster is a vivid example of such a 'worst case scenario'.

Somewhat ironically, while only major industrial accidents on land (such as mine disasters or chemical works explosions) attract large-scale media interest, even relatively minor offshore incidents can attract the same level of media coverage. The reason for this lies, at least partially, in the inherent nature of the industry itself. Ever since oil was first discovered on the UK continental shelf the industry has been big news. The high technology involved, the hazardous environment, the fact that the oil industry is peopled by true characters like Red Adair, all combine to excite media interest in events offshore. As a result, accidents inevitably become news – perhaps local news, national news or even international news.

The oil companies operating offshore have to be alive to this fact and have in place procedures for handling the media response to any incident affecting installations or the personnel working on them, in order to ensure the coverage afforded to any incident is both factual and fair.

PR Consultants Scotland were appointed by Unocal UK Ltd to review their existing emergency procedures for handling any offshore incident and to implement an action programme. This case examines the development of this crisis management plan and provides an insight into the complex issues that have to be taken into account and the meticulous attention to detail that is required.

Unocal UK Ltd and its North Sea facilities

Unocal UK Ltd is the British subsidiary of the Union Oil Corporation of Los Angeles. The company is the main partner in the Heather Field which lies in Block 2/5 of the UK sector of the North Sea about 90 miles east of the Shetland Islands.

Oil was first discovered in the Heather Field on 23 December 1973 and is extracted and pumped ashore via the Heather Alpha platform. The latter stands 770 feet from the sea-bed to its highest point (the top of the drilling derricks) in water almost 500 feet deep. The structure is secured to the sea-bed by means of twenty-four steel piles, each being 6ft in diameter and over 315 ft long, and the total weight of the topside facilities exceeds 22,000 tonnes.

Analysis of the existing emergency plans

The starting point in preparing a revised emergency response plan was a thorough analysis and review of existing procedures. This revealed that although Unocal had a well-defined emergency response plan covering evacuation, safety, fire-fighting, liaison with rescue services and other physical measures for handling an incident, little thought had been given to any public relations activities that would be needed in the event of a major incident.

The need for public relations in an accident/emergency situation

It is sometimes difficult for companies to realize the need for a well-rehearsed public relations plan for emergency situations. A failure to respond to media inquiries can often be misconstrued and is usually taken as an admission of some form of guilt on the part of the company. The withholding of information, either totally or partially, can encourage speculation, false assumptions and worse – misinformation. It can also lead to allegations of complacency or cover-up. Hence, perhaps the worst response in such situations is 'no comment'.

Not only must a company recognize the importance of responding to the media interest in an incident, but it must recognize the potentially damaging effect on its reputation of a failure to communicate effectively with other audiences with a vested interest in the incident:

- relatives of employees;
- government and its agencies;
- local MPs;

- local authorities;
- the police and emergency services;
- insurance and financial interests;
- environmentalists;
- special interest groups, for example, fishermen.

During an emergency it may be impossible to communicate directly with all potentially interested audiences. It is therefore essential for the company's reputation as a *professional* entity that it establishes and maintains effective communication with the front line communicators – the media.

By providing factual information about an incident and the steps taken to remedy the problem, the operator is more likely to achieve recognition for being in control of the situation. At the same time, the incidence of speculation and misinformation can be reduced or totally eliminated and the company itself becomes established as *the* authoritative source of information about the incident.

Objectives

As a result of the initial analysis of Unocal's emergency plans, the operational objectives for the programme became reasonably straightforward. Namely:

- to ensure that Unocal had a pool of staff who were fully conversant with the differing needs of the various sectors of the UK and international media in the event of a major incident;

- to ensure that Unocal's senior management were capable of undertaking sensitive TV and radio interviews;
- to ensure that the pool of staff who would be called upon in the event of an incident, had the relevant background information on hand to deal with the inevitable vast number of telephone inquiries from the press and distressed relatives that would result from a major incident.

Although in summary, this may appear a straightforward task, it involved considerable effort and careful attention to detail to ensure that the planned emergency response procedures covered, as far as possible, all eventualities. Not only was it vital to ensure that the pool of staff received the appropriate training that would enable them to understand the media, and how to respond to their inquiries, but it was equally important that the full range of emergency response procedures were fully understood by those who would be called upon to implement them. Of course, a vital part of the programme involved the testing of the emergency response plan in order to identify any oversights or potential problems that could occur should it have to be put into effect.

During an emergency situation it is often necessary to call upon staff who may, otherwise, have little or no experience of handling the media or very limited appreciation of the workings of the media. It is therefore vital to provide the designated staff with the necessary information and training to enable them to quickly slip into their 'emergency roles' if called on to do so. This involved providing detailed briefings to staff on all aspects of emergency communications.

The key elements that have to be considered in putting together an emergency response plan for public relations can now be examined.

The media

The first step was to clearly define the range of media whose attention any incident would attract. These were classified for the UK news media as follows:

- Regional newspapers, for example, *The Scotsman, Aberdeen Press and Journal, Newcastle Chronicle.*
- National daily newspapers – both the 'quality' and tabloid press.
- Wire services – Reuters, PA, API.
- Local TV and radio – BBC Aberdeen, Grampian TV, Northsound.
- National TV and radio – ITN, BBC Network, IRN network.
- Trade and Technical and Specialist press – *Offshore Engineer, Oil and Gas Journal, Aberdeen Petroleum Report.*

It is not simply a matter of chronicling these for the company's emergency staff. It is important that the staff are made aware of their different deadlines. For example, the 'wire services' whose function it is to 'sell' news to the other news media, seek to constantly update their stories on a round-the-clock basis. Frequently, they will be transmitting information overseas so that news deadlines for papers or broadcasting stations in, say, Los Angeles, can be met. Local and national radio also seek to update their information constantly since they are providing, in many instances, early news bulletins.

Television stations work principally towards deadlines for their lunchtime, early morning and mid-evening news broadcasts, with the last named being the most important nationally and the early evening being the bulletin which is of most importance to local stations, such as Grampian's 'North Tonight' and the BBC's 'Reporting Scotland'.

The advent of breakfast television means that 'running' stories – those with news 'milage' still left in them, will be updated on early morning television by reporters who have started their calls at 4 a.m.

National daily newspapers rarely update stories after their last edition deadlines (around midnight) and, in particular, the pressure from national and regional dailies for information eases considerably after 9 p.m.

Evening newspapers have early morning deadlines and seek information most actively in the period 8 a.m.–noon.

The trade and technical press tends for the most part to publish monthly. They, naturally, tend to be more knowledgeable about the technical aspects of the oil industry and will often seek to produce more in-depth retrospective articles.

Unocal personnel were provided with detailed briefing about the various media to enable them to be aware of their different deadlines and news interests, thus allowing them to be better prepared to handle the flow of inquiries in the event of an incident.

The role of the emergency staff during an incident

At any time, and particularly during an emergency, a company's employees play a critical part in maintaining the reputation of the company. During an emergency the company involved in the incident is inevitably placed under the media 'spotlight'. A vital part of any emergency response plan is, therefore, the training of staff as to how to respond to the numerous inquiries that will inevitably be received. It was stressed to the emergency response staff that unguarded comment, in response to a seemingly innocent telephone inquiry, can be potentially very damaging and may be misinterpreted.

The main sources of calls to a company, other than those from bona fide outside agencies, are likely to be from journalists or relatives anxious for news. The important guidelines set for handling inquiries can be summarized as follows:

- It is vital that such calls are handled courteously and accurately.
- Employees must avoid the understandable tendency to try to be helpful and discuss the situation with callers.
- All communication during an incident must be channelled through the official media or personal response teams. Callers should be passed to the appropriate public relations or employee relations staff to handle their inquiries.
- Where the pressure of calls becomes too great for the available staff to handle, or when calls are received before the crisis teams are in place, a 'holding' statement may be required, and callers should be asked to call back when the appropriate staff are available or free.
- Courtesy and tact must be the watchwords in handling all inquiries and, at all costs, speculation must be avoided.

Sources of inquiries

During any emergency inquiries will come from a number of different types of caller, and each category of caller may require to be handled differently:

Inquiries from relatives of employees

It is critically important that these are handled sympathetically. In the event of information not being available or unconfirmed at the time of the call, it is vital that relatives do not feel they are being deliberately 'kept in the dark'. Relatives may naturally feel anxious and frustrated if there is a lack of information and this may lead them to contact their MPs or the newspapers, creating the impression that the company is failing in its duty to its employees.

Inquiries from the news media

It is equally critical that the company provides the media with factual information as quickly as possible, and where necessary supplementary inquiries should be followed up and answered. During the early stages of an incident a good deal of misinformation may abound. However, once in print, such misinformation may assume a cloak of veracity and may be difficult to correct. Hence, it is vital that a company should, at least, prepare a factual holding statement, until fuller details of the incident are available for release.

Inquiries from other interested parties

These can be classified as to whether they have a direct interest in the incident – police, coastguard, and so on – and those with no obvious direct interest – non-priority callers, for example, members of the public expressing their sympathies. In all cases, inquiries must be handled in a common-sense manner and routed to the appropriate office of the company. If, as is often the case, the crisis response teams are under considerable pressure, non-priority callers must be still be handled with courtesy, but requested to be patient. Those callers with a direct interest should be noted and either called back, or asked to call back themselves, at a less difficult time.

The role of the team handling calls to a company is therefore of fundamental importance. They must have clearly established guidelines and know exactly where to route the different types of call. They may also be faced with many very distressed and anxious callers and therefore they must be trained to cope with this type of caller. Inevitably those answering calls may suffer from the stress of the situation themselves, particularly when called upon to work for prolonged periods without relief. The selection and training of the response teams must therefore be made very carefully. Whenever possible, a pool of back-up staff should be identified to help relieve the pressure on the front-line response team during a serious incident, particularly if the emergency lasts over several days or weeks.

It is equally important to recognize the need to prepare a response to inquiries during the immediate aftermath of an incident. Even when the immediate effects of an emergency have been dealt with, the company may still continue to receive inquiries from both the media and other groups during the days or weeks following a 'stand-down' from emergency status. These again must be carefully handled and routed to the appropriate office.

Defining an emergency

While Unocal itself has its own classification system for activation of an appropriate operational response to an offshore incident, activation of a media response team would obviously depend on the seriousness of the incident. A generalized and simplistic classification which illustrates this point is as follows:

Incident classification A – possibly serious injury or damage to installations

An incident involving injuries to personnel or damage to an installation, but not requiring shut down or evacuation. Casevac and repairs may be needed but the incident is over – there is no 'running' problem or potential for the incident to develop into something more serious.

Implications for the media response team

In these circumstances it would normally be appropriate for media inquiries to be handled by a designated individual within the company rather than calling in a full media response team and/or the outside PR agency. Inquiries from relatives would be handled by the personnel department with police assistance as appropriate.

Incident classification B – fatalities and/or serious damage to an installation requiring shut down

An incident involving fatalities or serious damage to an installation requiring shut down and evacuation of non-essential personnel. A probability that the incident is 'running' and may develop into an even more serious event.

Implications for the media response team

In these circumstances a media response team, trained to handle media inquiries under pressure, and co-ordinated by a designated individual within the company or appointed PR professional would be activated. Inquiries from relatives would be handled by the personnel department in close liaison with the police.

Incident classification C – potential catastrophe

An incident of potentially catastrophic proportions involving fatalities, emerᵤₗcy evacuation of an installation and potentially long-term consequences for the operation involved.

Implications for the media response team

In these circumstances the full media response team with PR co-ordination would be immediately activated.

Guidelines for handling media inquiries

The next stage of the programme involves developing a set of guidelines for the media response team as well as providing training for the designated personnel to prepare them to handle the various categories of incidents with which they could, at some stage, be faced.

The media response team guidelines included the following key points:

- Where an incident occurs in the B or C category, media interest is likely to be intense – the volume of telephone calls received by the media response team will be very high and consequently they are likely to be under considerable pressure.
- The first news of an incident normally reaches the media from their routine check on their own information sources. These checks normally operate between 8 a.m. when evening papers are preparing their first editions and 2 a.m. when the last editions of the daily newspapers are 'put to bed'. In the case of the radio stations and early morning TV, routine checks may start at 4 or 5 a.m.
- The sources used by journalists are the police, hospitals, coastguard, marine radio, helicopter traffic contacts, and other contacts maintained with personnel working in the off-shore industry.
- These various sources often provide journalists with some vague details of an incident offshore even before the essential facts are known by the operating company itself. Thus the story may 'break' quickly, and this can pose a serious problem. For example, if a story breaks close to the deadline for a news broadcast or newspaper edition, the journalists concerned may use whatever fragmentary information they have, before verification of the story has taken place.
- A 'no comment' response from a company will only tend to confirm to journalists that the company has 'something to hide' and it will tend to fuel speculation. It is essential, in an emergency, to take all steps possible to make the facts (as far as known) available in response to media inquiries, or inquiries from other interested parties.
- A holding statement should be prepared and held in readiness as a stop-gap until a fuller statement has been cleared for release.
- The response team should accept and log all media inquiries, and advise them when to call back for information would be appropriate.

- Similarly, supplementary inquiries should be logged and every effort m to have answers to them prepared.

Telephone-answering techniques

The guidelines for the media response team placed considerable emphasis on telephone-answering techniques. During any emergency most of the contact with the media will tend to be by telephone and it is important for the media response team to be aware of the limitations and problems of communication with the media by telephone. The staff involved were given training in tele-phone-answering techniques, and 'standard responses' to inquiries were prepared and rehearsed. The training stressed the importance of adopting a calm, helpful and genuine 'tone of voice'. However, it was also stressed that care is needed to avoid conveying a bland and complacent impression to callers.

'Dos and don'ts'

A set of basic 'dos' and 'don'ts' were prepared for the response team:

Basic 'dos'

- Give out *only* information which is authorized for publication/broadcast.
- If in doubt, check with the PR co-ordinator.
- Obtain additional information *only* from the PR co-ordinator.
- Avoid speculation on any aspect of the incident.
- If asked, give your name.
- Describe your function as 'a Unocal spokesman/spokeswoman'.
- Be courteous, as helpful as possible, and stay calm.
- Log all questions together with the name of the questioner, the medium represented, the time of the call and the call-back number.
- Suggest callers ring back rather than you call them.
- Refer relative inquiries to 'next-of-kin desk'.
- Assume everything you say to a journalist will be printed or broadcast.

Basic 'don'ts'

- Do not give out any unauthorized information.
- Do not assume anything.
- Do not give information on an 'off the record' basis.
- Do not answer any questions unless the answer is contained within the cleared information.
- Do not disclose your 'normal' role within the company.

● Do not lose your 'cool'.

Using background information

Throughout any emergency there are likely to be many requests for either general background information about the company or for specific technical data. An important part of the emergency response programme includes the preparation of background information on the company's offshore operations in the form of background fact sheets. This information has to be pre-cleared for release to the media, and all members of the response team must be made familiar with it.

During the early stages of an emergency the media will tend to be anxious for every piece of information regarding the company and the installation involved in the incident. The ability to provide journalists with this type of background information can help relieve the early pressure on the response team.

Face-to-face contacts with the media

Although during the early stages of an emergency most of the contact with the media will tend to be by telephone, as an emergency develops there may be requests for face-to-face interviews (or telephone interviews) with operations management. The media response team were trained to refer all such requests to the PR co-ordinator for a decision.

In some cases journalists and photographers may attempt to gain entry to the company offices or may even 'camp' on the doorstep in the hope of gaining an interview or to try to interview staff as they leave the building.

A part of any emergency response plan has to include security measures to prevent any unauthorized persons from gaining entry to the company's offices during the emergency. Journalists are, however, at perfect liberty to wait outside the company's buildings. Therefore staff must be briefed as to how to respond to requests for interviews.

In general, the same principles apply to face-to-face inquiries as for handling telephone inquiries, namely, staff are trained to be courteous and remain cool. However, they must be instructed not to disclose any unauthorized or 'off-the-record' information, no matter how seemingly innocuous. Staff must be instructed that the correct response is to simply state that they are not authorized to give interviews on behalf of the company, and to refer journalists to the press office.

It was pointed out to the staff that they must recognize that if confronted with microphones and cameras they are, at that point, essentially representing the 'public face of the company'. They must stay calm, confident and collected.

Working with the police

It is a statutory requirement that the Grampian Police be informed in the event of a serious incident offshore. The police will then designate an officer to move into the operations office to help co-ordinate the flow of information between the company and the police information room.

The police have a key role to play in handling relative inquiries and informing the next of kin of those dead, injured or missing. The police will post press information notices at the police headquarters and will update these as the situation develops. Close liaison is therefore required between the company PR co-ordinator and the police information room, to ensure that the information being issued in both centres is accurate and, above all, consistent.

The police will normally provide a number to which all relatives and next of kin can be directed, thus relieving pressure on the company PR function.

Handling non-media inquiries

Easily the most sensitive area of non-media inquiries during an emergency are those that come from relatives. These are generally best handled by the personnel department or the police. Wherever possible it is best if these are handled by company representatives, as this demonstrates clearly the company's involvement and concern for the well-being of its employees. However, the sheer volume of calls may require many to be re-routed to the police number.

Inquiries may also be received from MPs, local authorities and perhaps environmentalists concerned about possible pollution. The basic principle applied must be to distinguish the operational from non-operational inquiries. Calls from the Department of Energy, Ministry of Defence Search and Rescue, from the coastguard, lifeboat, or other bona fide emergency services, should be routed to the appropriate co-ordinator in the company. Non-operational inquiries should be passed to the PR co-ordinator who can then decide quickly on the importance of the inquiry and how it should be handled.

The importance of testing the plan and training staff

Although it may be unlikely that a full-scale (category C) emergency will affect a company operating offshore it is, nevertheless, always a constant possibility. It is therefore essential for all operators to have an appropriate emergency plan in place. However, just as it is normal to regularly test the working of emergency equipment on the offshore installations to ensure it is working efficiently, it is equally important to periodically test the public relations emergency response plans.

The pool of staff who may be involved in handling an emergency may obviously change over time, and new staff may be required to be trained. The standard background information that would be made available to the media in the event of an emergency will need to be periodically updated, and the media response procedures must be tested and revised where necessary. In some cases, changes in communications technology will affect the way information might be disseminated. For example, the recent expansion of facsimile equipment offers new ways of communicating 'hard copy' information such as fact sheets, photographs and press releases.

As part of the project for Unocal, PR Consultants Scotland undertook the training of the response team, and developed a number of emergency response exercises to test the effectiveness of the emergency plan and to update the skills of the company's staff who would be called upon to assist in the event of a real emergency.

The training for the media response team involved full-scale simulations of an emergency situation, which enabled staff to practice their skills and to identify any possible problems with the response plan. As part of this training, the media response team were given 'exercises' to help them appreciate the type of questions with which the media might confront them, together with the types of information that the media would be seeking from the company.

An example of the type of exercises given to staff to help them prepare for handling an emergency incident are shown in exhibit 1:

Exhibit 1
Information likely to be required by the media (exercise)

Listed below are a range of questions likely to be asked by the media during any major incident. Please put them in order of importance you feel a journalist will give to them assuming that the incident has resulted in death and injury to personnel.

This is not a *test*, but it will give you an idea of the type of information any media person will be looking for.

1. What is the company's safety record?
2. Where is the platform?
3. What time did the incident occur?
4. How many injured/dead?
5. How far is the platform from Aberdeen?
6. What are the arrangements for relatives?
7. What caused the incident?
8. How many personnel are there on the platform?
9. Are any other installations in danger?
10. What evacuation measures have been undertaken?
11. Has the platform been shut down?
12. Where is the company based?
13. How long has the company been operating in the North Sea?

14. How many staff work for the company in the UK?
15. What are the company's areas of operation?

Summary

Although this case provides only a general overview of the extensive and detailed emergency response plan developed for the company (confidentiality prevents precise details of the plan being revealed), it does provide an insight into the very detailed planning and attention to detail required in preparing company personnel to handle what may be, in the event of an offshore accident, a very traumatic situation.

Companies operating in potentially hazardous industries cannot afford to ignore the potential damage to their reputation that can result from a badly-handled incident. Although companies may have well-rehearsed and tested operational emergency plans, it may be more difficult for them to fully appreciate the importance of a carefully prepared emergency media response plan. In recent years a number of serious incidents in the offshore industry has alerted companies to the need to put such plans in hand, in order to avoid the potentially damaging effects of misinformation being promulgated in the media. The Piper Alpha tragedy is perhaps a prime example of the damaging effects that speculative media coverage can have on the reputation of a company.

An offshore incident, particularly when involving serious injury or death to company personnel, calls for very sensitive handling by company spokespersons, many of whom may be friends or even relatives of those involved. A difficult balance may have to be struck between the professional and efficient handling of inquiries both from the media and other interested parties, and conveying an impression of clinical disinterest in the human tragedy involved. Without professional training it may be difficult for management and other company staff to appreciate how their responses to questions from the media may be interpreted.

During an emergency there may be little time to obtain the potentially wide range of information that the media, in particular, may request. The failure to produce information will often tend to fuel speculation, and at worst may be interpreted as a sign that the company was ill prepared for the crisis now facing it. Often the company itself may not be fully aware, during the early stages of an incident, of the full extent of events. However, it must have plans in hand to respond to the pressures for information that may rapidly build up. This may involve the release of interim holding statements and background information that can, at least, serve to reassure callers and the media that the company is endeavouring to co-operate and trying its best to clarify the situation.

The key aim for any company faced with a serious emergency, must be to control the flow of information and to establish itself as the single authoritative source of information on the incident. This can only be achieved if the company has an effective emergency response plan in place, and its emergency procedures are regularly tested and updated in the light of changing circumstances.

Public relations professionals can bring their experience of handling the media to the assistance of companies who may become involved in an emergency. They can help the company to develop an appropriate emergency response plan, help train company staff to respond to media and other inquiries and help establish the necessary background information materials that would be required during an emergency.

Case discussion

'Crisis management' has become an established term for the emergency response plans that many larger companies have come to accept as an essential insurance policy against the potentially damaging effects of a major incident affecting the company. This case illustrates something of the detailed preparation that is required in preparing a company to handle an emergency.

At the heart of effective emergency or crisis planning, is the realization that it is concerned with meticulous attention to detail and the preparation of a responses that take account of all possible contingencies. However, it may be difficult to predict the full extent of any incident that could affect a company, and even planning for the 'worst case scenario' may not fully prepare a company for the impact of a major catastrophe, should it happen.

The emergency response training for Unocal recognized the need to extend the training to employees other than those making up the 'front line' emergency response team. Since a crisis can strike at any time and vary in its seriousness, it is essential to have a sufficient number of people who are capable of either assisting the expert emergency team or who can 'hold the fort' until they can be mobalized. Equally, as the case illustrates, emergency procedures must be up-dated and tested regularly. This up-dating must obviously include knowledge of the media. A vital part of preparing for an emergency must include training the people who will act as spokespersons on behalf of the organization, as they may be exposed to extreme pressure from the media during any crisis and will be seen as representing the views of the organization as a whole. Obviously, those chosen for this task must be very carefully selected and prepared for the likely pressures a crisis can involve.

This case also highlights the value of preparing a detailed background 'fact file' about the organization. This can prove invaluable during a crisis as a source of reference to handle specific media inquiries or to help compile a holding statement while the full extent of the crisis is being assessed.

As the case suggests, perhaps the most important principle of effective crisis management is the need to maintain control over the flow of information. This involves not only controlling the information emanating from the organization itself, but also ensuring that the information being released by the other emergency services is consistent and accurate. Effective crisis management requires clear responsibilities to be established for the processing of information and for the authorization of its release to the media or other interested parties. All staff involved in the crisis team must be trained to realise that, ultimately, the reputation of their organization may be at stake. The key lessons for crisis management teams are that they must maintain a professional, yet sensitive, approach to communication throughout an emergency if their respective organizations are to emerge from any incident without long-lasting damage to their reputation and relations with their various publics.

Student discussion questions and exercises

1. Draw up a list of key questions that the media might ask in the event of a crisis/emergency incident affecting either British Rail or British Airways. Place these in a likely order of priority.
2. Examine the media coverage of any recent emergency incident, and evaluate how well the organization involved appears to have handled the incident.
3. For a selected organization compile a basic background fact file of information that could be used by the emergency response team in the event of crisis affecting the organization.

Suggested further reading

The following additional readings are suggested, in particular, for student readers or those with limited experience of public relations:

Bernstein, D. (1984) *Company Image and Reality*, Holt, Rinehart & Winston. This provides some interesting insights into the thinking behind corporate identity programmes and in particular corporate advertising.

Black, S. and Sharpe, M. (1983) *Practical Public Relations*, Prentice-Hall. A useful and concise introduction to public relations for students and new entrants to the industry.

Broom, G. and Dozier, D. (1989) *Using Research in Public Relations*, Prentice-Hall. One of the few books to address the important role of research and evaluation in public relations and is essential reading for all those interested in furthering their understanding of the application of research techniques in the field of public relations.

Cutlip, S., Centre, A. and Broom, G. (1985) *Effective Public Relations*, Prentice-Hall. A useful basic primer on all aspects of public relations practice. It also provides some useful case examples of public relations work.

Grunig, J. and Hunt, T. (1984) *Managing Public Relations*, Holt, Rinehart & Winston. This provides a comprehensive review of some of the important management theories relevant to public relations work.

Hart, N.A. (1987) *Effective Corporate Relations*, McGraw-Hill. An interesting collection of articles by leading practitioners which examines the different roles for public relations within the corporate or business environment.

Johnson, G. and Scholes, K. (1988) *Exploring Corporate Strategy*, Prentice-Hall. Although not specifically devoted to public relations, this book provides a very useful review of the process of developing corporate strategy in general, as well as the strategic decision-making process to which public relations can make a valuable contribution.

Olins, W. (1990) *The Corporate Personality*, The Design Council. This is one of the few recent books to examine in any depth the development process involved in a corporate identity change. It provides many useful examples of organizations that have undergone a change of corporate identity.

Periodicals

Students of public relations or those practitioners wishing to keep in touch with the latest research and thinking about the practice, are recommended to subscribe to the following periodicals:

IPRA Review, Whiting & Birch Ltd, 90 Dartmouth Rd, Forest Hill, London SE23 3HZ.
IPR Journal, Institute of Public Relations, Gate House, St John's Square, London EC1M 4DH.
Public Relations Quarterly, 44 W. Market Street, Rhinebeck, NY 12572, USA.
Public Relations Journal, Public Relations Society of America, 845 Third Ave, NY 10022, USA.
Public Relations Review, 7100 Baltimore Boulevard, College Rd, Maryland 20740, USA.

Students and other readers may also find it useful to refer to articles relevant to the subject of public relations and corporate communications that appear from time to time in the following UK periodicals:

Management Today

Business

Marketing

Campaign

Marketing Week

The Economist

Business Week

Index